Through the Fire – From Intake to Credential

Constructing Knowledge: Curriculum Studies in Action

Series Editors

Brad Porfilio (*Seattle University, USA*)
Julie Gorlewski (*Virginia Commonwealth University, USA*)
David Gorlewski (*Virginia Commonwealth University, USA*)

Editorial Board

Sue Books (*State University of New York at New Paltz, USA*)
Ken Lindblom (*Stony Brook University, New York, USA*)
Peter McLaren (*Chapman University, Orange, USA*)
Wayne Ross (*University of British Columbia, Canada*)
Christine Sleeter (*California State University, Monterey, USA*)
Eve Tuck (*Ontario Institute for Studies in Education, University of Toronto, Canada*)

VOLUME 18

The titles published in this series are listed at *brill.com/ckcs*

Through the Fire – From Intake to Credential

*Teacher Candidates Share Their
Experiences through Narrative*

By

Cleveland Hayes
Kenneth Fasching-Varner
Hillary Eisworth
Kimberly White-Smith

BRILL
SENSE

LEIDEN | BOSTON

Cover illustration: Drawing by Luis-Genro Garcia

All chapters in this book have undergone peer review.

The Library of Congress Cataloging-in-Publication Data is available online at http://catalog.loc.gov

Typeface for the Latin, Greek, and Cyrillic scripts: "Brill". See and download: brill.com/brill-typeface.

ISSN 2213-722X
ISBN 978-90-04-38816-1 (paperback)
ISBN 978-90-04-38818-5 (hardback)
ISBN 978-90-04-38819-2 (e-book)

Copyright 2018 by Koninklijke Brill NV, Leiden, The Netherlands.
Koninklijke Brill NV incorporates the imprints Brill, Brill Hes & De Graaf, Brill Nijhoff, Brill Rodopi, Brill Sense, Hotei Publishing, mentis Verlag, Verlag Ferdinand Schöningh and Wilhelm Fink Verlag.
All rights reserved. No part of this publication may be reproduced, translated, stored in a retrieval system, or transmitted in any form or by any means, electronic, mechanical, photocopying, recording or otherwise, without prior written permission from the publisher.
Authorization to photocopy items for internal or personal use is granted by Koninklijke Brill NV provided that the appropriate fees are paid directly to The Copyright Clearance Center, 222 Rosewood Drive, Suite 910, Danvers, MA 01923, USA. Fees are subject to change.

This book is printed on acid-free paper and produced in a sustainable manner.

Contents

Foreword   VII
    Brenda G. Harris
About the Artist: An Example of Critical Teaching Enacted in
    the Classroom of Luis-Genro Garcia   x
Notes on the Authors   xv

1 What Is Going on in Teacher Education in the United States
   An Introduction   1

2 Tried and True   9
    Geoffrey Jaynes

3 Bianca: New Footprints on the Well-Trodden Path   10

4 Cecilia: Wisdom Is Earned through Experience   19

5 Covington: A Journey through the Hundred Acre Wood   27

6 George: The Last 100 Meters   39

7 Hillary: Teaching Is a Lifestyle   51

8 Jasmime: What Teacher Educators Can Learn
   from Teacher Candidates   58

9 Ximaroa: All Things Considered   68

10 Miquel: The Great Emancipator of Education   75

11 Owen: Is Math that Terrible?   83

12 Vijay: Education and the Pursuit of Happiness   93

13 Wade: A Teacher's Last Step before Game Time   103

14 Mary: The Bell Rings … The Journey Begins   113

15 Kaitlyn: Three Things I Learned during My Student
   Teaching Experience   121

16 Lauren and Patricia: An Elementary Prison   128

17 Jordan and Catherine: Realizations about Classroom Environment   137

18 Through the Fire: A Critical Race Perspective toward
   Preparing Critical Educators   145

   Afterword   163
      Kerri Tobin

   References   167

Foreword

Brenda G. Harris

In *Through the Fire – From Intake to Credential: Teacher Candidates Share Their Experiences through Narrative*, the authors of this volume have created an important opportunity and space for future educators to share their experiences of navigating the often treacherous terrains of teacher preparation and credentialing. Future teachers are typically the passive objects, not the agentive subjects and participants, of immense amounts of research and practice-based change or reform endeavors related to U.S. public schooling and the importance of teacher quality and teacher preparation for multicultural and equitable educational outcomes and opportunities for all learners. It is rare to have the opportunity to explore the preparation of future teachers from the perspective of future teachers themselves. Since there is no teacher preparation process without future teachers to prepare, teacher candidates and their experiences in teacher education are central to any understanding of how individuals become effective teachers in today's socially diverse classrooms and how to best go about improving contemporary teacher education toward equitable education for all.

By applying an auto-ethnographic approach in this volume to share and explore the experiences of prospective teachers as they navigate the preparation and credentialing processes of teacher education, we – as those who have gone before the future educators in this text and those who will come behind them, gain first hand insights from these young women and men about what it means and how to better prepare prospective educators to become a teacher against a backdrop of historical inequities in schooling and prepared for the multi-culturally diverse classrooms of today. Teacher educators, school and community leaders, and others committed to pushing toward more equitable social domains and forms of living and learning hence would do well to take up the opportunity provided in this text to learn from the narratives included in this volume and those of other teacher candidates; indeed, the narratives of teacher candidates herein and elsewhere are, in part, reflections of ourselves as teacher educators and evaluations of our work in teacher education and the professional preparation of those who will carry on our professions after us and for rising generations. What we as teacher educators teach, or think we are teaching, in teacher preparation courses may, or may not, be what prospective teachers are learning about being a teacher and successful teaching and learning for all learners, particularly those students historically underserved.

Each of the prospective educators who share their narratives in this volume are striving to become critical educators capable of promoting equitable educational and social opportunities, outcomes, and experiences for all learners. While their journeys are each distinctive and unique to them personally, the teacher candidates who share their narratives in this volume highlight some of the challenges and opportunities they have encountered in teacher preparation courses to learn about the functioning of social structures that sustain society's existing hierarchies and develop the skills and knowledge requisite to identify, implement, and assess critical learning strategies aimed at challenging inequities and promoting more inclusive forms of education. Specifically, these future teachers included in this volume are sharing with us, their readers, their attempts at learning to unhook from Whiteness and to disrupt the pernicious and historical school-to-prison pipeline that has long existed in the US between the nation's prison system and schools serving learners and their families and communities identified as racially not White, economically poor, and otherwise not members of the White, middle-class, primary English speaking, heterosexual, patriarchal mainstream.

Importantly, it is because of the directness and frank honesty of the future teachers who share their narratives in this volume that we as readers are able to witness their failures and accomplishments in learning to unhook from Whiteness and disrupt the school-to-prison pipeline in today's US public schools. If, for instance, future teachers view themselves and the children and youth of color they work with as individuals isolated from historical context, rather than as members of differentially positioned groups whose lives and opportunities are unequally structured by the historical privileging of traits, values, histories, accomplishments, and interests of Whites, then their teaching practices are not likely to challenge or transform the factors that function in schools and elsewhere to maintain the continued racial dominance of Whites. These understandings carried within the prospective teachers' narratives thus highlight points of potential engagement needed to push toward increasing the capacity of teacher preparation realize educational equity for all.

Like myself, readers will find it an honor and appreciate the opportunity to explore the narratives of the prospective educators who have contributed to this volume and opened themselves up to share their experiences and understandings of the teacher preparation and credentialing processes in their respective communities and institutions of higher education. The authors of this book have enabled us as readers to explore the viewpoints and understandings of the educators who will soon be taking on the precious task of educating our nation's children and youth in our public schools; they help us to critically consider what the teacher candidates are telling us about the process of teacher preparation.

It is of the utmost importance that we in teacher education not fail in preparing all future teachers to successfully teach all students. With future educators goes our future in education and the educational future of so many children and youth dependent on quality schooling for opportunities in a society and world deeply structured by inequities of every kind. This volume highlights these connections between education and past, present, and future generations.

About the Artist: An Example of Critical Teaching Enacted in the Classroom of Luis-Genro Garcia

Luis-Genaro Garcia, PhD, is an artist and high school art teacher in South Central Los Angeles. Dr. Garcia has a PhD in education at Claremont Graduate University. His work uses the CRT tenet of experiential knowledge. He uses his experiences growing up in a single parent household and schooling experiences to challenge traditional approaches to art education.

As an artist, Luis draws from the socio-political subject matter of Jose Guadalupe Posada and David Alfaro Siqueiros to paint in a "Social Surrealist" style that depicts working class people through metaphorical concepts. As an educator, in turn, he teaches the arts through a social justice curriculum that accounts and validates the ethnic, personal, and historical experiences of working class students. Dr. Garcia states,

> Rather than teaching students how to improve their artistic skills and abilities, a meaningful art education should teach students to use the arts as forms of resistance to current institutional barriers that exist in working class environments.

Resistance is a form of negotiation directed towards the hegemony that exists in schools. Luis's use of art as a form of negotiation to challenge the limitations faced by urban youth is a form of resistance he, with his students, negotiates to push against and challenge the existing hegemony and social hierarchies.

We, the authors of this text, take this space in our manuscript to focus on Dr. Garcia and his work as an artist-educator as an example that teacher candidates and others may find useful in considering a practical application of critical education in an actual classroom with students. Luis' classroom is an example of what critical education looks likes at a grassroots level. It is an example of what we, as teacher educators and teacher candidates, talk about in education foundation courses at both universities and other educational spaces. Dr. Garcia's classroom serves as evidence that a critically informed approach to teaching and learning is not some type of "pie in the sky" ivory tower idea that is unrealistic for actual teachers with "real" students. Rather, Dr. Garcia's classroom illustrates that a critically oriented form of education that is grounded in and relevant to students and their lives and communities can and, in some cases, is being implemented by educators.

We thus use the narrative[1] shared by Dr. Garcia to introduce and explore the possibilities provide by and through art and a connection to students' lives and communities toward more equitable forms of living, learning, and developing as individuals and groups. Often, in the teacher preparation courses we – the authors of this text, teach we hear from students that the practices of critical education will not work in schools. Our teacher education students frequently tell us that there is too much of a disconnect from the reality of schooling and what is being taught in Schools of Education such as a culturally relevant, critical form of teaching and learning.

This section provides evidence supporting a counter to that argument that education relevant to students and critically oriented is not practice or possible. The work that Dr. Garcia is doing in his classroom with students is real and, accordingly, if teacher candidates put in the effort to create their own teaching practices and perspectives toward culturally relevant, equitable education, they too can have these same real experiences.

As we – the authors and the artist, define it, the teaching-and-learning cycle is cultural work; it is a way of thinking about and thus approaching life and its many domains including education. It is not a technocratic, rational, objective, and mechanistic process or procedure. We already have a plethora of narrow curricula, scripted pedagogies, and standardized assessments that are proven failures despite the good intentions that may have produced them (Hayes, Juarez, & Cross, 2012; Ladson-Billings, 1994; Quijada Cerecer, Alvarez Guiterrez & Rios, 2010). In the paragraphs below, we introduce the artist-educator Luis-Genro Garcia. Dr. Garcia then discusses how he developed and implements a critical form of education grounded in art and based on his students' life experiences.

Dr. Luis Garcia

Dr. Garcia explains how he creates an environment in his classroom that allows for the students to make use of their lived experiences in their learning and life at and after school. He states,

> I am in my eleventh-year teaching. I think my cultural background has developed me, and helped me to grow as an educator. Because as an art educator, I started with, 'we're going to learn patterns,' 'we're going to learn, design methods' right.
>
> But, the reality of it, I realized, is that none of this is helping students. None of this is going to resolve the social and economic inequities faced by my students. So, little by little I just started developing a unique

art method. I developed my approach to art where I was introducing students to systematic and socioeconomic processes that limit working class families from accessing resources.

So, through the arts, I introduced them to how the social structure works, living in a capitalistic society, how labor and housing policies have targeted people of color, and the impact of environmental racism. I do this all through the arts. And so it's not just, 'oh, we're learning about the arts,' we're learning about how our environment works, specifically for people of color, and it's done through the arts right. That way – an actual benefit is students learning through the arts when it's connected to where they live and how, how that environment works. You know, get them to navigate through or around the limited environments that they live in. I didn't start taking my students out into the community to do art projects until after I received my Masters degree in public arts.

At that time, when I finished by degree, we were already doing projects in the classroom. However, after being exposed to different public art projects and to public art, it occurred to me that we need to do public art projects where it counts for them, with regard to students and doing arts projects in their own communities.'

My activist experience was started when partners of mine introduced me to Paulo Freire's (1970) text entitled *Pedagogy of the Oppressed*. They told me that I need to read this book especially if you're going to be working with urban youth. And that's when I also read the *Communist Manifesto* (Marx & Engels, 1848) and looked at how the social structure works, that is, how social hierarchy works, and how it related to some of my experiences.

I really did not start being politically active until my third or fourth year. But I was already thinking some of these things like social structure as an artist as well. I think that that's a very unique position of being artist/educator.

I started doing that around 2009 when I begin to get involved in demonstrations, citizen engagement introducing students to talking and expressing topics that were hitting them at home. These topics include immigration issues, gentrification, and the school-to-prison pipeline. And so, now that I'm completing my doctoral studies – I'm able to bring even more theoretical concepts together. Where I am using critical education methods to bring the arts to students in working class and underfunded art programs.

I don't get any flack from my school administrators. They see that I do have a revolutionary approach to education, and they see how students respond to it. They see that I do connect them to the classroom. It's my way of really making a difference in my community and thinking about the learning experiences of the students. Bottom line I try to empower students through art.

For example, taking these empty lots that have been left ever since the '92 riots. We say this. OKAY, what can we do for the best of the community? Right now, my students are working with the Trust of Republic Lands to developing that avenue of networks. It's not necessarily their project, but the murals they make are part of the class.

Creative Resistance in My Classroom

By situating resistance within the educative realm of daily visual experiences, students, and teachers can begin to meaningfully assess, interpret, and attend to the social, political, psychological, and cultural struggles that occur within the multiple sites of the everyday. (Darts, 2004, p. 318)

I define creative resistance as more of an action rather than a theory. Creative Resistance is; any creative forms of expression that contests or challenges systematic-oppressive; structures, actions, misconceptions, stereotypes, political agendas, or inequalities that diminish the development of a group of people or community through fine or performing art productions. I have introduced the idea of arts-based critical pedagogy with urban youth. During a recent service learning project my students and I used culturally relevant art instruction in a way that incorporated the historical and cultural experiences of socio-economically challenged students, while linking them to civic participation. I think this type of project can open opportunities for students to challenge the limitations they encounter in urban schools and communities. (Garcia, 2012, 2015)

As I see it, after completing an art course where the curriculum focused on the environments and experiences of the immediate neighborhood through concepts of social justice were able to reflect on issues of gentrification and a broken school system based on their understandings and the implications of living in a socio-economically challenged area. I saw several of my students develop a richer political awareness and the influences it had in understanding their circumstances and why it was difficult for them to navigate their academic endeavors.

The idea, to develop student awareness, to develop student confidence and really having invest with their own persons and voicing out their own opinions, because the first day of class is always ... okay, let's look at this art period and tell me what you think? They don't want to answer because they think it's wrong. I told them sometimes, I tell them, "Look man, that's your opinion; it's not right or wrong. An opinion is what you think and the problem is that you've been told that tree is green. You've been told that when you paint the sky it's probably blue. No. It doesn't. Little by little your imagination is deteriorating because teachers tell you what to do. So, you're just used to being told what to do. In my class, your opinion is what you need to do. So, I tell them why, because you guys need to be proactive about what you think and that's the start of being opinionated; that's the start of making changes; that's the start of thinking about certain situations. But, my teaching philosophy is how I can teach students ... and teaching students to look at their environment and improving it through the arts.

Note

1 This narrative is written from data collected from a larger study that Dr. Cleveland Hayes is conducting on Latino teachers and not written by the artist.

Notes on the Authors

Cleveland Hayes

Ph.D., is a Professor of Education Foundations at Indiana University Indianapolis. At Indiana University – Indianapolis, Dr. Hayes teaches science in the elementary school, education foundations and qualitative studies in education. He is also affiliated with Africana studies and teaches various courses. In addition, Dr. Hayes is an affiliated faculty member in the Center for Education Equity and Intercultural Research at the University of La Verne. Dr. Hayes's research interest includes the use of Critical Race Theory in Education, Historical and Contemporary Issues in Black Education to include the school to prison pipeline, Teaching and Learning in the Latino Community, Whiteness and the Intersections of Sexuality and Race. Dr. Hayes is an active member of the American Education Research Association (AERA) at the Division Level, SIG level and committee level. He currently, as a program Co-Chair for Division K and is a member of the Special Interest Group Executive Committee. He is also the vice president of the Critical Race Studies in Education. Dr. Hayes's research can be found in Democracy and Education, Qualitative Studies in Education, and Gender and Education, Urban Review, and Power of Education. In addition, he is the co-editor of the books titled: *Unhooking from Whiteness: The Key to Dismantling Racism in the United States* and *Unhooking from Whiteness: Resisting the Esprit de Corps*.

Kenneth J. Fasching-Varner

Ph.D., is the Shirley B. Barton Endowed Associate Professor at Louisiana State University. Varner's areas of scholarly expertise and interest center on the intersections of identity in globalized contexts. Varner examines the nature of White Racial Identity (WRI), Critical Race Theory (CRT), and Culturally Relevant Pedagogy as well as international education, neo-liberalism, and educational foundations within global contexts. He has published articles in the journals *Teacher's College Record, Educational Foundations, Democracy in Education,* and *Social Identities: Journal for the Studies of Race, Nation, and Culture* among others and has edited and authored over 10 books related to these areas of expertise. Varner studied Language, Literacy, and Culture with a focus on Critical Race Theory and Culturally Relevant Pedagogy at The Ohio State University in Columbus Ohio and is a faculty member of the Curriculum Theory Project as well as the African and African-American and Women and Gender Studies programs at LSU.

Hillary Eisworth
Ph.D., is a faculty member in the PK-3 Early Childhood Teacher Education Program at Louisiana State University. She teaches courses on the development of young children and pedagogy in early childhood. Dr. Eisworth earned her PhD in Curriculum and Instruction, with a specialization in early childhood education, from The University of Texas at Austin. Before joining the School of Education faculty in 2007, Dr. Eisworth taught pre-kindergarten, first, and second grade in Las Vegas, Nevada, and in Portland, Oregon. Her areas of interest include multicultural education, teacher education, and teacher inquiry. Currently, she is the faculty advisor for Score a Friend, a campus organization whose mission is to promote and provide opportunities for Unified Friendships through school and community-based sports and clubs.

Kimberly White-Smith
Ed.D., is Professor of Education and Dean at the University of La Verne's LaFetra College of Education (LFCE), which houses more than $10 million in grants and donor monies to create innovative programing and scholarships for students. She is the intellectual force behind a number of scholarly endeavors that foster academic justice for traditionally underserved students through enhanced educational environments, policies, and teaching strategies. She has authored articles and book chapters on diversity, inclusivity, and leadership, such as, *The Struggle for Identity in a Teacher Community*, in Etta R. Hollins' latest book, *Learning to Teach in Urban Schools* and *"That's Why I Say Stay in School": Black Mothers' Parental Involvement, Cultural Wealth and Exclusion in Their Son's Schooling* and *"Just as Bad as Prisons": The Challenge of Dismantling the School-to-Prison Pipeline through Teacher and Ccommunity Education*, co-authored with Quaylan Allen in *Urban Education and Equity and Excellence in Education*. She is part of the national conversation on Teacher Education through her leadership positions such as Program Chair of Division K, Teaching and Teacher Education (2013–2016) and member of Program Committee, American Association of Colleges of Teacher Education.

CHAPTER 1

What Is Going on in Teacher Education in the United States

An Introduction

The twenty-first century education generally, and schooling specifically, are complex sets of contradictions that make navigating a pathway from student to teacher a complex endeavor. Teacher preparation programs play a major role in the quality education PK-12 students receive. Teacher education programs continue to look for ways to best prepare teachers. Key players in the development of quality teacher education programs are the teacher candidates and how these programs impact those candidates' thoughts on teaching (Nuangchalerm & Prachagool, 2010). According to Banks (2014), teacher education programs are continually scrutinized for a variety of reasons many students in credential programs come into teacher preparation buying into misconceptions about the landscape of learners and learning. These misconceptions often become roadblocks to understanding and embracing the complex nuances of becoming a teacher. Two prevailing misconceptions are that (1) some people are born to teach and (2) most of the learning about teaching occurs while teaching.

The Educational Testing Complex

Educational coursework appears too often provide diminishing return on investments; several studies have indicated that teachers with advanced subject matter degrees, rather than advanced education degrees, produce students who perform better in math and reading. A credential in education may be sufficient to produce basic student learning, but greater content knowledge has been found to affect learning as much as advanced education degrees (Beare, Marschall, Torgerson, Tracz, & Chiero, 2012).

The importance of greater content knowledge in teacher preparation generates the following question: To be an effective teacher capable of implementing successful, equitable forms of education for all students, especially those learners historically underserved, is it sufficient for teacher candidates to simply, or just, pass exams like the CSET, in the case of California, or the PRAXIS, in the case of Louisiana, and many other states throughout the US? In this book we explore the narratives from two institutions, the University of La Verne and Louisiana State University and consequently a little context seems appropriate.

Many of the students at the University of La Verne are in a holding pattern toward obtaining teaching credentials. The students in this holding pattern have been in the program upwards of 30 months because they cannot pass the CSET. In 2008, when the economy tanked in California and there were very few jobs in teaching and the jobs that were in teaching were in secondary math and science. The program at the University of La Verne saw many who had degrees in something else other than math and science attempting to pass the CSETS in those content areas.

At Louisiana State University nearly all students pass the PRAXIS testing, but many find themselves competing for jobs with under skilled and wholly under qualified teachers from alternative certification programs who are not held accountable through a rigorous process like those who attend the four-year teacher preparation program at LSU. These complexities provide for unique and daunting challenges for both University of La Verne and LSU students.

A Tale of Two Schools

This project, as previously noted, is focused on the experiences of teacher candidates as they themselves discuss their understandings and participation in teacher education's credentialing processes at two different universities. This book, therefore, is situated within the context of two teacher education programs at two different universities in two different parts of the country.

The first school is the University of La Verne, located in Southern California. The University of La Verne's College of Education has a long tradition of preparing teachers. The students enter the teacher education program from colleges and universities from the entire state.

In California, the teacher education program is a post-bachelorette program, where the teacher candidates have bachelor's degrees in something and as the chapters in this book will illustrate that causes some point of concern in terms of being able to teacher advanced placement for example. A student can have a degree in Sociology, but if they can pass the CSET in math then they can become a math teacher. However, on the other hand, there are students who have degrees in the content area in which they want to teach and, yet, they cannot pass the CSET for their content area.

Miguel, for example, in chapter four shares, "You know I think I will be a pretty good teacher. I have several lived experiences that really shape my love of teaching but I cannot get over this CSET hurdle – which really frustrates me about this process." Miguel sees himself as a teacher; he feels he will be an excellent teacher. However, the testing complex of teacher education at present serves as a barrier to Miguel's path forward toward realizing his dream of becoming a teacher because, to date, he has not been able to successfully complete the intake to educator credentialing process.

LSU, in turn, is a flagship university for the state of Louisiana. Elementary and Secondary teachers can obtain licensure through the traditional undergraduate programs or through a Master of Arts in Teaching. The emphasis in the secondary teacher preparation programs is on disciplinary content as evidenced by the fact that secondary student degrees are conferred by the colleges of their academic disciplines and not the College of Human Sciences and Education. The elementary teacher preparation program has a much more pedagogical focus as most of the teacher preparation happens within the College of Human Sciences and Education.

The teacher education programs at both the University of La Verne and LSU follow clinical models. Students of elementary and secondary education are provided with opportunities for breadth and depth of classroom experience with master teachers throughout their preparation programs. For students from both institutions, the clinical model is based on emphasizing reflective practice, collaboration and classroom based inquiry. In addition, the fieldwork supervisors collaborate closely with the program faculty to ensure a strong balance between theory and practice.

While supportive in many ways of future teachers' learning and development of skills and knowledge needed to become a successful teacher, the clinical model does present challenges for not only the students but also for the institutions, programs, and faculty. For instance, finding meaningful sites that meet institutional and state goals for diversity with master teachers who engage sound pedagogical practices is daunting to say the least. In both contexts of University of La Verne and LSU, many of the local schools that serve diverse student populations are labeled by their states as underperforming and therefore not inhabited by educators who have evidenced successful teaching for diverse and all learners. Specifically, many of the teachers in low-performing and culturally diverse K-12 schools do not consistently demonstrate the pedagogical strength needed to mentor a developing new professional educator. Second, when the master teacher and the teacher candidate have philosophical difference, as teacher educators, we find that the experience is less meaningful for the candidates. Accordingly, many teacher candidates exit their teacher preparation programs suggesting that they learned most about in their coursework and field experiences is 'what not to do' as opposed to having had meaningful experiences to observe 'what to do' and thus observe, begin to develop, and engage in culturally relevant, critical praxis in the classroom and school.

As authors of this book, we also have served as faculty teaching in and directing the programs in our respective institutions. Hence, as teacher educators ourselves, we are committed to helping teacher candidates understand the overall significance of the curriculum and the context or learning/living landscape in which the curriculum is delivered. As teacher education faculty, we are focus in our teaching and content in teacher preparation coursework upon interdisciplinary themes as well as on the relationships between the curricular, teachers, and learners while engaging and critiquing the social order. We feel that it is important that future teachers learn about to identify, assess, and act on the many factors of the socio-historical context that dictate in many ways our own as well as the life chances and opportunities afforded to or taken away from PK-12 public school students.

As part of having a relevant and intellectual defensible standard in teacher preparation programs, candidates at both La Verne and LSU are required to document their progress toward the learning standards set out by Associate of Childhood Education International, the accrediting body of Elementary Education. Candidates at both institutions are also expected to gather evidence throughout their credentialing programs that connect to the professional standards expected by the specific state offices of education. While engaging those state credentialing-required learning standards in our coursework as teacher educators, we expect teacher candidates to think reflectively and analytically on course readings and activities in their field experience classrooms and on their past experiences in schools. This emphasis on critically and recursively considering requisite teacher knowledge in relation to context and student learning continues during the student teaching year to encourage and support the development and continuation of reflective practices in teacher candidates' teaching approaches and throughout their teaching careers (Fasching-Varner, Eisworth, Mencer, Linbom-Cho, Murray, & Morton, 2013).

Through the Fire: This Book Project

Developing a culture of evidence to assess and improve teacher preparation programs is a critical issue in United States education. Teacher education has been struggling with the challenge of preparing and retaining high-quality teachers who can work effectively with students from all cultural and racial backgrounds. Researchers Beare, Marchall, Torgerson, Tracz, and Chiero (2012) make the case that teacher education programs should incorporate new cultures of evidence and inquiry in teacher education with the hopes of providing transformational experiences for those who want to become teachers. They continue to make the case that teacher education programs need to include the nuance of culture and include a situated understanding of the role human interpretation in the use of evidence.

The teacher candidate narratives in this book reflect the coursework they have taken while on the journey of becoming a teacher for some while for others focuses more on their clinical experiences. We see both trajectories as critically important for teacher education programs. The candidate reflection is geared towards two audiences. The first audience is fellow teacher candidates and the second audience are those who prepare teachers. The purpose of the book is aimed at improving teacher preparation. Accordingly, as Beare, Marschall, Torgerson, Tracz, and Chiero (2012) point out, improvement in teacher education is fundamentally linked to several factors that include candidate knowledge, skills, and dispositions, and the candidate's actual practice in the classroom.

In the quest for any improvement in the process of preparing and credentialing teachers, the education community often looks to what we, the authors, consider to be very sterile results. The results of TPA test results, PRAXIS and CSET scores, adequate yearly progress (AYP), and the matter of how many boxes on official forms that teacher candidates are able to robotically check off are typically seen as evidence of improvement in many contemporary teacher education programs. Yet, test scores can be and often are realized without looking internally to what these test scores actually represent about teacher education programs and how they are doing in terms of effectively preparing future teachers to be successful in contemporary classrooms and schools. Test scores, and even the perspectives of teacher educators about those test scores, while to some degree very important, they do not represent the very audience they are supposed to represent as evidence of successful teacher preparation – the future teachers themselves.

Indeed, test scores do not reflect or carry the voices or knowledge derived from the lived experiences of teacher candidates who must successfully navigate through the teacher credentialing process to become teachers in their own right recognized by their states. Test scores do not represent those who are experiencing the program and are actually the focus of teacher preparation programs and the teacher credentialing process. Test scores likewise do not reflect what the teacher candidates who will come through teacher education in the future can learn from the teacher candidates who are currently navigating through teacher education today as well as those who have already gone through the fire of the teacher credentialing process.

Teachers' lives and careers must be studied in the context of their whole lives with attention given to the routes they have taken toward becoming educators. In this regard, studies of teachers' lives, and ideas about what it means to be a teacher, reveal life experiences prior to formal teaching. The experiences include teachers reflecting on being students themselves and how previous life experiences, as they relate to education and teaching, are more influential than other factors (such as preservice teaching education programs) that influenced beginning teachers' actions in the classroom (Ball & Goodson, 1985; Hayano, 1979; James, 2002).

Pointedly, a teacher's background and experiences influence the expectations the teacher holds for students and the perceptions and motives for teaching. The voices in this book will hopefully shed light on the culture-related perspectives in teacher education that give rise to a social change agency and educational opportunity for students in schools through the effective preparation of future educators (Dingus, 2003).

The Importance of This Volume

What can we learn from those teacher candidates who have made the journey in teacher education through the teacher credentialing and preparation process from intake to teacher? Many enter teacher education program across the United States and many of these candidates take the traditional route while others take the route of becoming a teacher through alternative teacher education – a disturbing yet growing trend. The candidates who contributed to this volume have taken the traditional route. In this volume we share the lived experiences of teacher candidates from two different universities in two different regions of the United States.

Sometimes poetic, sometimes painful, these compelling personal narratives of novice teachers in this volume provide a poignant view of the struggles, fears, and celebrations developing teachers traverse on the journey of induction into the profession. Teacher educators and teacher candidates alike will find much to explore and discuss in these chapters.

The journey of becoming a teacher is a complicated, emotional, and often intricate endeavor. Much has been written about pre-service teachers but rarely do we understand the journey through their own voices. Join the pre-service teachers in this book as they share their experiences, challenges, and victories through a series of powerful narratives. Committed to making the process more transparent for those embarking on a similar journey, the chapter authors share honest, personal, and heartfelt viewpoints about what it means to become a teacher. No stone of learning to teach is left unturned!

Putting to practice critical perspectives about what it means to teach in the 21st century, teacher candidates expose their vulnerabilities with a range of literary approaches including metaphor, reflective journaling, and storytelling. *Through the Fire* is, then, framed by teacher educator insights about the contexts and complexities of teaching. This text is by design intended to help both candidates and programs make sense of completing course work, subject matter and teaching methodologies. How to have relationships with their master teachers and university supervisors and what happens if the relationship goes south?

We believe it is also critically important for teachers who leave our programs to be prepared to teach the racial and linguistic diverse students in schools throughout the whole of the United States America, where being culturally responsive is more than just having a picture of Martin Luther King or Rosa Parks hanging on the wall. We also feel it is important for those reading this book, as well as who have completed or will complete teacher education programs to have the ability be blend theory with practice, and there in that intersection is the place where the journey of becoming a teacher is born.

Again, we caution against reading the narratives in this book as a recipe cookbook, how-to-guide, or other kind of source for magic bullet-type formulas on how to successfully become a teacher. The idea here in considering the narratives of novice teachers is to make connections to and draw on the idea of learning from the lived experiences of those subjected to our official processes in teacher education to improve the preparation of future teachers. We hope that by exploring and learning from the narratives of the novice teachers in this volume those individuals considering entering teacher education can also benefit by considering what it might look like to be supported to spend less time navigating the teacher credentialing process and teacher education system and more time learning how to become a successful teacher capable of implementing successful, equitable teaching and learning for all learners.

Reading This Book

This book is organized as a series of 15 narratives written as composite stories. While the names are fictitious the experiences of the candidates are real as told to us the authors of this book. Often, in narrative inquiry, composite stories are used to protect the confidentiality and anonymity of participants (Lindsay, Cross, & Ives-Baine, 2012). In our case, the purpose of the composite story is to represent the synergy of our collaboration while giving voice to each person. We authored these chapters using a composite approach and to craft chapters that read like auto ethnographic narratives so that readers better resonate with the experiences and that the chapters were formed drawing upon a multiplicity of real experiences, narratives, prompts, and interviews. The names are not the real participants, but are pseudonyms intended to help provide readers with the opportunity to better connect with each of the stories as they link the lessons to their own experiences.

What unifies the narratives in the book is that candidates while in their respective preparation program wrote them. While the journeys are different they do share some similar experiences. We have organized the chapters by student. We looked for a cross section of students based on race, class, gender, and sexuality and other lived experiences. The lived experiences that others can use as they begin their journey to teacher hood. The different lived experiences are also important for teacher educators. Teacher educators and teacher candidates the two are not mutually exclusive, a bridge that we are trying to merge with this book.

We are at a crossroads currently. Students in public school settings are not provided with a transformative education that situates them as competitive players in society. This is particularly true for students in urban and rural settings as well as racially, ethnically, and linguistically diverse backgrounds. This work, consequently, is important if we are to take serious preparing teachers who can enter a system that works against most of its constituents and engage students with a pedagogy that breaks cycles of poor education. We hope that in these narratives you find a renewed energy in the endeavor of becoming a teacher or preparing those who are becoming teachers.

CHAPTER 2

Tried and True

Geoffrey Jaynes

Back in the day, when I was young, Times when things were carefree and fun.
One day a trouble toiled my mind, An answer I truly struggled to find.
When my grandpa approached me, old and wise, Left me with a saying he said held no lies.
He said, "Son, when you struggle with something that makes you blue, Tried and true will always pull through."

Days would pass, and eventually would he, A hero and idol he was to me.
Eventually school came, a new world to explore, Creativity and fun, everything to adore!
But years would pass, it wasn't to be, That creativity and fun vanished from me.
Lectures and work, no time to play, The world turned dark, a solemn gray.

I refused, I wanted to fight!
This tried and true didn't seem right.
I crafted my wings, I wanted to be free, I wanted to fly, that would be me!

So I showed them my wings, but they called it defiance, I was beat and torn for my lack of compliance.
My wings shredded, replaced with a label, A heavy burden, that said I was unable.
They said, "Tried and true might pull me through" But that wasn't who I was, I wanted something new.
Hope and smile, I began to lack,
My wings had been torn, from the flesh on my back.

I once gazed upon the stars with a future so bright, But now I can't even see their light.
My dreams have faded, all but gone, Like water from a dry and old, cracked pond.
I look at the stars and cry, "I wish they only knew!" That tried and true, doesn't always pull through.

CHAPTER 3

Bianca: New Footprints on the Well-Trodden Path

I chose this title because I am currently a teaching credential candidate who is both eager and anxious to begin in my unique teaching journey, as others have done before me. I have a Bachelor's degree in English Education and a Masters in English Literature, so it probably comes as no surprise when I say that my content area is English. I have always had a deep-seeded passion for all things English and so I have made it my goal to help students see the value in what our language and literature have to offer them. I want students to see how language and literature can be and are used to impart social experiences and change in our world.

There are many reasons why I, and others like myself, want to teach. Some of us want to teach because we gain satisfaction in seeing others learn, because we want to make a significant contribution to society, because we want to impart our subject matter expertise, or, perhaps less respectably, because teachers are given many days off throughout the year. Many of us want to teach to make a difference, to improve things, to participate in a profoundly human and social experience, to change the world, sometimes one precious life after another (Ayers, 2010).

The reality of teaching is that there are many challenges that come with the various roles we are expected to fill. One of our most important roles is to make connections with all students, especially those with different backgrounds and cultures, because each child comes to the classroom with unique desires, abilities, intentions, and needs. Somehow, we must reach out to each student; we must meet each one (Ayers, 2010). While this is arguably the most important role a teacher will play in the life of a student, this is also one of the greatest challenges. It is necessary that teachers learn about the communities, cultures, and interests of their students so that a connection is even possible.

Another challenge for new teachers is just to figure out their own preferred methods and styles, and to accept that this might take time and a great deal of hard work. To make a life in teaching is largely to find your own way; to follow this or that thread; to work until your fingers ache, your mind feels as if it will unravel, and your eyes give out; and to make mistakes and then to rework large pieces again and again (Ayers, 2010).

In my own credential program so far there has been content that I found both helpful and unhelpful. The most helpful includes the course on how to teach English Language Learners, how to create a five-day unit, and when we focus on student-teacher relationships. The course that taught us how to teach ELD students was crucial because it taught us how to create lesson plans and use materials that will benefit both native English speakers and those for whom English is a second language. One main component of this class was implementing specially designed academic instruction in English, or SDAIE. The argument for using SDAIE and its approaches to teaching ELD students is that when limited-English-proficient students ... participate in well-designed, well implemented programs of instruction, they can successfully acquire English and they may reach satisfactory levels of competence in academic areas as well (Genzuk, 2011). What we learned in this course about what benefits ELD students, such as using realia, focusing on academic language, assessing prior knowledge, building new knowledge, collaborative problem-solving, and modeling, is beneficial for all students and can apply to every lesson we teach.

In addition to using these concepts in our lessons, I found that creating a unit lesson plan was helpful for me in multiple ways. So far in the program, I have been asked to create two five-day units and at first this was really tough because before this we had only ever been asked to teach the odd lesson here and there. I found this to be quite the learning curve for me but now that I have done it, I find it more fun to focus on something for a week, rather than the standalone lesson because it allows for more opportunities and projects to really get the students engaged. It also allowed me to go into more depth with the content so that I was more knowledgeable about the topics covered.

Lastly, I found that the focus on student-teacher relationships this term to be helpful because I know that there will be times in the future when I am having trouble connecting with students. In my current classes there is a strong focus on student relationships, communities, and culture; all things that will help us connect with our students if we make the effort. It is important for teachers to find out as much about their students' lives as they can, but it is also important to create your own sense of classroom community. Establishing respect for your students will in turn result in respect for you from them. Additionally, by being honest and authentic with your students, the seeds of trust will be sown, and classroom community can grow and flourish (Burant, Christensen, Salas, & Walters, 2010).

The parts of the program content that I did not find helpful include parts of the literacy in the disciplines course and the heavy emphasis on technology that this program contains. While I enjoyed the literacy course that taught us all how to teach reading in our specific content areas, I do think it was a little bit redundant for my discipline. I understand that teaching English and teaching how to read various English texts are different, but prior to that class it had never occurred to me that a teacher would not teach students how to read a poem, a speech, a play, informational text, persuasive text, etc. I have always understood that students need to be taught how to read these things with an English lens so I thought that holding an entire course on it was less helpful for me than perhaps for some of the other content areas.

I also found the emphasis on certain technology assignments to be unhelpful. I agree whole-heartedly that teachers need to implement technology for these twenty-first century learners, but some of the assignments required of us, such as making videos, do not necessarily seem to make me a better teacher. Again, I think it is necessary to know about the different technology assessments we can assign but holding an entire course on technology, coupled with the diversity and interactions course (which I did perceived to be a useful class), and various other video projects seems to be unhelpful at times to make me a better teacher. I think that time would be better served teaching us how to teach media literacy, because media literacy education "requires active inquiry and critical thinking about the messages we receive and create," and it "recognizes that media are a part of culture and function as agents of socialization (Media Literacy Ed). I think it is very important to implement technology into my future classes because students are constantly using technology in their everyday lives, but they are also bombarded with media advertisements and underlying stereotypes that I believe we should be teaching more about. There are certainly benefits to implementing technology in the classroom, but I felt that the overemphasis on it in this program was unnecessary and would be better spent on teaching media literacy.

With the current education trends today, it is also important for me to be aware that I will come across teachers who are excited and willing to implement these new changes as well as others who are apprehensive or even doubtful. I have already noticed this separation when it comes to Common Core. I have only encountered one or two teachers that have admitted they will be slow to implement the Common Core Standards, but I have also heard complaints from parents about Common Core and their concerns with how this will affect their child's learning. Some think the CCSS are only about repetition and rote memorization but there is actually room for freedom and creativity in the content because there are "ways in teachings for creativity supports learning the skills and knowledge of the ELA Common Core and ways in which teaching to the ELA Common Core can also nurture students' creativity" (Beghetto, Kaufman, & Baer, 2014, p. 61). I am personally excited about Common Core and have so far found it to be a successful form of teaching.

Along with the understanding of how Common Core can be a gateway for more interactive teaching and project-based learning comes change in the sciences with the Next Generation Science Standards (NGSS). I think the new science standards will work nicely with Common Core since the goal is help students learn how scientists work, not just how science works. The vision of NGSS "is to use scientific and engineering practices as a means for students to show evidence they are able to apply knowledge," or in other words, we want students to integrate practice with content (Pruitt, 2014, p. 146). The NGSS argue that it is through this "integration that students are able to show their mastery of content, but also an understanding of the accumulation of scientific knowledge" (Pruitt, 2014, p. 147). Having an understanding of the way these new standards work, both Common Core and NGSS, can help me as a teacher as I plan possible cross curricular lessons, units, and projects.

My advice to students who want to teach would be to make sure they have spent time in classrooms to figure out how they interact with students and what age they are best suited to work with. Observing in a classroom reveals much more than I first thought it did. When I originally discovered I wanted to be a teacher, I thought I wanted to work with elementary students, but three weeks into my first semester as a Liberal Studies major I realized I wanted to work with students who were able to hold deeper conversations about the content. My observations helped me realize that I wanted to major in English and then become a high school English teacher. I was also a high school track coach so I knew I could connect with students that age. So, to those wanting to become teachers, I would first ask them why they want to be a teacher, encourage them, honestly explain to them what the credential program is like, and what the first year of teaching is like.

One piece of advice that I often refer to myself is to make sure we, as teachers, set realistic expectations for ourselves. Coming fresh out of a credential program we are full of enthusiasm and energy to create the best lesson plans we can think of. However, the more time I spend in the classroom the more I realize that not every lesson will be smooth sailing, and not every lesson will be your best lesson. When this happens, we have to give ourselves a break and we can be honest with the students by admitting to them the lesson didn't quite go as planned. It is important to remember this because a "common experience of teachers is to feel the pain of opportunities missed, potential unrealized, students untouched" (Ayers, 2010, p. 21). This will happen to us, but we must remember that we are doing our best. All we can do is accept the situation, and learn from it.

I would like to tell credential students that one of the most important components of a successful classroom is respect. We must make "respect central to [our] classroom culture" because the only way to hold students to high and rigorous expectations is to gain their respect and their acknowledgement that your class will lead to real learning that will benefit them (Burant et al., 2010).

This is something that is reiterated to us throughout the program, but it is also something that I have always been very passionate about. We cannot expect to gain students' respect if we do not give students the respect they deserve. The second point here is about making the content relevant to their lives because life in school must be thought of as life itself, not simply preparation for later life (Ayers, 2010). This is their life right now so we need to treat it as such as we create our curriculum.

Lastly, I would like to point out to these credential students that often teachers are not viewed in the brightest light when it comes to national education plans and reform.

While working through my teaching credential I have met a few challenges. Politicians tend to blame poor teachers for our nation's education troubles, such as education gaps, and parents tend to agree, but if educators had gotten to the podium first and demanded change from the politicians, parents would have likely nodded their heads in agreement to that as well. Conclusions being drawn from a growing number of researchers argue that 30 years of test scores have not measured a decline in America's public schools, but are rather a metric of the country's child poverty … and the broadening divide of income equality (Raden, 2015). We all want what is best for our students, but we should be aware that we are often the ones to blame for the education gaps are likely a much larger problem in America.

In my first term of the program we needed to give lessons and complete observation hours and the teacher I ended up with had a very different teaching style to mine. It was difficult to watch her do things one way when I would have chosen the opposite. It did not affect my lessons, but it made it tough to go to her for help. Despite this hardship, this was the first time I realized I had a teaching style, which helped me as I continued to give more lessons and move to other classes. From this experience I could recognize the things I wished to avoid as a teacher and the specific ways in which I would do it differently. Working with this teacher not only showed me what I disliked, but it forced me to come up with alternative methods to reach the students. This is an experience I can now look back on with less frustration and more appreciation as I reflect on that term.

I can say with confidence that I have come a long way from when I began this program. Although I have yet to complete my student teaching, I recognize the growth in myself in my confidence, my knowledge, my lesson planning, and my delivery. I have been able to find the balance in a lesson between what they need to know and what they need to discover on their own. I am now also less rigid when teaching and feel that I more comfortable facilitating discussions with my students.

The program at the University of La Verne has been wonderful when it comes to preparing us to teach all learners. We have learned how to teach English Language Learners and meet their needs, including being able to identify the levels of second language acquisition. For example, we are taught that comprehensible input is of the utmost importance; meaning we need to speak at an appropriate pace (not too fast or too slow, which results in unnatural speech), enunciate clearly, and use gestures and body language, when appropriate, to reinforce your point (Vogt & Echevarria, 2006). Our classes have prepared us very well for teaching English Language Learners, which will be constantly helpful, given the demographic changes in the country and especially in California.

The La Verne Program has also taught us how to teach both special needs students and gifted and talented students. For example, I did a project on GATE were I learned that it is crucial for teachers not to assign more work for their gifted students, but to hold them to a higher expectation. It would be unfair to give them more work because of their intelligence, but it is fair to hold them to a higher standard than that of their classmates. Teachers of gifted students should provide differentiated curriculum through the use of depth and complexity, acceleration, tiered assignments, and independent contracts as well as provide both collaborative learning with flexible groupings and opportunities for independent study (GATE Teacher Certification).

Lastly, the program has taught us how to reach students of different backgrounds and cultures, including students from urban schools. What this program first taught us was how reflect on our own lives, values, and beliefs so that we can be aware of them before walking into any school because as teachers we must come to understand ourselves-who we are and what we know and value-as well as what we believe about teaching and learning (Richert, 2012). Once we come to terms with our own beliefs and values, we can then better understand and hopefully better connect with students from different backgrounds. When creating curriculum for students in urban communities, it can be difficult but a teacher needs to learn to balance what is 'required' to teach with what he or she believes she 'ought' to teach given what he or she knows about the students, including who they are, what they already know, and what is valued in their communities (Richert, 2012). One of the most important ways to successfully teach diverse students from urban schools is to really learn about their culture and their community so that we can create the content to be, even slightly, more to their interests and opportunities.

I want to be a teacher because I have a passion for the content and a passion for sharing that content with others. I want others to be as excited as I am about English, or at least parts of it, and I want others to see the value in what this content has to offer. I want students to know the power of the written word and of the spoken word. I want them to see my class as a form of expression and as a place to analyze the expressions of others. I do not expect students to love everything about my class, but my goal is for them to discover what they do like about my class. If I approach the material with enthusiasm and provide them with various outlets to demonstrate their knowledge I think they will eventually find that book they love, or even better, a genre they like so that they can continue to read in the future or produce work of their own. I genuinely care for others and I want them to share in the happiness that English brings to me though for them it might be another subject altogether. Being able to answer this question important because I think our answers often change throughout the program as we become more knowledgeable about the complexities of teaching and reaching students. This is a question that teaching candidates should ask themselves every term because it requires reflection. One cannot help altering his/her answers based on the new views and appreciations they have gained throughout the most recent term.

Prior to beginning the credential program my teaching philosophy was centered mostly on wanting to share my subject matter with students because of my enthusiasm for it and the importance it holds in our world. Now, however, my philosophy has expanded quite a bit over the course of the program. My philosophy still consists of maintaining the enthusiasm and value of my content, but it now also encourages inquisitiveness and personal connection. I believe students should be interacting closely and deeply with various works in various forms in order to ask personal, political, and cultural questions that will lead to new views about our world. I want students to walk out of my class with a newfound perspective and knowledge about their world that will, ideally, help them grow. The growth I have shown here are something teacher candidates and teacher educators can use to help reflect on their own teaching philosophies and how they may have changed over time. I think it is important to discuss these things because it shows that the program has made an impact on me as a person and through my views on teaching. We must continue to challenge ourselves and by reflecting on our experiences and our teaching beliefs we are doing just that.

My lived experiences are also a point of reflection for me. I am a White female from a White family in a predominately white city. Because of this, I am concerned that I will have a hard time connecting with students from diverse backgrounds, and similarly, I am concerned that I will demand of the students what I grew up thinking was important. To my family, family is important, grades are important, sports are important, and, when old enough, holding a job is important. However, this is not something I should project onto my students because I may have students that are juggling much more than I did in their homes lives so that they don't have time to work or play a sport. I recognize that I was only able to do all of the things I did because my family was able to afford for me to be in sports, help me with my homework, and take care of the household and my younger sisters so that I could hold a part-time job after school and on weekends. Not everyone has this luxury. Additionally, it was always understood in my house that we should strive for college. However, for some students, college may not feel like an option. It might appear to be too far of a reach or too difficult to take out a loan for school. As a teacher I want to encourage students to go to college, but I do not want them to feel alienated if college appears to be less possible for them. It is for reasons such as these that teachers need to get to know their students, their students' communities, and what they want for their future.

I have accepted my lived experiences for what they are and have moved forward to focus on allowing students to show me their lived experiences, rather than projecting mine onto them. My experiences can be used as an example of someone who was afraid that connecting with diverse students would be an issue. Now, however, I have accepted my background and where I come from and I choose not to let it affect my future relationships. Students might look at my face and see someone who cannot connect with them, but when they see that I truly care about them they will realize a connection can be made. We all have unique backgrounds and lived experiences but it is important to remember that these "are the makings of our personal identity and the foundation on which we build the professional identity that will guide us in our work (Richert, 2012). Once we accept our lived experiences we can remind ourselves of the values and beliefs we maintain, and we must use these to expand our values and beliefs in order to become better teachers. We need our own experiences at the forefront of our minds so that do not push these experiences on others and so we can be reminded that the student who just walked through the door has a very different life experience to ours.

The Authors' Response to Bianca

Bianca's chapter provided some problematic statement for us as the authors of this book and we want to end her chapter with some advice to her as well as others who may share some of these well intended non malice thoughts about children who did not grow up with their White middle class values. This is advice is not meant to be mean spirited or attacking her and others in anyway but to give her and others something to think about moving forward and we also think these parting thoughts will erase some of the concerns that have been expressed in the last part of the chapter.

Bianca and others, it is important to unhook from Whiteness because it may hinders the preparation of teachers to effectively teach all students. For teachers to be successful teaching all students, you and others must learn to be warm demanders who engage in culturally responsive teaching, learning, and assessment practices. Following Ware (2006), warm demander pedagogy is a component of culturally responsive teaching. "Culture is variable that is often overlooked as a function of student success" (Ware, 2006, p. 428). Teachers who adopt a warm demander pedagogy are responsive to the culture of students and thus recognize and address the ways that race and racism structure the lives of all individuals as beneficiaries or targets of the systemic privileging of Whiteness. Teachers who are warm demanders engage and prepare the students for the White middle class norms of dominant society while simultaneously drawing the students' backgrounds into the classroom as a valued source of knowledge that belongs in the curriculum. Teachers who are warm demanders thus view teaching as a political, not neutral, act.

Pointedly, most teachers today – a predominantly White, female, primary English speaking group, continue to enter the classroom knowing little about their own racial identity development or any other group other than their own and unable to identify, implement or assess teaching and assessment strategies that are culturally responsive. Most teachers today continue to enter the classroom best prepared to teach students from the increasingly non-existent normative standard of White, middle-class, primary English speaking, two – parent families. What we want to leave you and others with who are reading this chapter is to make sure future teaches enter the classroom prepared to teach all learners and unhook from the paradigm of White superiority and Black and Brown inferiority (Hayes & Juarez, 2012; Hayes, Juarez, & Cross, 2012; Juarez & Hayes, 2012).

CHAPTER 4

Cecilia: Wisdom Is Earned through Experience

What we learn through school, work, and life experience adds to the wisdom we acquire. I have been fortunate to implement my knowledge of art and education through teaching as an adjunct art instructor. In addition, I have taught high school courses in child development, career training, and graphic arts. Throughout my professional experience within the higher educational setting, I created a syllabus, selected books to incorporate within the curriculum, and assessed student work. For the high school classes, I created lesson plans, selected the curriculum, planned fieldtrips, and coordinated student events. However, I feel that it would be fair to give me and other credential students, credit for previous teaching experience. In addition to teaching experience, I have a California Adult Education Clear Teaching Credential and a Master of Education. This program requirements need to take into consideration the education and experience of the teaching credential candidates in order to avoid unnecessarily starting everyone from square one. For example, some of the fieldwork requirements and the introductory courses could be waived for those who have at least two years of teaching in a public school setting.

My experience included teaching students of all backgrounds, socio-economic levels, and mixed abilities. Incidentally, I decided to get a single subject teaching credential in art to continue working in education and to become a full-time teacher. I enjoy learning and teaching in the subject areas I have studied. My students have told me that they like attending my classes. I find teaching meaningful, especially, when students become motivated to succeed in my class and gain a hope for their future. Rather than facilitating only teacher-centered instruction, I seek to motivate by giving students some choices. Reeve, Bolt, and Cai (1999) support this instructional practice by emphasizing the importance of creating a learning environment, which promotes autonomous learning.

Throughout my teaching experience, I have reflected on what I need to change or revise in order to meet the challenges that are sure to arise. Although I have earned my Adult Education Teaching Credential, the best way I have learned to teach is by having my own class, coupled with supportive administrators. In my experience, clear and positive communication with colleagues and administrators is one of the most important keys to successful teaching. Conversely, without this support teaching can become extremely difficult. Administrators that support their teachers will help provide staff with resources, professional development, and help them resolve issues. Above all, on the job training has led to wisdom I have gained throughout my teaching career.

During my seven years teaching, I have learned to work with administrators, colleagues, students, parents, and the community. At first, it was a steep learning curve and I spent much of my time trying to figure out the school culture, policies, and getting acquainted with students and teachers For example, at times I did not know who to ask for books and materials because it was unclear if the school district would provide them or the Regional Occupational Program. I had asked the secretary and she told me I could order them through her office. By the way, I later found out that I had to order books from my supervisor, and not the school district. As a result, my students did not have books for a month and were not taking the class seriously. Thus, I had to plan activities and lesson plans on a daily basis and I felt that much of the class time was not as productive as I had intended. Finally, when the books arrived I was able to create a structure where students were learning and provided a framework for the course. The teachers' workbook edition included a wealth of activities to enhance student learning through projects such as posters, plays, and other activities. Hence, students were engaged in the learning process and their behavior improved. When students created posters, they can practice and improve their presentation, artistic, and writing skills (Newbrey & Baltezore, 2006). Furthermore, I learned that it was important to know who to ask for materials, and information, and most of all support.

Generally speaking, excellent communication and interpersonal skills are necessary when working with the people; especially, in education. According to Sindhi (2013), it is very important for principals to demonstrate excellent interpersonal skills when speaking to teachers and students. Doing so could contribute to the creation of a positive learning atmosphere and safe school climate (Sindhi, 2013). Additionally, teachers have to be comfortable talking to parents and administrators when solving problems or making recommendations. Timing is important when communicating to parents; especially, when their child is at risk of getting low or failing grades. This gives the parents a chance to find out how their child can improve and also discover the cause of the problem. Authors described ways educators could develop solutions when faced with the problem of numerous failing grades. For example, Sanchez (2007) stated how parents were relieved to hear that monthly parent workshops would be available. Furthermore, these parents were so happy to hear that additional volunteer opportunities would be discussed throughout the year.

Parents don't like to hear that their child is not doing well at school, but they usually would rather know before it results in a permanent grade on the child's report card. Likewise, teachers need to let the parents know when students are achieving their educational goals. Keeping parents involved in their child's education is vital to student success. According to a study conducted by Wang and Sheikh-Khalil (2014), results indicated a positive correlation amongst parental involvement, educational success, and the emotional well-being teens.

Additionally, I have had parents volunteer for many school events. This included chaperoning field trips, contributing to fundraisers, gathering canned goods for food drives, and assisting at special events. Whenever I contacted the parents, I liked to let them know that I appreciate having their student in my class. Positive interactions between parents and teachers also helped students know that we all support their academic success.

The courses I have taken towards the teaching credential program have been a good review of some of my existing knowledge and also have provided information pertaining to the changes that will be taking place. For instance, the implementation of Common Core Standards and Smarter Balance testing are new methods of teaching and assessment. Rather than attempting to remember numerous facts, the Smarter Balance testing will assess students' research skills (Sarles, 2013). This is a dramatic shift in testing methods when comparing previous ways of assessing. How to assess students' progress has been an ongoing conversation between teachers, students, parents, and administrators. Currently, we are preparing to try improved ways to assess student's skills and abilities that will better prepare them for success after they graduate from high school.

I have had conversations with teachers currently working in K-12 grades who have expressed their concern about these changes. They have told me that they do not feel that they are well informed and are not prepared to implement of these programs. As a result of my current courses in the credential program, veteran teachers have asked me to give them any resources and information regarding Common Core Standards. Although the school districts are in the process of training their teachers through professional development, some teachers do not feel prepared for such vast changes. According to Williams (2014), both "the National Education Association (NEA), one of the country's most powerful teachers' unions," opposed Common Core standards" (p. 1). Although opposing opinions exist, supporters of Common Core are also voicing their opinion. These people seek to refute what they believed to be a false representation of the curriculum (Ujifusa, 2013).

In contrast, I'm excited about the gradual implementation of Common Core, and have had the chance to understand the changes and apply some of the strategies during my fieldwork. For example, I have created and implemented lesson plans for art, where students work with a partner, or form teams, to brainstorm ideas. These group dynamics lead to incorporating the creative process in the most efficient manner. By collaborating, they practice speaking and listening. Likewise, students also learn to think and work independently by having time to think before they contribute to their group. They learn to contribute ideas, work together as a team, sharpen their social skills, and give constructive feedback. Providing opportunities for students to solve problems, listen to each other, write their ideas, and present to the class, are all part of developing skills that prepare students for their future. According to Pavlov (2013), incorporating an aesthetic mode of enquiry can help students improve their creativity. In addition to developing fine arts skills, students who are taught art in this manner are likely to brainstorm creative solutions pertaining to everyday situations. The visual arts are an excellent platform for creative expression and communicating by using images, text, and current trends in technology. In addition, summative assessment is a natural aspect to the creative process as affirmed by Andrade, Hefferen, and Palma (2014), "As the teachers saw improvements in student engagement and the quality of art making, they embraced formative assessment. They made seismic shifts I their assessment practiced, moving from end-of unit assessment critiques that mirrored their experience with studio practice, to ensuring that assessment is informative and ongoing by having students review and talk about their works-in-progress" (p. 36).

Generally, art students do not have opportunities to practice their writing skills in K-12 grades; however, college art classes require incorporating assignments which require reading and writing. For example, when I taught college art courses, I included a text book in my syllabus and assigned chapters to read. In addition, students had to write a report about a famous artist. Likewise, high school art teachers can incorporate the Common Core language arts standards by having art students write artist statements to accompany their artwork. This is common practice when preparing for an art exhibit. The art exhibit can serve as a summative form of assessment. As a result, students will be able to talk about their artwork in a manner that shows their understanding of the language and skills unique to the visual arts.

Furthermore, my technology class in the teaching credential program has kept me current in the latest trends in using computer technology in education: social media, resources for online collaboration, and internet safety for students. In the past, I have been confident in working with computer technology as an art tool; however, I was not sure if social media had any place in the classroom. My instructor in Technology for Educators has led the way in demonstrating how to use the Internet applications including social media in K-12 grades. Vickers, Field, and Melakoski (2015) stated that teaching students about social media resulted in positive learning outcomes. Consequently, I am more confident in my knowledge and skills using computer technology for education and instruction. For this reason, I have been selected to assist with the first Smarter Balance testing at the high school where I work.

Contemporary Issues/Foundations and Introduction to Teaching/Single Subject has provided me with an additional perspective on the social issues in public education. I have been able to build on the information and experiences I gained throughout my career in education. My Associate of Arts in Social and Behavioral Sciences had touched on many of the issues we have discussed. In particular, through this course, I have had a chance to reflect and elaborate on my current observations and research. This class emphasizes teaching in public education and urban schools. I have enjoyed learning how to incorporate social justice issues into my curriculum. Art has traditionally been a gateway to reflect social issues in our culture. Teaching students how art could reflect social issues helped them express current discuss and express that they encountered throughout their social lives (Kirlew, 2011). It has emphasized our role as advocates for the economically disadvantaged in the surrounding communities and possibly where we work. It emphasizes our responsibility as educators to become socially critical teachers, as stated by O'Donoghue and Berard (2014),

> While socially engaged design offers opportunities to change aspects of the world for the better, we must be mindful that it might also eliminate other socially empowering practices in its efforts to "improve" perceived living conditions or ways of being in the world. Socially engaged design practice's investment in the future, then, might not always be as enabling as it appears – something to be mindful of when advancing this form of design as a means of enlarging one's capacity to live in the world. That said, socially engaged design enlarges the possibilities of living and world making by promoting living practices that are mindful, expansive, and collaborative. (p. 7)

On the other hand, although the teaching credential program has enhanced my readiness to teach art in the high school setting, it has been somewhat repetitive for me. I already have teaching experience, an Adult Education Credential, and a Master of Education; furthermore, I have implemented and studied a majority of the subjects that are presented in the teaching credential program. For instance, I have taken the following courses in my previous graduate work: Global Learning/Cross Cultural Classroom; Instructional Design/Development; Curriculum Foundations; Advanced Educational Psychology;

History and Philosophy of Education. These upper division graduate classes should count towards my teaching credential but were not considered for equivalency.

My previous graduate education, coupled with my teaching experience, could have been applied toward the teaching credential program. The university's role is to formally recommend teacher candidates to the California Commission on Teaching Credentialing, and has the authority to waive courses based on proof of equivalency. Although teaching is not a career change for me, I had to start at the beginning of the teaching credential program. I would recommend that those who have teaching experience consider applying for an administrative or pupil services credential so that they can get credit for their teaching experience. These are programs that require five years of teaching experience to get accepted. This is one solution to advance in a career in education and not repeating basic teaching courses.

As I reflect on my choice to apply at this private university, I know I will have to repay at least $25,000 by the end of my program. Although I appreciate the student loans, I have struggled to buy the course materials and pay my bills; moreover, I am a substitute teacher do not have any family support. This is a large cost I have incurred and I constantly feel a sense of buyer's remorse because I did not investigate the details of their limited scope of financial assistance in the Title V funding, specifically, towards financial assistance for the Latinos in graduate programs. Those funds have been allocated towards creating tutoring programs and professional development for current faculty and staff.

For this reason, I would recommend to new and prospective students, who want to apply for a teaching credential, especially at a private university, ask all the right questions regarding financial assistance and that they read all the information before making a commitment. I have discovered that each college and university decide how to allocate their financial aid opportunities to students. Colleges and universities receive government funding based on meeting specific criteria and meeting the needs of the student population they serve. Schools have many choices on how they want to spend the funding as long as they keep records that they used the funds for the intended purposes. In hind sight, I would have been a better consumer if I asked the right questions before signing up for the program. Generally, private universities are structured to recruit students' who have strong financial support from their families, such as upper middle class and wealthy international students. In the teaching credential program and for graduate school, private universities do not overtly discriminate towards low income students; however, they do not participate in state or federal programs that would make it more affordable, such as Cal Teach, which applies Cal Grant A or B financial aid towards earning a teaching credential. Most universities do not consider a teaching credential to be graduate studies because it consists of 400 level courses, in comparison to the graduate course that are 500 levels. Not all colleges or universities participate in Cal Teach, although, in California one cannot teach without a teaching credential. Student loans are the only source of financial aid available for most graduate studies. Although I am grateful to be able to receive student loans, I would have appreciated having scholarships or grants instead.

Incidentally, in a recent press release, Stanford University announced that they will be giving free tuition to incoming students whose families make $125,000 per year or less. In addition, room and board will be free of charge for students whose families make less than $65,000. I was please to know that such a prestigious private university would provide such generous financial assistance to those in the middle class and especially to lower income students. They are leading the way in true social justice by giving all students a fair chance at succeeding in higher education.

After having taught as an adjunct art instructor at the community college and university level, I have appreciated the teaching methods of higher education. First, I had to specialize in my subject matter. One way I proved my subject matter competence is by showing proof of experience in graphic design. I presented my portfolio of professional projects I had designed. Second, I was required to have a bachelor's and master's degree. Being an expert in my field was the main requirement for becoming an adjunct instructor. There are some fields in higher education that do not require the instructor to have a master's degree, but instead they must have a bachelor's in that field and at least five years of work experience in that field. Instructors must have extensive knowledge and experience when teaching the following certificate programs: applied arts, auto technology, cosmetology, drafting, water technology, and performing arts. Likewise, single subject, middle and high school teachers must be experts in this subject matter in order to properly prepare students for their careers. As stated by Stewart (2014), curriculum planning involves an assessment of student needs, interests, and questions; local considerations; institutional mandates; and a host of other factors, including the passions and expertise of the teacher.

My teaching philosophy has continued to develop as I continue to learn new issues relating to art, computer technology, and educational requirements. My education and teaching experience have helped me to build a strong rapport with students, parents, faculty, and staff. Elementary and secondary programs need aim to prepare students for higher education, and for their careers. For example, the Westside Unified School District is facilitating a series of free college workshops for parents of elementary students (Pittenger, 2015). These opportunities are presented by the College Academy for Parents (Pittenger, 2015). Additionally, authors suggest the integration of curriculum, which actively discusses college and career opportunities throughout students' high school experience (Livingston, 2010).

We can begin by implementing rigorous programs, financial support, and opportunities that will build on their strengths. In addition, art teachers need to let students explore their creative expression through trying new ideas and incorporating new mediums, including digital technology. This is supported by the Common Core Standards as illustrated by Jarvis (2014), there should be an associated emphasis on the value of expressive making and a move away from the focus on 'copying' and 'representation.' In addition there needs to be much more of a critical approach to the looking at and understanding of art, craft and design and its place in the cultural fabric of a society. It is essential that teachers and students stay current on technology trends, grasp a global perspective, and attain specific skills in their major area of study. Helping students understand the educational requirements, financial resources, and their options are the initial steps in assisting students. Setting high academic standards, coupled with parental teacher support, can provide students with a positive learning environment. Keeping students accountable and motivated is vital in all helping students succeed (Jarvis, 2014).

In summary, my experience in the teaching credential has been both exciting and educational. This teaching credential was the missing link in my resume and hopefully will lead to more job opportunities in the future. The Adult Education Credential I already have is limited and is slowly phasing out due to state budget cuts. Teaching as an adjunct art instructor has been an opportunity of a lifetime; however, it does not generate enough income for my family and me. Hiring adjunct instructors has been a strategic means for colleges and universities in an effort to meet their budget. As an artist and educator, my teaching credential will allow me to teach a subject matter. My teaching experience along with my education will be an asset to any school district who recognizes talent and professionalism. I command excellence in my students with an intellectual and gentle manner. I am devoted to the education of our youth and also infuse a sense of humor. Above all, I am highly motivated and eager to get involved in the classroom helping students succeed.

CHAPTER 5

Covington: A Journey through the Hundred Acre Wood

My name is Covington Richardson and I am currently in the process of acquiring my California single subject teaching credential for social studies in secondary education. In all honesty, education was something I had never really thought about until I had become disillusioned early on in the process of working toward my *Juris Doctorate*. This disillusionment caused myself to really weigh my options since I was already burnt out with the field before I had even really gotten there. I used to get extremely excited at the thought of litigating a case, but once I saw the unfortunate realities of my chosen legal field my feelings of animosity and resentment increased ten-fold. It was actually my wife who had suggested taking two summer education courses at the University of La Verne. She thought that I would make a good social studies teacher because of my love for the field and my ability to communicate boring historical information in a way that was actually interesting. I decided to take the two courses and I was instantly hooked. In a sense, the way I feel as an educator in the classroom is the same feeling the thought of being a lawyer used to give me so long ago.

There are a variety of reasons why individuals decide to enter the field of secondary social studies education. Laura Robb (2003), author of *Teaching Reading in Social Studies, Science, and Math*, identifies a key reality that some teachers become dispensers of knowledge, while others integrate storytelling and projects, and orchestrate activities (Robb, 2003). I personally found my own niche within the confines of dispensing knowledge and orchestrating meaningful activities that are fun, interactive, and content driven. My love of social studies, primarily with my educational background in law and history, drives my development as a social studies teacher forward because I am able to share my knowledge in a way that is meaningful to the students, along with providing a platform for culturally reflective social studies instruction that promotes inclusiveness and creativity.

When I first began my journey in education, I did not really have any teaching beliefs that guided my curriculum development because it was an entirely new experience for myself personally. I had no experience in the field of education nor did I understand the skills required to deal with the complexities of student personalities, curriculum development, culture, and educational bureaucracy. Some of these early obstacles were rather easy to overcome because psychologist and neuroscientist have learned a lot in the past few decades about where these skills come from and how they are developed (Tough, 2013). These obstacles were easy to overcome because I had the necessary guidance and instruction through the social studies credentialing program at the University of La Verne. I was able to apply the necessary strategies to anticipate, mitigate, and correct many of the problems that I would be faced with as a secondary educator.

I quickly decided to complete the credentialing program and enter the field of social studies because it's the most effective and most enjoyable way to change the world. That's the bottom line: We need to change this world, and this is the way I'm choosing to do it (Aguilar, 2013). This philosophy has become the foundation of why I teach. I have the ability to use historical, political, and economic information in a way that is student-centered and culturally reflective of the students and their experiences. Similarly, this philosophy promotes the ultimate goal of correcting injustices by intertwining the content material with meaningful student-center activities that have culturally reflective and critical pedagogy embedded into the foundations of the curriculum. I also have the ability to scaffold my culminated knowledge in a way that is meaningful and interactive. It is important to also understand that most ... students seem desperate to blend in, to look right, to not make a spectacle of themselves (Edmundson, 2014). This is an aspect of institutional suppression that affects both educational instruction and student interactions because the students are attempting to conform to an established set of values which are not their own. However, through the implementation of critical and culturally reflective pedagogy in my social studies classroom I believe that I can mitigate and correct these trends through awareness, promotion of creativity, application of knowledge, and involvement in the community.

The Credential Program: A Journey through the Process

My experience in the University of La Verne education-credentialing program started with my completion of Diversity Interaction and the Learning Process and Theories and Methods of Education for Linguistically Diverse Students. These two courses, as identified in the preliminary meetings with my academic advisor, were the introduction courses to the single subject credential program. Diversity, Interaction, and the Learning Process was extremely beneficial to my understanding and ability to effectively reach and communicate social studies content material to the students while taking into account the cultural background of the students in question. We learned the fundamentals of education in both multiple and single-subject format, along with learning certain strategies that can enhance the learning environment of the classroom. I took Theories and Methods of Education for Linguistically Diverse Students, during the same session and it was with this course that I was introduced to many teaching concepts and requirements that would be seen in corresponding education courses. Some of these concepts and requirements included ELA and Common Core Standards, along with the strategies to achieve the required learning objectives throughout a unit or lesson. This course was extremely important to my development as a social studies educator in a secondary classroom setting because I was able to study and learn about the numerous teaching hurdles that accompany academic instruction, along with having the opportunity to develop and present my skills as a social studies educator in a classroom environment. Gary Fenstermacher and Jonas Soltis (2009) identified that perhaps it is necessary to adopt such an approach to teaching that capitalizes to well on structural and organizational features of contemporary schooling (Fenstermacher & Soltis, 2009). This approach enhanced my ability to run through mock lessons, develop an understanding of Blooms Taxonomy, understand how to organize a lesson plan, and the numerous strategies that are available for ELA instruction in a social studies classroom. These two courses, along with the motivation that I had personally culminated, significantly contributed to my willingness and enthusiasm to enter the field of education.

During my next semester, I enrolled in Introduction to Reading for Single Subject, Teaching Strategies, and Learning Technology for Educators. This semester proved to be more difficult than I had anticipated because I had to make up my observation hours for my summer courses and transfer them into my observations at North Ontario High School. Even though I had this obstacle to overcome, the material provided in these three courses significantly enhanced my effectiveness as an educator, as well as contributing to my successful completion of the observed lessons requirements. The Teaching Strategies course significantly improved my abilities to communicate lesson objectives and content material in a way that was coherent and understandable. Similarly, the technology course also has contributed to my development as a social studies educator because it completely opened my eyes to the possibilities of technology application in a social studies classroom. The most beneficial experience, however, came in the observation portions of my Introduction for Reading in Single Subject course. Many teachers know that teenagers are struggling with their reading skills, and that there are very specific reasons why ... and if content area teachers and those teaching English and social studies want students to become proficient in reading, we need to integrate comprehension strategies (McKnight, 2013). I was able to observe what not to do in the context of classroom instruction. Nearly all of the positive educational elements that I had learned up to this point were completely dismissed by this teacher and the students' performance reflected this reality. I was able to see how the reading and teaching strategies that I was learning could actually improve the retention rate and educational ability of the students in my classroom.

The two classes that probably have engaged me the most has been Introduction to Teaching Single Subject and Teaching in Content Area. These two courses have actually offered the most benefit to my development as an educator and my ability to reach the students in a meaningful way. Both courses introduced the importance of critical pedagogy in the field of education and provided ways to incorporate critical pedagogy, such as application of theory, into a secondary classroom environment. My content area teaching course has significantly improved my cultural and demographic awareness of the school in which I teach; an aspect that I had previously been completely oblivious too when growing up. This has helped my ability to reach the students on a meaningful level in my American Government classroom, along with contributing to my scaffolding abilities that communicate new information in a relatable and relevant way. The Foundation and Introduction to Teaching course, on the other hand, immensely improved my understanding of the minority experience within education through the analysis and application of critical pedagogy. This understanding has not only developed my sense of awareness regarding disproportionate allocation of educational tools, it has also increased my desire to work in urban schools in order to curve the trend of unequal access to education.

Education and Common Core

In terms of education and current trends that seek to improve the way teachers instruct their students, there is no greater debate than the current one over the Common Core State Standards Initiative. The CCSS standards, as identified by Harriet Porton, represents an organic outgrowth of the standards movement, easily integrated into the fabric most states' curriculum, and part of the national dialogue regarding how students, schools, school systems, and teachers will and should be assessed (Porton, 2013). I personally believe that much of the backlash, which is directed at this policy, stems from ignorance, misunderstanding, lack of education, and most importantly, politics. Bob Riley, author of *Why I Support Common* Core, makes the argument that put simply, Common Core does not allow the federal government to prescribe what our children learn. Much of the resistance to the program stems from this single misperception, which is itself rooted in a deep distrust of the president (Riley, March 25, 2014). Each one of these outside forces impacts education and the implementation of Common Core in different ways. It is important to understand, however, that Common Core is not a new system and with any big government program there will be push-back.

The problem for myself lies within the intersection of ignorance and politics. Parents across the country have begun a campaign to eliminate Common Core education from existence, but the reality is that most of these parents have no comprehension of the actual standards or what the requirements are. Certain politically based entities then prey on this ignorance, asserting that national education should be abolished and returned to the state and local level. So, in a sense, parents are letting an educational issue become a political one and the benefit to the student becomes minimal at best. I personally find the Common Core Standards for literacy and writing to be extremely open-ended and easy to achieve when implemented properly. The standards allow for creativity and personalization, effectively eliminating a singular approach to educational instruction. The inherent reality is that creativity and learning thrive under conditions of intrinsic motivation (Beghetto, Baer, & Kaufman, 2015). I personally believe that the CCSS program has the potential to transform a classroom into a relevant and student-centered learning environment, but the program's success rests on the premise that educating the public on Common Core will negate the perpetual fear of big government control over the institution of education.

Words of Wisdom

The field of education is filled with ever changing variables that involve both personal and professional interactions with students, parents, and collogues in the field. Before anyone enters the field of education, however, they must first come to the understanding that educational instruction in secondary classrooms is extremely complex and involves a variety of variables that affect educational instruction. No matter how the issue is presented, it is important to understand that the bottom line is that teachers are overwhelmed when the difficulties of society enter their classroom, and teachers are at a loss as to what to do with many students (Martinez, 2008). These variables are often times outside of the teachers control and it is important to assess whether or not one can function as an effective educator in such conditions, or even if motivation to do so exists in the first place. It is important to understand that there are a whole bunch of other things, important things, that you may not know yet. You need to be open to that and ready to learn new things (Burant, 2010). Motivation and flexibility are two of the most important personal qualities an aspiring educator can possess. It is with these two factors that an educator can overcome the ever-changing conditions of secondary educational instruction and provide the students with the best possible classroom environment and the highest form of intellectual development.

Starting the education credentialing program can seem daunting to an outside observer seeking to immerse themselves in the profession of teaching. I have personally seen countless individuals start the program only to drop out shortly after because their determination and personal aspiration simply not correspond to the realities that exist in the field of education. There are a variety of requirements, such as the TPA assignments, that are incredibly work intensive and require a great deal of time and attention. An aspiring educator must be aware of this fundamental reality in order to mentally prepare and motivate themselves for the educational requirements that accompany a credentialing program. Similarly, a teacher credential candidate is also required to complete observation and teaching requirements in an actual classroom. This is done in conjunction with all of the TPA and course requirements that exist within any given education course at the graduate level. A teacher credential candidate must be aware of this reality and possess the necessary motivational strategies and skills to guide them through the credentialing process.

Motivation is one important quality to have for an aspiring educator, but flexibility is another equally important element that must be applied in order to successfully complete the credentialing program at the highest level possible. I have personally refined my own personal and professional methods of flexibility throughout my journey in the credentialing program. I began with a general attitude of getting what I wanted, or what I thought I deserved. I quickly realized that this mentality led to a diminished capacity to learn, impeded my ability to work with others, and limited my abilities to be open minded and understanding. I was able to reverse this trend, however, by constantly assessing and modifying my personal and professional goals in the field of education. I was able to make this transfer because I allowed for flexibility in my journey through the credentialing program. Instead of becoming even more rigid and unworkable, I decided to become more understanding and flexible with issues and requirements that are outside of my control. This mindset is incredibly important to have in the field of education, especially for new educators, because so much of education is uncontrollable with moving variables at every turn. It is important to incorporate a flexible and understanding approach to professional and personal development in the classroom in order to mitigate many of the uncontrollable problems that arise with secondary education.

Moving through Difficult Situations

One of the major impediments to the field of education lies within the process of navigating difficult situations that arise from direct instruction in the classroom. Difficult situations, like in any profession, can arise in a moment's notice and can involve numerous elements with varying complexities. Anna Richert (2012) asks the reader to consider the impact of poverty as an example. It is difficult to understand the experience or consequence of poverty when one has not been poor oneself (Richert, 2012). When I first entered the credentialing program, my biggest fear was with interacting and negotiating with hyper-controlling parents regarding classroom material or content, not dealing with the impact of poverty. Even though I have yet to run into the problem of hyper-involved parents, I have encountered the impacts of poverty on a daily basis when doing my observations for the credentialing program at the University of La Verne. This program has provided the appropriate tools and techniques to professionally deal with the current teaching dilemmas that I have experienced, along with providing strategies to mitigate problems from arising in the future.

Even though my biggest fears have never manifested themselves in a classroom setting, there are still a variety of difficult obstacles that a teacher candidate must overcome, especially when working towards receiving a clear teaching credential. For myself personally, the biggest hurdles in the credentialing program have been with the TPA assignments. I have not had a problem with passing my TPA requirements but the level of time and effort that must be invested for success is immense. Each of the tests provides scenarios for the teacher candidate to move through in order to demonstrate competency as an educator. These tests, however, are not something one can sit down and complete in a few hours. This is a long and complex process that involves the application of numerous skills and strategies that have been learned throughout the teacher-credentialing program. In order to complete this test without the need for revision, a teacher candidate must invest the appropriate amount of time to complete these extremely difficult and complex tasks. Similarly, a teacher candidate must implement the appropriate time management strategies in order to complete the TPA tasks before the assigned deadline.

In order to move through difficult situations, one must be prepared to encounter such situations in the first place. It is an inherent reality that teacher candidates will face at least one or more difficult situations that are beyond their control in the context of the education-credentialing program. It is important to understand that preparation, time management, and mitigation protocols can help turn a difficult situation into a manageable task because the teacher has invested the time to appropriately address such situations. I have personally implemented these strategies of time management, preparation, and mitigation protocols; all of which significantly contributed to my success in the credentialing program. Lisa Delpit (2012) reinforces this reality by identifying the solution for ensuring the implementation of these essential practices, now echoed by others in the field, is the creation of teams of teachers who will work together in professional learning communities (Delpit, 2012).

The Credential Program and My Ability to Teach

The complexities of education are diverse and immense. When I first began my journey in the education credentialing program, I began to realize how ill-prepared I was to deal with many of the student-centered issues that arise with secondary educational instruction. The benefit of the credential program is that the credential candidate, through a systematic process, learns the appropriate strategies to deal with such issues as English Language Learners or ELA's, special needs development, and the difference between suburban and urban education. Learning the various teaching strategies, such as those associated with direct and collaborative based instruction, have improved my abilities to communicate social studies content material by implementing the appropriate recall and relevance based strategies that include the experiences of the students. The credentialing program offers a wide variety of support mechanisms and Teachers have at their disposal a variety of ways to differentiate spoken English to make it comprehensible for our diverse English learners (Echevarria, Vogt, & Short, 2013). Each course in the credentialing program provided a guide on how to properly develop a lesson plan that incorporates learning strategies that address the various learning needs of the students in the class.

Learning the numerous instructional strategies that address the varying levels of proficiency can be extremely beneficial in the field of social studies education. I have done my entire program at the same urban school, North Ontario High School, and the strategies that I have learned throughout the credential program have helped immensely in my ability to reach and teach the students in my classroom, especially students in poverty. These strategies and learning theories have taught me that If I really want to understand my students in poverty, I have to understand this key aspect of their experience: not only do they not have access to computers or the Internet, but they carry the weight of shame for not having that access in a society that equates technologies with social evolution (Gorski, 2013).

The constant emphasis on the ELA and CCSS requirements was extremely beneficial because I was given tools that help address the learning gaps that exists within any classroom environment. The emphasis on critical pedagogy was also extremely beneficial to my personal development as an aspiring social studies educator in a secondary classroom environment. By incorporating culturally relevant elements that reflect the students in my classroom, I have been able to increase the participation rates among the special needs students that I am teaching. This is a process, however, and I had to learn the fundamentals of learning and applying critical and culturally reflective pedagogy into a classroom environment. It is important to understand that many strategies may not work or may not transfer from class to class because each situation is unique. If one relies on the strategies and knowledge gained in the teacher-credentialing program, such as I did, then the possibilities of achieving successful instruction in the classroom will increase dramatically.

Why I Teach

I personally never wanted to be a teacher growing up. In fact, I do not remember the though ever entering my mind. It was something that was recommended before I went for my graduate and doctorate degree in a similar field. It was not until I received placement at North Ontario High School, teaching American Government and Economics to high school seniors, that I knew teaching was for me. I was able to see how teaching high school students, especially in urban environments, could be a desirable career path because I simply love what I do. I teach for a variety of reasons, some personal and others professionally based. I teach because I have witnessed the disparity in access to education which I have the ability to change. I want to be a teacher so I can share the knowledge that I have gained through my own educational journey in hopes of motivating my students to achieve the same goals in higher education. Many of the students that I have worked with and come to know personally have been written off by the majority of the education community. Being at a "ghetto school" has provided the reinforcement that I needed in terms of secondary social studies education because I have witnessed the dramatic improvements made by students whom simply received the proper support. Even though I had not planned to enter the field of education, I know consider it one of the best and most rewarding decisions that I have ever made.

Before entering the teacher credential program, every teacher candidate should assess their personal motivations for entering the field of education in order to establish the legitimacy of their quest. If the primary focus does not include a student-centered approach, then the profession is not for you. It is important to ask this question because it can provide the candidate with an indication of how successful and motivated they will be in the credential program. I personally believe all conscientious teachers need to ask themselves what they need to know in order to be successful with this kid and with this one and this one (Ayers, 2010). However, it is extremely important for new teacher credential candidates to evaluate their responses to this very basic, yet incredibly complex question in order to determine whether entry into a credentialing program is advisable.

My Teaching Philosophy: Then and Now

Upon entry into the teacher-credentialing program, I had a very basic and undeveloped teaching philosophy that was primarily teacher-centered. It was not until I started moving through the process of obtaining my credential that I learned the importance of student-centered educational strategies and philosophical approaches. Having a teaching philosophy is incredibly important because having a solid teaching philosophy is a significant contingency in goal setting that is often overlooked (Parsons & Schroder, 2015). I had personally witnessed the disconnect that inherently exists with teacher-centered educational philosophies and I have learned the importance of implementing and refining a student centered-teaching philosophy in order to provide effective and meaningful educational instruction. Learning the various instructional strategies that accompany collaborative, inquiry, and direct instruction have been extremely useful in my ability to achieve a student-centered teaching philosophy that is reasonable and applicable in a classroom environment. Also, the reading strategies that I have learned, such as read-aloud and you're the teacher activities, have significantly improved my teaching abilities in the field of social studies education because they allow for student development with the teacher's assistance, thus achieving the student-centered philosophical goal. This teaching philosophy can be adapted and incorporated into any classroom setting. The primary goal, however, is to keep a student-centered approach in the development of professional teaching philosophies because these very philosophies will be applied directly into a classroom environment, all of which directly affects student retention and performance.

My Experiences: A Learning Curve

One of the most important experiences that has influenced my development as a social studies educator lies within culturally reflective teaching that reaches the students in the classroom. When I first began my classroom lessons, both observed and unobserved, I had a problem of talking over my students by using complex vocabulary they were unfamiliar with, along with providing examples that were not reflective of the students experiences outside of school. I had to constantly modify this impediment in order to provide more effective educational instruction. In simplistic terms, the problem was communication. I was using white, elitist language that the students were completely unfamiliar with. My culpability in this area may seem minimal, simply because it was all I knew and was what I grew up with. However, the fact that I took the time to refine and improve my communication skills has lessened my culpability in this area, along with dramatically improving the participation and retention rates of my students because I am talking to them, not over them. The hard reality is that the concrete conditions and circumstances have changed; we are now required to make our own contributions in our own time and place (Ayers & Ayers, 2011). This is an important learning experience to infer from because many teachers seek out schools or classrooms that fit their personal preference, running at the first sign of diversity and unpredictability. By taking the time to learn about the students and having the flexibility to formulate a teaching strategy to reach them, a teacher can drastically reduce their stress level and increase their competency in reaching all learners, at all levels.

My Future Classroom

What will I future classroom look like? This is a question that has manifested itself numerous times throughout the teacher credentialing program. The structure of my classroom, especially within the confines of social studies, is incredibly important to the development of my students and their engagement with the content material. I must take into account the academic learning environment which refers to the learning content specified in state content standards (Garrett, 2014). By creating a classroom environment that reflects the content standards that will be covered throughout the course, such as poster boards, state standard lists, and student expectations, I will create an environment of inclusion and interaction because the students would be constantly engaging with the academic material in a visually meaningful way.

In order to make my classroom effective in a universal sense, I must incorporate elements of social-emotional learning which promotes growth in social skills and the ability to express emotions maturely (Garrett, 2014). This could take the form of displaying student work or structuring a classroom to reflect collaborative or student-centered instruction. I have personally witnessed the benefits of structuring a classroom to emphasize social-emotional learning in order to enhance the effectiveness and retention of the academic instruction that is provided every day by the teacher. I have come to realize that there are many benefits and pitfalls of having students work in small groups or with a partner. In order to capitalize on the benefits and avoid potential pitfalls, remember that students need to be taught how to work in groups (Garrett, 2014). By moving the students through the collaborative process and structuring my room in a way that promotes meaningful engagement and comprehension, I have the ability to reach all students, in all proficiency levels, and with a student-centered approach that incorporates relevance in civic-mindedness.

My Goal as a Teacher: A Conclusion

The main goal that I have as an aspiring educator is to always be open-minded with the willingness to develop and refine my skills according to the most current research and analysis of the field. I have come to the realization that if educational research is to have an impact on practice, and be seen to have an impact, it is decisions if this sort that it must influence. Hence, it is on this issue, of the current influence of research on teachers' everyday practice and how it might be increased (Millar, 2006).

By constantly staying up to date on the current educational research that offers improvements in the way content material is communicated by the teacher and retained by the student, I have the ability to provide the best possible student-centered education to my students because I understand, at a fundamental level, the best possible instructional methods and how to apply them into a classroom setting. This reality, along with many discussed in this chapter, have to do with motivation and flexibility in the classroom. By constantly refining my teaching abilities and having the professionalism to allow for a critique of my own instructional methods with the purpose of making improvements, I will meet the ultimate goal of providing the best possible student-centered social studies instruction to my high school students.

CHAPTER 6

George: The Last 100 Meters

It took me well over thirty minutes to come up with a title for this chapter. I have always put a lot of thought and effort into the heading of my work. A truly great title can sometimes communicate just as much meaning as the sentences following it. I would say the title to this paper belongs on my top-ten list because it has an array of meanings. Coming from an athlete who ran track for eight years (both in high school and college), the last 100 meters mainly refers to the final steps one must endure to complete their race; it is the home stretch.

I am using the title in this paper as a sort of metaphor that accounts for my journey as a teacher candidate. This paper is my last 100 meters in the sense that I have not entirely finished my credential and master's program but am approaching the finish line. During this race I have endured the trials and tribulations of a lifelong student, learned about myself as an individual, challenged myself as a thinker, built relationships with my peers, and prepared, to the best of my ability, to becoming an educator. The last 100 meters of a race can cause one's vision to become somewhat blurry from all of the fatigue; keeping this in mind, I hope that I can leave years' worth of thoughts knowledge in this chapter.

A serious competitor always has goals set in mind when running a race something that provides the athlete with purpose. Without a purpose it is much more difficult to self-reflect and assess one's overall performance. That being said, I would like to give this paper a purpose; an avenue for reflecting on my experiences as a teacher candidate in a credential program.

A journal article entitled *Providing Adequate Teachers for Urban Schools*, the author makes the argument that U.S. credential programs made a rather alarming observation when noting: "teachers participating in alternative certification programs lack adequate training and coursework when they enter the teaching profession" (Burstein, 2009, p. 25). I read further to find that issues of inadequacy within credential programs stem from an overemphasis on theory, frail linkage between coursework and fieldwork, and poor quality of student teaching experiences.

Though this article was written in 2009, I could not help but relate to some of the dysfunctions being analyzed. I, for example, have witnessed first-hand just how disconnected the relationships between university and fieldwork sites are. Given each state's standards for obtaining a teacher's credential, are universities really utilizing these values and preparing teacher candidates as efficiently as possible?

As I approach the last 100 meters in this race to obtain my master's degree and teaching credential I hope the story that comes along with it provides useful insight for past, present, and future educators. While I love to share moments of self-accomplishment and triumph, I want to also spend some time investigating the question of how we can make credential programs more efficient in the realm of fieldwork. The biggest challenges I have faced as a teacher candidate are not with students themselves, rather, these issues originate in the disconnection existing between university and fieldwork.

My particular credential program has created a scenario where I am in catch-up mode because of their inability to assign me fieldwork in a timely fashion. So, I propose: what may be done to ensure that each new teacher walking into class on the first day knows that they were trained properly?

The History Teacher

My California driver's license states: George W. Merrifield, Age 22, Male, Brown hair, Hazel eyes, 5'11, 150 lb. I have always looked at this state-issued piece of paper and thought to myself: "they sure make you look like a really ordinary person on these things." Though this information does in fact describe me, it does not describe *all* of me. I am George W. Merrifield, the 22 year-old student from California studying to become a history teacher.

As a young child, before I knew "history" was an actual thing that people could study professionally, I fell in love with the art of story-telling. The oldest recordings of history were stored in peoples' heads and passed down along through generations orally. Much like this, my earliest interactions with history came from stories that my father told me during long car rides or before bed. My journey to becoming a history teacher thus stems from a passion developed long ago. Teaching is a way for me to pass along my father's legacy and also maintain the Earth's most ancient way of passing along knowledge.

Though I have wanted to be a history teacher since seventh grade, I feel as though my journey to becoming an educator did not start until junior-year of college. This is where I departed from years of fantasy and truly began weighing the realities of being a teacher. Having been studying education as a subject for over two years now, it really blows my mind that none of my K-12 teachers ever showed any evidence of battle scars acquired from their credential program. Studying to become a teacher is no walk in the park. There is a big difference between one loving to help people and being 100% dedicated to helping people and loving it. The credential program is a place where I witnessed, for the first time, just how vast the world of education really is. However, it also the place where your education reaches a checkpoint and all of the passion I have for promoting a more just world is ignited.

If one has put themselves through enough trouble to get into a credential program, answering the age-old question "why do you want to teach?" should result in a much more thought-out answer than: "because I love to help people." I would like to think that everyone is born with an innate capacity to want to help others; it feels good. However, for any teacher candidate preparing to enter class on the first day of school, "I love to help people" is probably not going to be enough firepower for withstanding the whirlwind of madness one faces in a nine-month period. If there is any one phrase that one will hear the most in a credential program it will be: "the first years are always the hardest." As I sift through teacher articles recounting their first years it is somewhat bone chilling to hear things like: "The reality of a teacher's work week is directly correlated with physical illness, mental ill health, and strained relationships with significant others and families" (Baig-Ali, 2012, p. 71). Or even worse is Erika Daniels admitting: "I cried every night and second-guessed my career choice" (Daniels, 2010, p. 6). These types of statements definitely make one deeply consider why they want to pursue a profession such as education. However, underneath these cringing confessions lays a second layer of truth. Why putting up with the early years are worth it to teachers.

I haven't much to say in terms of how hard a teacher's first years are; I am still trying to attain my credential. However, I can say that despite hearing such grueling stories, the classroom is where I want to be. I can still vividly remember writing my first statement of purpose at the University of Central California (UCC) after declaring education as a minor (undergraduate studies). There was a point in which so much emotion filled my body that I had a difficult time typing up my response. My statement of purpose read: "I want to teach because I want to give something to someone that maybe they didn't have before." These very words have withstood the test of time despite being denied acceptance to UCC's graduate program, hearing frightening stories from teachers on their early years, and even reading studies compiled by the Children Trends Database that notes how despite teaching efforts, 8,300 students will drop out of school daily (Statisticbrain.com, 2015). I am smiling as I write this because there is a feeling of certainty deep down that tells me how beautiful it is to provide for others. Dr. Jason Raley (2013) once pin-pointed the beauty of teaching so elegantly when he told the story of Eddie; a child diagnosed with ADD. Raley (2013) noted how Eddie's "disruptive behavior" was completely eliminated by simply giving him a piece of gum to chew on during class. Actions like these that are so simple, yet so constructive are precisely why I want to teach. Finding ways to have a positive effect on someone's life regardless of whether it has something to do with your subject area is an awesome thing. I whole-heartedly agree with William Ayers (2010) when he says: "they become teachers because they love the world or some piece of the world enough that they want to show that love to others" (p. 20).

It is critical that any teacher candidates regularly ask themselves why they want to teach. Though my statement of purpose has yet to change, my overall attitude towards teaching is constantly evolving. There is always some sort of new statistic being presented, or story that your professor confesses, challenging you to remold your understanding and approach to teaching. For example, if you plan to teach high school, by the time student's reach your door on the first day of school more than half will be reading below grade level (nces.ed.gov, 2013). What are you going to do about this? Since beginning the credential program I have kept my personal values close and held an open heart. This is I feel, is the best approach to following the path of becoming a teacher.

The Ever-Evolving School

The trends of education that this nation has witnessed within the last three decades are rather overwhelming when investigated. As I write this paper, America is in the middle of making a monumental shift between educational policies for future generations. Though I do not intend to specifically talk about educational trends, they do in fact play a crucial role in understanding the way credential programs are operating today. Just as William Ayers (2010) called himself a "crusading teacher" (p. 19) in his first professional years; we are all a new age of reformers in the credential program. The *Common Core* educational policy seems to be sweeping the nation by large, challenging schools to rethink their way of preparing children for being successful in post-high school years (Common Core States Standards Initiative, 2015). Our credential programs have been directly affected by this new educational policy, as I myself have been trained to carry out these new methods. However, as the nation tries to shift its way from older policies such as *No Child Left Behind*, some states are biting back. As Dennis Van Roekel (2013) has mentioned, coming closer to the implementation of a new standards is a cause for "anxiety" ... "Change is hard" (nea.org). This begs the question: if we as a nation do not agree upon a singular educational policy, are theory-based classes amongst different states setting up all teacher candidates for success?

I would like to think that Common Core is the right direction to go for schools across the nation. According to Sarah Boslaugh (2014), the US, unlike other industrialized nations, has never had a national curriculum for K-12 grades. In an ideal world it would seem nice to at least have a single set of organized standards for states to work with. Furthermore, Common Core offers a handful of inventive plans such as implementing more computer technology and collaboration-based standards that are well-suited for the fast-paced society we live in today (Boslaugh, 2014). One thing however strikes me about all of this. As I navigate through my credential program to become a history teacher, there has yet to be a set of Common Core standards written for social sciences. Professors in the University of La Verne credential program base many of their educational theory classes around Common Core, yet I have been left in a state of limbo, just as this nation has. As social science teacher candidates in California await new standards to which they can put into practice before becoming employed, credential studies consist of utilizing old content (California State Board of Education, 2015). This particular situation is much like being in a class where half of the students have brand new, updated computers, and the other half has outdated ones. While the teacher and students know that at some point everyone will be working in sync because more computers will be delivered, there is a phase where some students are limited to the ways in which they can study newer material.

Any good teacher should have the ability to be flexible and adapt. Not having official Common Core standards for social sciences is thus not a tragedy by any means. However, as a teacher candidate I have seen how California's state of transition into the Common Core has stirred some confusion for professors. As Mike Kirst (2014) has said, "We have come a long way since the State Board of Education adopted the Common Core standards in 2010," however, as evidence by a lack of new standards for subjects like social science, the new educational reform still has a handful of kinks to work out. Professors are therefore left to make assumptions about the new educational trend or simply tell teacher candidates "I don't know." When will new social science standards come out? "I don't know."

The professors in my credential program have clearly been doing their best to prepare me for my first day of school. However, because such a large shift in educational policy has befallen upon California, my professors have been left with the task of not only decoding the Common Core as it is still in the process of being made, but also preparing teacher candidates to implement it as well. This age of transition has consequently resulted in in some gray area within the credential system. With professors imparting half of their knowledge about Common Core standards and yet still referring to older standards as well, there lies a contradiction in the university requirements teacher candidates must meet in order to obtain their credentials.

Where there lies confusion in the Common Core's implementation, opportunity also exists. From my own observation I have found that the debate between the Common Core's advantages and disadvantages drowns out conversation about what California will actually do with its new educational vision. Rather than get caught up in debate and speculation over Common Core, credential professors and teacher candidates should be collaborating. If the foundations of California's educational system are bound to change what smoother way to establish a sturdy vision than with candidates in our credential programs? There is no longer a need to teach candidates about the very schooling system that they all grew up in (No Child Left Behind, etc.); there is a need to actively engage the puzzle that has been set before young educators. I feel that adequate time needs to be set-aside for teacher candidates to become scholars of the Common Core system. If I could, I would propose a course be taken on applying these standards so that new teachers are not second-guessing their formal approach with students. Whether one agrees or disagrees with the Common Core, there is little use in only talking about it; students are the main focus, and they need confident mentors. My advice for new teacher candidates would be to quickly familiarize and engage in new educational policies like the Common Core. See the Common Core as a new frontier unto which endless possibilities may pave the road for our fast-paced school system. Everyone in the educational field is on the same playing field right now; trying to make sense of America's future in schooling. Do not let negative remarks about the Common Core steer you away from understanding it at all; collaborate with peers. Studies have shown that young students are often responsible for innovating within older social systems (Fisher, Frey, & Lapp, 2009); teacher candidates should thus take it upon themselves to begin establishing and promoting the new age of education.

Beginning the Race

"If you can get yourself through undergraduate studies, you can definitely get yourself through a credential program" (Vaster, 2013, personal communication). Those were the words of advice my neighbor, a former graduate of The University of La Verne (ULV) master's and credential program, gave me amidst the whirlwind of graduate applications I faced senior year of college. My original "plan" for graduate school was not to attend ULV. After being denied an invitation to my undergraduate institution's credential program (UCC) I set my sights on a Cal State University. I gladly accepted their offer of admission May, 2014 and began preparing for a new chapter in my educational career.

It was from my initial point of acceptance to this Cal State however, that I realized graduate programs are not always as clean-cut and organized as people make them out to be.

I was offered admittance to La Verne's master's and credential program two days before school began in the Fall of 2014; I frantically accepted. Just as abruptly as I switched topics between this paragraph and last, my decision to switch credential programs did too. In a conversation I had with my good friend Sofia Moonie (personal communication, 2014), a recent California credential program graduate, she stated: "get used to having to take control of the situation ... credential programs are just disorganized like that for some reason."

It is important to note that while I would, and should find academic research to communicate Sofia's message, little, if no such material exists to my knowledge; what credential program would volunteer to name themselves as "disorganized"? It took months of trying to contact the Cal State credential program I was originally accepted by before I was left with little choice but to revoke my intent to enroll. Countless phone calls and emails trying to access information about my financial situation, living accommodations, and class enrollment were left unanswered by the very program who told me they were "pleased" to have me aboard.

There is almost little to say about the details of this unprofessional act because I was only given my acceptance letter and an email regarding the first day of classes. By the end of summer I found myself enrolling at ULV both frustrated and desperate.

Thankfully, I was welcomed with open arms and immediately began my post-baccalaureate journey to the finish line. This episode of inefficiency and neglect I experienced with the university system however has not been my last personal encounter. My good friend Sofia (2014) surely made a valid observation about the credential system that is worth investigating. Issues of inefficiency within the credential system should be identified and examined.

Life as a Teacher Candidate

If grade levels were still used in college I would be in 17th grade by now, working on 18th. That's a lot of years schooling, seeing as I am only 22 years old. The point of all of this is that most of my life has been dedicated to the theory of general education. If we take a look at the Common Core Initiative's main goal (the same goal I am being taught to convey in the classroom) I have successfully been "prepared for higher education" and am now working on the "employment" aspect (Boslaugh, 2014). To me, the credential program is a lot like trade school; I have reached a threshold in my educational career where I now need to use the knowledge accumulated from years of schooling and physically practice the trade I intend to dedicate myself to. University of La Verne's credential program specifically emphasizes the act of *practicing to teach* as the home page of their website (2015) states: "students must successfully complete teaching methodology courses and fieldwork" (ULV Teaching Credential Program Catalog, 2015). My studies in the credential program may thus be seen as two halves; one consisting of understanding how to teach and the other, putting these methods to use in the classroom. Balance in this educational system of training is therefore extremely important, as teacher candidates must apply methodology just as much as they are receiving it. I attend university classes each week and receive all of the necessary educational theory required. My discussion of the disconnection between university and fieldwork starts with observing what the credential program looks like when the equal balance between methodology and practice in the classroom is disrupted.

In a keynote address dedicated to newly-graduated credential students, Dr. Lynn Gordon (2012) of Occidental College stated: "the teacher is the most crucial variable affecting student achievement – not the school, not the curriculum, and not the pedagogical method/philosophy/or reform flavor-of-the-year being promote" (p. 2). Here, I would like to point out that the teacher themselves, not the methods they utilize on a daily basis, are more vital to a student's personal success. The classes I have taken at ULV have been a huge help as my understanding of the necessary methodology for conducting a positive classroom atmosphere has drastically evolved. Finding useful approaches to guiding EL students or devising structured lesson plan templates for example have proved to serve both practical and personal purposes. In 2009 it was estimated that 43% of students in California's K-12 educational system spoke a primary language other than English (Aminy & Karathanos, 2001); methodology in this area is critical for teacher candidates, especially for those like me who only speak English. Developing lesson plan templates and systematically selecting them for appropriate lesson objectives also has a major independent impact on student achievement (Marzano, 2003). The balance between understanding these methods and using them in practice however has been rather uneven during my time in the credential program. Giving my time in a classroom environment and learning how to be a teacher has been overshadowed by university theory. I have observed that this disruption in balance is seeded in the university's ability to efficiently place teacher candidates at fieldwork sites. In other words, I have spent a majority of my time in the credential system learning theory rather than actually going out and practicing it. If this problematic situation cannot be addressed, the credential program is at loss of one of its key attributes: developing a well-rounded educator that is prepared to teach on their very first day of class.

On my first day of school as a teacher candidate a syllabus was laid out in front of me for inspection. Much like any other class, the syllabus stated class objectives, a break-down of course content, and of course, classroom requirements. My 'EL Methodology' course required that I not only participate in classroom activities but also complete fieldwork hours and teach two lessons at a K-12 school. A fieldwork director from the university came into our classroom and discussed how they would be in charge of finding each teacher candidate a school to conduct their required volunteer hours and lessons. We then filled out paper forms that listed our preferences for school districts, grade levels, and subjects. I can recall thinking to myself how convenient it was to place a university representative in charge of my fieldwork relations; an act that almost seemed too good to be true. I came to find that in some ways, it was. During my first semester of graduate school I found myself cramming thirty hours of volunteering and giving two lessons within the span of two and a half weeks. The university had nearly failed to find me a placement within a 16-week semester and this had a direct effect on me as I needed to complete its course requirements. On top of this, I was placed at a middle school after specifically mentioning that I wanted to intern in a high school setting. My master teacher also gave the impression that she did not want a teacher candidate observing in her classroom. Since this slip-up by the university, a large portion of my focus and energy in the credential program has been dedicated to seeking balance between fieldwork and university classes; an act proving to be extremely strenuous.

I know that I am not the only credential student to ever be in a situation of displacement with regards to their fieldwork. However, the role that fieldwork plays in any credential program is elemental and must thus run efficiently for students; especially if the university takes responsibility for placing teacher candidates. How might we make this aspect of credential programs more efficient? In the article "Bridging the Gap between Theory and Practice," David Allsopp (2006) proclaims that in order for credential students to fully benefit from their program, the university must develop mutual standards, trust, and strong communication with surrounding schools. In an experiment conducted to develop a mutual link between universities and surrounding schools, Allsopp (2006) mentioned that most successful programs: rearranged class schedules to conveniently aid teacher candidates, developed an orientation segment to notify candidates in advance about upcoming requirements, created specific schedules with candidates at the beginning of each semester for their required teaching lessons, and collected data from schools to see if their relationship was beneficial to teacher candidates. In my own experience, I can recall professors and the fieldwork director describing how the university lacks strong relationships with a number of surrounding school districts. It is because of this disconnect in professional rapport that the university has a difficult time placing teacher candidates in classrooms at times. Is this the reason why I have been put in the difficult situation of fieldwork displacement? In order to maintain an efficiently-ran credential program, one might suggest that universities make a serious investment in building relationships with surrounding K-12 schools.

I have managed to navigate through La Verne's credential program with satisfactory performance in both theory and fieldwork thus far. With each semester's requirements becoming more demanding however, (about 80 hours of fieldwork, five lessons, and university coursework) the issue of fieldwork placement from my first semester seems to have a lingering consequence that is surprisingly becoming bigger. One of my highest values as a future teacher is the importance of relationships. I believe that the best type of learning occurs when a teacher has a strong bond with his/her students. As Neslihan Saltali (2013) has noted, one of the most vital relationships a student develops in school is the one with their teacher; it is important for both social development and learning. By having to switch schools for my fieldwork requirements, I have missed out on quality time that could have been spent building a good relationship with my master teacher (one whom actually wants a teacher candidate in their class) and their students. It is my hope that with the last school transfer I have made for fieldwork things will remain intact. In this way I can focus my efforts on developing a sturdy relationship with a master teacher; someone that may physically help guide me through the practice of teaching.

Finishing the Race

There is always a point in the last 100 meters where you must reach beyond what your body wants to do and find the strength to finish racing. You know deep down that you will finish the race; you just don't know exactly how. I am very much in the same situation with my credential program at the moment. I am close, but not done; there is still plenty left to see, feel, and experience. Graduation day is coming into sight and I am now reflecting on how I got here; wondering how other teacher candidates before me got to this point. It is here where making an example of myself and sharing some advice seems most appropriate.

I would be lying if I said I was not mentally battered and bruised at the moment. The credential program up to this point has truly tested my patience, ability to think, and interact. As mentioned before, it truly blows my mind that none of my K-12 teachers ever showed any battle scars from their days as a teacher candidate. Despite these bumps and bruises, I am still here; and there is a reason for that. I can still wake up every day, despite my conditions, and feel that same spark I did in seventh grade – when I decided to become a teacher. I would say to those who plan on teaching, find your spark. Whatever it may be, there has to be something inside you that is unbreakable; once you find this you cannot let go. The beauty of teaching may sometimes be lost in actually *learning how* to teach because of the challenges credential programs present. In my case, having to deal with fieldwork displacement on top of coursework has caused loads of stress I find rather frustrating and unnecessary. However, by reminding myself of why I am here in the first place (to give something to someone that maybe they didn't have before) I have been able stay focused and work past these factors.

In regards to the biggest challenge I have faced yet, which are catching up on fieldwork hours, I suggest to any future teacher candidate that they always remain proactive in accomplishing their objectives. If my unfortunate experiences with getting into graduate school and this fieldwork dilemma have taught me anything, it is that credential programs are not perfect. Always take initiative and stand up for yourself. I have managed to remain successful in this program by staying communicative with faculty and administrative members. Remember that despite its imperfections, your school community is not out to see you fail; we as members of the education community are surrounded by people who have dedicated their lives to enriching others. Also, seek support in your peers, as I have found that teacher candidate struggles are similar. The credential program sets itself apart from other forms of schooling in that your peers are not in competition with you, they are there as friends and resources. Delanie (2015), a good friend of mine in the credential program once brought up a useful point: "Don't hesitate to ask me for anything; the only way we are going to get through this program is if we all use each other" (Dunn). Statements like these are a great reminder that my niche of teacher candidates has played a significant role in keeping me emotionally intact. Your success in the credential program is reflected by your ability to be presented with challenges and accomplish them while still maintaining a passion for teaching. Approach these challenges with confidence in yourself and the confidence of knowing you are not alone in this race.

As I part from this paper and continue on my journey to the finish line I would finally like to say that I am thankful for where ULV's credential program has brought me thus far. Despite the disappointment I have felt from being displaced in fieldwork, my desire to become an educator is stronger than ever. It is interesting to note that episodes such as my late transfer to ULV and being behind in fieldwork have caused me to think much more critically about the education system as a whole. Instead of focusing my frustration on the imperfections of our schools, I have been given an outlet to think about what best suits the needs of students; a more critical eye for what works and what doesn't. I have moved past thinking about school with a linear mindset, a black-and-white system that consists of giving a pre-selected lesson, which results in students simply regurgitating information. I wonder why things, such as the power of relationships, the understanding of cultures, and promotion of individuality establish such strong learning environments. ULV's program has given me the gift thinking beyond the surface; something that I believe gives so much more meaning to being an educator. As I inch towards the finish line, I am confident that my gathered experiences and deeper understanding of education as a system will leave me ready for the very first day of school.

CHAPTER 7

Hillary: Teaching Is a Lifestyle

If you are reading this and you are working towards becoming a future teacher, I want you to think about something before you start your journey as a student teacher. I want you to think very carefully for what your life is like RIGHT now. Think about all of your friends, your family, your relationships, your faith, your hobbies ... now, consider the balance that holds all of these entities together. How much effort do you put into all of these categories? How often do give time to these different aspects of your life? I want you to deeply think about all of this, because once you start on this journey that is teaching, your life will alter drastically. As you begin your quest as a teacher, you will be adding many more categories to your life, especially to your heart. You will soon learn, teaching is much more than an 8:30 a.m.–3:40 p.m. job. It is a lifestyle.

This year, I have learned that when someone chooses to be a teacher, that someone is deciding to change his or her way of living. You no longer only care about your own little world, you start to care about the worlds of 28 little second graders who depend on you every single day. As a teacher, you have to learn how to be selfless, dedicated, and proactive in EVERY aspect of our lives, in order to keep the balance that holds us together. This is absolutely vital in this profession, because ultimately, *we are the balance that holds our students together.*

This year has taught me many lessons about the selfless dedication that is required in this profession. During my year of student teaching, I was able to experience life with 28 new students, a wonderful mentor teacher, curriculum frustrations, administrative issues, political agendas, broken hearts, upset parents, kept secrets, lesson plans, and all of the work that goes into getting a Master of Arts in Teaching at LSU. Not to mention that at the same time I am planning my wedding, working a separate ten-hour-a-week job, and am preparing to move to another city entirely. I am also trying finding a teaching job of my own! I have found that each day I come home tired, exhausted, and stressed. What I also have found, though, is that my heart exploding full of love, pride, and angst to get back the very next day. I salute you if you have decided to join this profession, it is the most difficult and rewarding occupation there is.

I did not always want to be a teacher. Actually, I had some pretty bad experiences when I was younger, and I seriously thought of teaching as an M-R-S degree that required absolutely no intellect. (*I was so naïve.*)

I came to LSU in the Fall of 2010 majoring in Biological Sciences. I had no clue what I wanted to be when I graduated college. I had a wonderful biology teacher my senior year who gave me the confidence to pursue a degree in this subject. (I should have known from that moment how influential great teachers can be, but more on that later.)

As I started my first semester at LSU, I soon realized that biology was definitely a lot harder in college. I also realized that the professors were in no way comparable to the teacher that I had at my high school. I was used to the supportive environment that I had grown accustomed to. So the freshmen biology class where I sat among the 800 other students, was clearly not the case. I soon realized that this was going to be a miserable four years if I did not figure out what I wanted to do for the rest of my life.

My mother was the one who had always told me that I should be a teacher. I definitely did not agree. I had some bad experiences with teachers when I was in elementary school, and I did not want to be the one who repeated those same mistakes and make another students' school experience less than they deserve. I was the student who struggled in elementary school. I was not the brightest, did not stand out among the other students, and just sort of passed on through. Some of the only memories I had about my elementary experience were the negative aspects of it. Because of this, my opinion of teachers was skewed. My mom eventually convinced me to switch my major to Elementary Education, advocating that I was good with children, my holidays would be great, and when you get married it would be easy to find a job somewhere. I felt like I was signing up for the M-R-S degree that people tend to label this degree with. I was ashamed when people would ask me what my major was. Usually I would just brush it off and say, "This is just until I can figure out what I want to do with the rest of my life." God has a funny way of leading you in the direction that you never think you are going to go.

Before I even knew it, the profession of teaching had changed my life. It altered my path and led me to a new and unexpected direction. It began in the spring 2011 semester in my new EDCI classes. This is when my interest piqued about becoming an educator. I started to understand why people respected the profession, and I began to feel the same. I was exposed to classrooms where the teachers did more than just teach, they inspired. I was pushed by my professors to consider the teachers I had in the past, the GOOD and the BAD. I was able to pull from my past experiences and understand what makes a great teacher, and what I could learn from my not so great ones. I was no longer ashamed to say, "I am an elementary education major." I was proud. I still am proud. I believe that teachers are some of the most influential people there are. Teachers are the ones who ask the questions that make you think, they push you until you show them your best self, and they inspire students to be better for themselves. This year, I have been able to be that person for my students. I have learned how to inspire and motivate my kids. There have been days where I have had parents come to me and say, "You are a difference maker. Thank you for everything that you do for my child." How can you ever be ashamed of a profession with that kind of reward?

Teaching does alter your life, but it is in the most unexpectedly heartwarming of ways. Five years ago, I would never have imagined that I would be finishing up my Master of Arts in teaching degree. I would have never believed someone if they told me that I would be spending an entire year in a second grade classroom. My life has changed from what I expected, even coming into this year it has changed drastically! If you are a student teacher about to embark on the journey of student teaching, your life will do the same. Get ready for it, it is a wonderful ride.

When I started my journey of student teaching at the beginning of August, I had a lot of expectations for what the year was going to be like. I imagined that I would be crazy busy while I was at school, that I would fall in love with all of my students, that I would probably have some students who were a bit more frustrating than others, and I had expected to be a little tired. During my first couple of weeks at school, I had noticed a couple of things beginning to change. The first of these changes were my sleep patterns, spare time, and my social life. Before, I was able to stay up until about 11 o'clock each night watching Netflix or reading a book, never caring about when I was going to bed. I actually attempted this during the first couple of weeks, but soon realized the exhaustion that ensued the very next day when I woke up at 5:30 a.m. In a past journal entry from the third day of school I had written:

> *August 13*
> HOW *am I so tired when it is only 7:00 at night?? I literally have to keep up my energy for my students from 8:30 a.m.-3:40 p.m. I don't even notice that I am tired until I get home and sit at my kitchen counter. But, I love these kids already. They are just so welcoming and just want to please my mentor teacher and me. I really hope it gets easier to wake up and do this every day ...*

Luckily, it has definitely gotten easier, because I have started going to bed early and understanding the importance of a good night's sleep! I am happy to go to bed earlier in the night, because it will help me have enough energy for my kiddos every single day. You do constantly have to keep up a high energy level for your students so that they remain interested in the content you are teaching them. All students deserve teachers at their best. This was the first aspect of my lifestyle to change.

Another major factor in my life that has altered is my social life and the daily interactions I had with my friends and with my family. I love all of my students, but I have realized that they constantly are on my mind. This is not something I had expected to happen during my year of teaching. I had not expected to care about every little thing that happens throughout the day. I knew that I would care about them all, but I seem to be affected by everything these children do as if they are my own. When I come home from school, I am either talking to my mom, fiancé, roommates, friends (anyone who will listen, really) about what happened during the day. I have come home fretting, worrying, praising, laughing, and sometimes crying about all kinds of situations that happened with my students. My students all always have different days and are all in different situations, whether it be academically, socially, or emotionally. Sometimes there are great days, and sometimes I question my choice of joining this profession. One thing that my students have changed about my lifestyle, though, is the way that I look at others. Not just children, but the way I look at all people in the world. Just like my students, everyone in this world is on different and deserves to have someone help bring out the best in them. My students have taught me how to look at others in a positive light, and they have taught me how to be respectful in all situations with all people.

One day, I had a best friend of mine (who is also a teacher) say, "Whitney, you seriously need to find a new topic of conversation. I love you, but this is all that you have talked about today!" I thought about her comment, apologized, and we moved on. However, I always think about her comment. Why do I always talk about my students? Why can't I just turn off my thoughts once the school day is done? I catch myself when I am thinking about it and I always have the same answer: they are my hearts. I love these kids. I care if they fail a quiz, if they are sick, when they get angry, when they are happy, and especially when their world seems to be completely wrong and all they need is a nice comment to turn their day around. I want the absolute best for these kids, in every aspect of their life. I have a journal entry from November 11, 2014, where I am expressing my concern for all of the students who were struggling at one point,

> *November 11, 2014*
> *Today was not a good day ... we have 28 students in our class, one who is labeled with a mild form of autism, two who receive special services, a separate six students who are reading on a kindergarten or first grade reading level, and two who will* NOT FOR THE LIFE OF THEM *participate without us constantly redirecting them.* HOW *am I supposed to use all of my time and energy to accommodate all of them? How am I supposed to have the patience and the resources to get them back up to level, while I have the*

> *other students who are at or above level who need to be pushed? I am worried how they are going to survive this year. The material is just getting harder and harder, which creates more frustrations for them, which amplifies all of their current behaviors even more ...*

I'm not going to lie. I had a bad day when I wrote this, and was completely frustrated. Was it the last time I had a bad day? No. Have I had any good days? Absolutely. I am happy to say that ALL of these students have greatly improved in the areas they struggled with in November. This journal entry is just an example to show how teachers are greatly affected by how their students are struggling. I want to celebrate when they are doing well in school, and help them reach their potential when they are having difficulty. I want to give them a hug on a bad day, or a high five when they are proud of themselves. Teachers are difference makers. We don't get to choose the children who come to us every day. It isn't their choice to be there, they have to be. I want to make sure that every child in that room is loved and cared for.

One important lesson that I have learned about student teaching is the new way that you approach life. I consider my job and my kids when I make almost every decision each day. When I am going to the grocery store I think, "Will I have time to make this for lunch and bring it to school?" When I am going shopping for clothes I decide whether or not the outfit I am choosing would be appropriate if I saw my kids outside of school. When I want to have a negative opinion about a person or event I think, "Would I be proud of my kids if they said or had this attitude?" What my kids are teaching me this year without even knowing it, is how to be a better person. I want to be the model to show them what a good person looks like. As an educator, I do not believe that our job stops at teaching the students the content material. I want to teach my students how to respect others, and how to respect themselves. I feel like I am unable to teach those lessons if I myself do not practice what I preach. I have a student who has a very sweet heart. He sometimes has negative attitudes about the activities or subject matter we are working on for the day. One day we had a very important conversation. I started it out by saying ...

Me:	"Okay class, we are about to do centers that will help you practice counting money!"
Student:	"UGH! Miss Tidwell I hate centers!"
Me:	"That was not a respectful thing to say. We need to think positively about everything we do in this classroom, it will help you be focused and want to participate, and will help you produce great work!"

Twenty minutes later my mentor teacher and I were having a discussion about an afternoon meeting after school that we were very uninterested in ...

Mentor Teacher:	"Don't forget we have that meeting after school today!"
Me:	"UGH, I have so many other things that I have to do today after school, I am not in the mood to stay after for a meeting ..."
(Previous student I corrected for being negative):	
	"MISS TIDWELL! You have to think positively about everything you have to do in life!"

... He sure told me! It was a hilarious comment, but he really hit home. I cannot tell my students that I expect them to act a certain way when I do not do it myself. So, after that day, I make sure that if I tell my students that we expect a certain behavior, I model exactly what I want to see. I do not stop when I get home, I practice it as a daily ritual. Student teaching is a learning experience in a lot of ways, but who would have thought that the students would start teaching you as much as you teach them?

There are many aspects of student teaching that have been rewarding, yet difficult. One of the most difficult tasks I have found is trying to be everything for your students when you have such little time. I believe this is why teaching is a lifestyle and not just a job. If you want to do the job right and be the best you can for your kiddos, you have to constantly be working and thinking about your students. I think the best teachers are the ones who put their heart and soul into their kids. The best teachers are the ones who believe in their students when they are two grade levels behind, the ones who push their students to reach their full potential, the ones who are willing to stay at school until 6 at night in order to adjust the reading centers for the students who needed extra practice. These teachers are the difference makers, and they are who I aspire to be. This year has been a phenomenal, stressful, exciting, yet scary experience. I have read multiple articles on how to help my kids in different content areas that they struggled with throughout the year, and most of them always had the same piece of advice. All of the articles mentioned that, in order to be a great teacher, you have to be willing to use your time to research, study, listen, and find new ways to help your kids learn. Most great teachers have said that if students are struggling, it is most likely something that the teacher needs to change about themselves or the way that they are doing something. I recently read an article titled, "5 Great Teachers on What Makes a Great Teacher," written by Anya Kamenetz. This article was written to inspire current classroom teachers of all levels. The author of the article interviewed five established teachers, and asked them multiple questions that dealt with real world issues of teaching, and the advice that they give to new and veteran teachers. One of my favorite pieces of advice was from Ken Bain, who was a teacher for 50 years. When asked what advice he would give to teachers now, he responded by saying:

> I'd just say that we have to learn constantly, about our students, their learning, our subjects, their society and lives, and so forth, and we just have to take advantage of all the opportunities we have to learn. All of the things that my colleagues have mentioned are important, but I'd emphasize three: Read, listen and talk. Read everything you can about learning and about your subject. Engage in conversations with other people who are also exploring the questions, ideas and information.

I relate to his response, because I have witnessed and experienced the success in his words. Listening to our students and learning from them, will eventually help ourselves. As a teacher, constantly researching and finding new ways to reach are students is eminent in our field. If I had to give any advice to a future student teacher, it is to never stop believing in your students, and to do all that you can to be their support and their guide.

Will your life change when you become a teacher? I sure hope so. My students have created such an evident change in my lifestyle, and it has been for the better. My students have challenged me, praised me, and have shown so much love to me. They have done all of the things that I have hoped I have done for them. Being a teacher is the best life-changing decision I have ever made, and I wish for all future and current teachers to receive the same blessing that I have received this year.

CHAPTER 8

Jasmime: What Teacher Educators Can Learn from Teacher Candidates

I named my chapter *Revelation* because during the writing process I was able to reflect and develop somewhat of an understanding why I wanted to become a teacher. This was difficult to write, because I did know how to approach it, and when I started to write, I did not know when to stop. Throughout the chapter my culture and language appears and my intention in doing this it to let the reader know and unveiling my thoughts about being and teacher candidate and becoming a teacher. Enjoy and learn!

"¿Mija, asi te vas a ir?," "Is that how you're going to leave?" These were the words that came out of my father's mouth as I was leaving for another day of AVID tutoring. I had my usual shirt and jeans combination, nothing out of the ordinary. I looked at him stunned, why should he care? "Mija, tu eres el ejemplo para los alumnus," "You are the example for the students." This is when I realized that my father saw me as a teacher before I did. For the rest of the day, I considered my role as an AVID tutor, and a future teacher.

I am a math major at the University of La Verne, yes, Math. I often get "why?" or "you're brave" from strangers. I would often retort with "thanks" or "suicide was too easy"; the response depends on how cheeky I am feeling. I never thought that math would be the subject I would be most intrigued by, but it was the only subject, which required me to sit and study. It was a challenge, a puzzle for my brain, a time to recognize and discover patterns and anticipate the next move. Teaching math came to me at the end.

The idea of teaching came to me in waves. I decided I wanted to be a teacher in third grade, mainly because of the impact my third grade teacher, Mrs. Charlotte, had on me. Mrs. Charlotte was a known for being a mean old lady that screamed at her students, but in realty she was the most compassionate teacher I have ever had. She was strict and expected a lot from us, and in return we tried our hardest.

In contrast, Mrs. Charlotte did not use labels such as at-risk, high-risk, limited English proficient and poverty-impacted, all that point to and justify race-based oppression, to describe her students of color. These deficiency-based terms facilitate and justify systemic acts of oppression against students of color most often in the form of lowered expectations and victim blaming. Many teachers are quick to blame their students of color for low school performance, a symptom of race-based oppression (Bonilla-Silva, 2010; Leonardo, 2005; Mills, 1997).

Mrs. Charlotte's pedagogy and classroom practices can be described as "old school" in the sense of what she expects from her students. Gordon (2000) calls "old school" teachers those who are traditional, conservative, and demanding. Ware (2006) and Bonner (2009) would consider Mrs. Charlotte a warm demander. They define a teacher who is a warm demander as someone who engages students through high expectations, firm and authoritative classroom management and culturally familiar communication (Hayes, Juarez, & Cross, 2011).

As I grew up, I later debated the thought of becoming a teacher and started to pursue other ideas, all of which I found to dislike. Teaching came back into my life my senior year of high school when I was chosen to be a co-teacher. This opportunity led to me being hired as an AVID tutor, which sparked my teaching ambitions again. Teaching math came about with the help of AVID. I was the only one who would take the challenge of helping students understand a difficult subject.

While I choose to enter the teaching profession to help students, others have chosen to teach for different reasons. Those who have decided to take on the profession have many reasons for doing so. For instance, Johnson et al. (2010) found through an analysis, based off of his questionnaire, that 23% of teachers entered the profession because of the possibility of putting underprivileged students on the path to success. As a former underprivileged student I can relate to the importance of giving others a chance and spending time with them. Many people who decide to become teachers have worked with children and adolescents before. Through interviews, Johnson et al. (2008) finds that teachers who had interaction with students and enjoyed it were more willing to go into the teaching profession. There was also a theme of continuing schooling through teaching. An interviewee liked history so much that she decided to become a teacher to continue her love of history, while teaching students (Johnson et al., 2010). Another aspect to why teachers go into teaching is the time commitment. Many of the teachers during Johnson's et al. (2008) interview considered the time flexibility; they were able to have a balance between work and family life.

With these incentives to go into teaching there are also challenges that new teachers face in the profession. Linda Darling-Hammond, in an interview, states that new teachers that are underprepared can become burned out (Scherer, 2012). She recommends new programs that assist teacher candidates with professional development and training (Scherer, 2012). An additional challenge that new teachers face is the ability to construct student centered lesson. New teachers are allowing for student-centered lesson that come easy to student and are not very challenging (Sadler, 2012). Further challenges are the lack of ability to create questions for student, when to ask questions, and how to asses students; how to manage student behavior, and how to create task that target a specific session (Sadler, 2012).

These challenges should be addressed during the teachers credential period. Teachers should be taught how to make student centered lessons challenging. Student centered lessons create an environment for students to question their studies and gain intellectual growth (Oliver, 2011). Teachers who have difficulty creating questions should look at Bloom's taxonomy. Bloom's Taxonomy helps challenge the way students think and improve students understanding of the subject (Lord & Baviskar, 2007). Some of these concerns should be acknowledged during their credential program.

Throughout my teaching experience I have created some beliefs about teaching. One of which is that teachers do not get much credit for what they do. I do not refer to what they teach or how they teach – it is the non-education aspect. Teachers are more than just lecturers and paper graders. They are motivators, leaders, councilors, and advocators; the list goes on and on. Teachers cannot simply come into the classroom and not get involved with the lives of their students, even though some try. They eventually find that one student whom reassures what they have been doing.

Unfortunately, there are some teachers that do not have same beliefs as others do. I came across a teacher that works at Fountain Middle School. She has a preconceived notion about her students. The population in Fountain is predominately Latino and African American. She told me that she does not bother helping them because "the girls will end up pregnant and the boys will be in jail before they turn 18." Her preconceptions revolted me and I realized she was feeding into a stereotype. Riley and Ungerleider (2012) have noted that teachers' attributions and stereotypes contribute to the high dropout rates and students self-worth. I discussed with her the implications that this can have on the students, but she did not listen. I am glad that we touch upon some of this in the credential program. I am not sure if the teacher is current at that school, but I hope she realizes what she is doing to those students.

While going through the credential program the courses that I have taken so far have not met some of my expectations. I thought going into the program that I would learn how create meaningful lesson plans. I thought we would learn different classroom management techniques, but above everything else I wanted to learn more about education in California. Yes, I was educated in California, but I wanted to know the ins and outs of this new common core implementation; I wanted to know about how to approach English learners and Special Education students and what California is doing about it.

During my Theories and Methods of Education for Linguistically Diverse Students course, I learned more about why my English speaking and writing skills are subpar, rather than how I could adapt lessons to English Language Learners (ELL's). I found out little to nothing on how I can make math accessible to EL students, other than vocabulary. During Diversity, Interaction, and the Learning Process course, we learned about diversity and the acceptance of it. Hobbs states (2014), as teachers we must learn about poverty to connect with students and find ways to help them they will accept the challenges that we put forth (Marquis-Hobbs, 2014). At times, I felt that I was being doctrine to hate White people and any Christian based religion rather than to help students in poverty, or with disadvantages. During one of our lectures about acceptance, we spoke about religion in the classroom and the professor said "teach in a private school if you cannot accept everyone" I agree with his quote to a certain extent. I do not believe in preaching to students about religion, or personal beliefs, in a public school. Personally, I do not expect students to have the same beliefs as I do and I will not preach to them. The claim that he stated made me realize that even those who preach equality and justice for everyone will not be acceptant of others beliefs. I'm not White and I felt that I was being personally attacked because of my beliefs. Both courses had a main focus on multiple subject credentials, and I always had to think about adapting the multiple subject strategies to single subject strategies.

I did take the six-week writing course, which was ok. The teachers were straightforward with the fact that they were there to teach grammar and not writing styles. I did benefit from this course because we spent some time on why commas are put in their place rather than to place commas when there is a rest. I did become more aware of my grammar even though I know I lacked in the fundaments. I always passed grammar test in grade school because they were multiple guess. The Learning Technology for Educators class has taught me usable tools for the classroom. I have used many of the features and applications that were presented to me. I have used Snagit to make screencast videos and I now use Prezi for presentations.

This semester I am taking Introduction to Teaching of Reading for Single Subject Candidates. This course, so far, has not met my needs for how to teach my students to read math or choose the right type of math reading for the students. I try to adapt what I learn from the course to my subject matter and how I can interpret the lessons to my future students. I am hoping it will come around during the rest of the semester. In my Teaching Strategies class we learn and present strategies, there is a summary at the end for the adaptation for ELL's, gifted students, and special challenged students. I do feel that I am ill prepared for this class, but my professor has helped us find the different types of modeling for teachers. She also emphasizes the multiple intelligences and reviews them after the lesson is taught. Multiple Intelligences are important because they help students understand material in differ ways and teachers are able to reach students different strengths (Christison & Kennedy, 1999). In Foundations and Introduction to Teaching: Single Subject class emphasizes on social issues that educators will face. The course has observation reflections based upon what the teacher candidate has seen in the fieldwork. The readings are prevalent to the social issues and my teachers have held me to a high standard. These are the professors, I tend to I learn the most from.

At Pacific Railway a lot of what I here is about API scores, and Standardized testing. The student's talk about the district being a well performing school based on the score the school has. They even talk about other schools in the district that have low scores. It fathoms me how they talk about it, and how important the student take scores into account. As a student at Pacific Railway High School, API scores where just a thing. The school would bribe us with a week-long of events at lunch to help us relax before state testing, encouraging us to study and later rewarding us if our API score went up. We never worried about what the score was; we just wanted to beat the other school in the district.

With No Child Left Behind ending and Common Core beginning it intrigues and scares me at the same time. No Child Left Behind (NCLB) began when I was in middle school. I didn't know how it would affect me and I did not care about the politics of it till I noticed how it affected my teachers. I remember going into my second period US history class with Mr. Monroe; he was an older man, with a grandfather complexion. He always stood by the door and greeted us as we walked in. His lectures were filled with "grandpa" stories of his road trips and his upbringing in the Panama Canal. It may sound like a cliché, but he really made history come alive when he animated his stories. During one of our regular lectures, Mr. Monroe was reminding us of district test coming up. The district had mandated benchmark test to be sure that teachers were following the standards. As he reminded us, he was going over the topics that were going to be on the test. The class was frantically writing down the topics, but as we did, he realized he needed to move a few lectures around to accommodate a few topics he did not cover. This was the first time I saw the frustration of NCLB, he told us that we would not be able to do an upcoming lesson for WWII that we had all been looking forward to. As he told us this there was a sense of disparity in the room, it was shown more by Mr. Monroe, he told us that he was frustrated with testing and he missed when students would volunteer and be active in the classroom. He continued with not being able to teach fun inquisitive lessons, because he had to get through lessons that were on the test. His voice was filled with disappointment, disappointment for a school system that had changed the way a teacher had to accommodate for tests. As I heard this, I realized how much testing was involved in school. I knew how to play the testing game well; I sometimes forgot to study and end up with a "C" or higher because I knew how to eliminate answers and find clues in the questions. At that moment I know that I was not really learning, to this day the only thing I remember are the lessons that Mr. Monroe attached to his stories. It intrigues and scares me because I do not want to have that frustration. I am intrigued by what is to come of the public school system and I am scared to get so lost in following the rules that I completely forgot about my students. Mr. Monroe retired the following year and now works as a substitute teacher for the History teachers on campus.

Many students have approached me and tutees letting me know that they want to go into teaching, and after I ask "why?" I usually tell them to read up on education and the changes it is facing. I tell them to tread carefully because no one really knows what is going to happen with the system changing. I tell them to observe a classroom and see if they can do it for a day. I have them imagine themselves in the classroom every day and ask what they envision. I also tell them to read up on the politics of Education and the requirements to start teaching. I try to bring to light the different perspective of teaching to them.

I would not stop anyone from going into the profession unless they really had no clue what they were going into. I do advise for people to check the standards and the different courses offered. I do warn them about the students they will be encountering; I often say that students smell fear and they will take advantage of anyone who does not have a sensible hand to deal with them. I ask them "why" and listen to the reasons they state, and I continue asking questions till they have reached no answer. I do not push too much when I ask others about why they want to get into the profession because I am still exploring my own doubts.

I often have doubts about my own ability to teach, but I try not to let it affect me because I know it can hinder my teaching abilities. Teachers' self-efficacy can impact a students' learning because the teacher does not have confidence (Penrose, 2007). My doubts are often about my ability to teach, or the ability to stay true to myself. The one thing I know that will keep me from moving forward is my CSET. I have already taken it, and will have missed the first CSET by two points. I am currently trying to find time to take it again, which I can never seem to find. Another challenge I have is to resend my TPA 1; I went to review it with one of the advisors and as we were reviewing it she told me she did not know why they did not expect the explanation I gave. It was really frustrating. I do not like repeating myself when I am answering questions, but I guess it is something I have to do to get a passing score. I need to find the time to get everything done.

Time is another struggle, which I believe it is part of being a first generation student. As much as my parents encourage me, they think that school stops when I get home, and if I stay in school too long to get things done they complain that they never see me. It is a never-ending battle of responsibilities of school, work, and home, and neither side will ever win or come to a compromise.

Other challenges I face is the ability to help special needs or students in urban schools. I have never dealt with students who have special needs, but I will have to wait for my Special Education Course to see how to prepare for them. As for urban schools, I do not feel that I could relate to them. I was raised in a neighborhood that rang with gunshots at two and three in the morning, with my next-door neighbors being gang members. My elementary and middle school where close to home, but my mother drove us twenty minutes to get to Pacific Railway High School. My parents succeeded in getting us into a good high school. It was in a better neighborhood and had a good reputation. People may call my Alma matter Ghetto-Wanda, but it was not ghetto at all. It has a diverse population, but most of the students where second and third generation students. There were no real issues with racism, or bullying. Fights were a rare occasion at the school, and there was no fear. Reflecting back it feels that it was a whole other world.

These past weeks I have asked myself "why?" why do I want to teach so badly? It all comes down to wanting to help students. I want to be able to help students get to college or make a difference in the community and lives. I think about the politics and it worries me because I may not know how to deal with it, but after I do my observations and spend time with the students I see that they want to learn. I like the connections that the students make after I explain something or give them a hint to a problem. I want to give my students the ability to have opportunities I never had. In school, I always had the grades and dedication to study, but being a first generation student I did not know how to het to college. The only requirements I knew were the A-G state requirements, a good GPA, SAT or ACT score. What I did not know about was when and how to fill out the college applications. I did not know about the fee waivers or personal essays. I was in the top 5% of my high school and I did not know how to get to college. This is one of the reasons why I worked for AVID, they helped students meet their potential and get them in a four-year college, and it was the start of my teaching career.

I enjoyed my time as an AVID tutor, I see old students posting on Facebook about their college experience and having opportunities that they might not have gotten. There were a few students who gave up on AVID and dropped out early, but by their senior year they would come up to me and ask for help. I did not say no; fortunately, they were TA's in some of the classes I tutored, so I was able to help them start a pathway to what they wanted, even if their transcript did not reflect a "good" student.

By maintaining a relationship with these students I was able to help them even if it took them four years to ask. Students who drop out of school claim they do it because teachers did not care about them (Wilkins, 2014). These teacher-student relationships influence student academics (Wilkins, 2014). Teachers should make an effort to attain a relationship with their students, so that they are able to help them when they ask.

I also think that teaching may be in my genes, I know it cannot be proven, but after I told my parents I wanted to be a teacher, they said "Como tus tia," "just like your aunts." I found out my aunts in Mexico are teachers, and a few of my aunts in California where teacher in the Los Angeles school district. My father told me about my aunt and her husband who are now retired, were the activist for the schools in Mexico. My aunt was a superintendent of the schools in Aguascalientes and my uncle was a university professor. They started off in San Luis Potosi were they started a school from scratch in an old cornfield. They wanted to make education accessible to everyone in the area. I am proud of my aunt and uncle; though they are both retired they are currently still involved in the school districts, in Mexico, publishing books that could change the way schools and the government work. Their passion for teaching feeds my ambitions, but I also know that I have to be realistic about my teaching.

My teaching philosophy as I began was simple. I wanted to help students help themselves. I did not want to simply give them answers; I wanted them to learn how to find the answer. Now, I want students to ask questions, reflect, and discover the answer. I want them to become curious in the material. Socrates once said, "I cannot teach anybody anything, I can only make them think." I want my students to become reliant on themselves, this does not mean that I will not be their when they need help, but I want to teach them to learn how to think and ask questions.

Other teachers can use this to help students search for the answer and become curious about the subject they are taking. Teachers can ask student relevant questions to get their minds going. My philosophy is still developing, and it will change as I keep teaching, and learning from my students. Some of my best teachers, like Mr. Monroe, used their experiences for teaching. I feel I can bring my personal experience to some of my students. The elementary school I went to had a few lock downs when I was there, two of which I remember. One of the incidents happened while I was at recess; I was in the fourth grade. I was at lunch running towards the playground, and a friend and I saw a man hiding in one of the trees across the field. The lunch proctor called into the office and the bell was immediately rung. We went straight to our classrooms and continued recess there. We did not know what was going on, but all we heard were helicopters and a loud speaker. The guy in the tree had apparently stolen a car and had hid from the cops in a tree. I feel that if I ever experienced a locked down in my career, the important thing is to keep a level head for my students.

The worst lock down I experienced was at Pacific Railway in May of 2008. A "shit list," much like a burn book from the movie *Mean Girls* was going around in a text message. They exposed every secret about a few students on campus for three days, new secrets and names were on the list every day, by Wednesday afternoon while coming out from a club meeting the security guard started shutting the entire school down, "get out everyone we are closing, its after school," "call your parents to pick you up," what I did not know was awaiting the next day. A threat had gone out to the students who were on the list; they were going to be gunned down if they showed up to school the following day. Thursday seemed normal walking into school, until I saw cops surrounding every entryway, and students going to the front of the campus because newscasters were in front of the school. At this time I did know about the threat, so I went to the office, I was the switchboard assistant and I saw and heard what was going happening as it unfolded. Parents filled the entire front office, the line was heading out the door, parents wanting to know if the reports where true, and if the school was going to be shut down. The parents were in pure panic mode, demanding to know what is going on and pulling their children from class. I had to translate the entire time I was there. During my TA period I was running around campus helping to get off campus passes to students with other teacher on their prep period. It was awful; you would have a stack of passes, go into a classroom, call out names and see if the student was there. If they were there they had the ability to leave. If they were not there they most likely were waiting in the office for the pass. By fifth period there were three people in my class. The police had determined that there was no danger, but they still remained on campus. That did not stop the threat; it was continued for the next day. Friday came and the school was deserted. Only a few students came, five to ten per class with students leaning every period. Till this day, the freshman now, who were in elementary school when this occurred, know what happened.

Just this past fall semester we have had six bomb threats. The FBI is now involved in the investigation. These experiences may be intense, and unfortunately it has taught me a lot of what I will have to deal with. Teachers must know how to keep their cool during these situations. By keeping calm they are still able to have some sort of control when this occurs. Teacher candidates can use my experience that some days will not be easy. Teacher candidates must be prepared for any type of day when they are teaching.

With the challenges that schools are facing being critical is important. To be critical is to express the good and bad judgment of something. Being critical in uncritical times is to be able to reflect on what is happening now, asking "Why" is it that people are not changing? Why are they resisting to change? This saying can mean many things, we may want to change while others do not see it necessary, or we can evaluate what is going on to improve, even if things seem to be ok.

As for my teaching profession, this statement means making the right judgments during a time when no one notices that something is going wrong. At times it may be standing up for students to be given opportunities. It reminds me of when my government teacher wrote a letter to the district about the district testing. His letter berated the test, going through each question letting them know how poorly written the test was, and further stating why he thought the test was unnecessary. He was able to see the issue of the test when the district thought there was nothing wrong. The district made us take the test anyway, but our teacher let us know how the questions were written, so we could test better.

The teaching program so far has only one course that has make me think critically. It is Contemporary Issues, Foundation and Introduction to Teaching: Single Subject. I am constantly thinking about applications to the school, society, and questioning whether my practices, my master teachers, the schools, and the district practices are going to help the students. I have read more articles on education on my own because of this course. My only add on is how I will be able to make a difference without risking being labeled "that" teacher. I do not want to seem as if I am not a team player. I would like some advice on how to go about this. All of my teachers that have shown some type of judgment have been at the school for years and are taking their last chance to help the education system. I refer back to my father's comment that baffled me; I now see that if I start acting the part, in his case dressing the part, I can start to make a difference.

CHAPTER 9

Ximaroa: All Things Considered

The summer between my junior and senior year of college presented educational obstacles that were life changing; I began to question myself as an intellectual and everything I had worked towards to that point. For years, I was reluctant to talk about that time in my life. As I go about my journey in a teaching credential program, I often find myself reflecting on my past experiences, my passions, and strengths as a prospective educator. The more knowledge I gain in the field of education the more I realize that there are multiple factors that come into play when determining my potential success as a prospective teacher. For this reason, I present to you *All Things Considered*.

Throughout secondary school and college I did not envision myself as teacher, but I knew that I loved to learn and share innovative information with those around me. My high school Earth Science teacher sparked my interest in Geology; her passion was infectious and her knowledge in the subject was clearly reflected in her teaching. She was consistently enthusiastic and engaging. I gained a great amount of useful knowledge in the subject that year, which is not surprising considering that teachers have a significant effect on student learning, and content knowledge plays an important part in teachers' effectiveness (Darling-Hammond, 2000; Izumi & Evers, 2002).

I entered college with a romanticized view of receiving a degree in Geology in four years, going to graduate school, followed by finding an amazing job in the field. My first three years as an undergraduate studying Geology, with an emphasis in Paleontology, were full of rich experiences and an abundance of learning opportunities. I worked in an invertebrate paleontology lab for all three years where I worked hands-on with a specimen collection from the Himalayas and another from Colorado. This hands-on experience with specimen lead to my getting selected for a paid internship position, which was originally only for graduate students, in the curation department at the Western Science Center in Hemet, CA. One of the greatest opportunities I was presented with was assisting with a master's student research project, which was eventually published in the *Journal of Paleontology*, making me a co-author. I am very grateful that I was selected to participate in research being that undergraduate research has been shown to be a high-impact practice that benefits undergraduate students (Kuh, 2008; Manak & Young, 2014; Osborn & Karukstis, 2009). Studies also show that students who have opportunities to engage in undergraduate research have significantly better learning outcomes than similar students without those opportunities (Manak & Young, 2014). I believe this to be true being that undergraduate research not only allowed me to gain knowledge in the field, but also allowed me to master certain aspects of it to the point where I was able to present findings at undergraduate research symposiums. I also attend dozens of lectures given by experts in the field, which increased my literacy in the discipline. At this point I was not just accumulating knowledge about the discipline, but understanding the discipline's important theoretical ideas by being continuously exposed to them (Johnson et al., 2011).

By the end of my junior year of college, I had received multiple awards, grants, and scholarships as an undergraduate in the field, but I needed to pass a math class to register for senior year courses. I used grant money I had received to retake the class in the summer. I thankfully passed the class, but then something strange happened; when I tried to register for senior classes I couldn't. This is when everything changed. I quickly made an appointment to speak to my science advisor at the university who informed me that there was a new policy that required students to file a petition to retake a class. The petition had to be approved by the dean of science at the university in order for me to continue working towards my degree in Geology. The advisor had no explanation as to why I hadn't been notified before paying for and taking the class, but I forgave her being that it was her first year as an advisor. An article I recently read showed that meeting with academic advisors about course plans did not have a positive effect on degree attainment for students in STEM (Gayles & Ampaw, 2011); these findings do not surprise me. The petition was quickly returned to me. As I slowly pulled it out of the envelope, I read DENIED in large red bold letters stamped on it and a hand written note by the dean himself that said, "based on your previous academic history, I do not believe you will succeed in future academic courses in your field." I was devastated. I recently read an article that talked about the loss of women in STEM fields at critical junctures of the education pipeline and how the loss has received national attention over the past few decades (Gayles & Ampaw, 2011). The article also mentions that federal support has been earmarked for attracting and retaining women and other under-represented populations in STEM fields (Gayles & Ampaw, 2011). Another article presented a critical issue of concern in regard to the high number of women who enter college with an interest in STEM and the low number of women who actually complete a STEM bachelor's degree six years later (Huang, Taddese, & Walter, 2000). These articles focus on prior grades and student backgrounds, but I'd be curious to see if there are other factors that contribute to these shocking statistics.

Fortunately, the obstacle of not being able to complete my degree in Geology was not the end of my educational career. Towards the end of my sophomore year, I had decided to take a few Spanish Literature courses. Spanish was my first language, and I felt it necessary to strengthen my skills. I took the language placement test and placed into upper division language courses. That year, I began taking Spanish courses concurrent with my Geology courses. When my petition was denied, I had no choice but to leave the sciences and transfer to humanities. I played catch-up and took three to four Spanish Literature courses per quarter my senior year of college. My hard work paid-off that year and I was able to graduate on time with a B.A. in Spanish Literature. During that final year as an undergraduate in the humanities, I was successful in my courses and was able to meet knowledgeable professors. I did not participate in undergraduate research; however, I was invited to my last quarter. Although I enjoyed my experience as a Spanish Literature student, Geology continued to be my passion.

Throughout the teaching credential program we have discussed the importance of getting to know our students. Author William Ayers (2010) in his book that we read in my Foundations of Education Course makes the argument about the importance of viewing students for who they are and taking into account the skills and experiences they bring into the classroom. I share my experience as an undergraduate with you in an attempt to give you insight on the experiences that have shaped me into the person I am today.

When I started my credentialing program I was working towards a single subject credential to teach foreign language. I thought it would be best if I applied for a single subject credential to teach Spanish being that it was the subject I had a physical degree in. I figured I'd have a better chance of getting into the credentialing program this way since there are multiple articles presenting the belief that teachers should successfully complete an undergraduate major/course work equivalent to an undergraduate major/a graduate degree/advanced certification or credential, in each subject they teach (Tzur et al., 2011).

As I worked on lesson plans and assignments during my first semester in the program, I realized I would enjoy the process and perform tasks with much more enthusiasm if I were searching for content that was Earth Science related. At the beginning of my second semester, I switched my credential focus to single subject Earth Science, which is my current topic of study. When I told my supervising professor about my decision to switch content focus his eyes enlarged and his expression suggested I was making a poor decision. He didn't say much or ask me why; all he said was that I would need to pass the CSET. He does not know much about me other than what is stated on paper; therefore, I did not judge his reaction.

The discussion on whether or not a teacher should be able to teach outside of their content area of expertise can be quite controversial. In Theories and Methods of Education for Linguistically Diverse Students, there was a heated debated among students on whether or not students who did not major in a subject should be allowed to teach it. I do not remember what stance the professor took, but I do know that the discussion greatly affected a student in the program. After class, she talked to me about what another student had said that upset her and how she was unhappy with how the credentialing program was being run. It was our first semester in the program and we had the same professor for two classes. I must admit that I too was questioning the program at that point; the classes seemed unorganized and I didn't feel that we were covering the content in enough depth. Unfortunately, she dropped out of the program shortly after that class session. The student was extremely knowledgeable in liberal studies, gender studies, and literature and always made positive contributions to class discussions; I believe she had the skills and potential to have become a great teacher.

I frequently come across the phrase "highly-qualified teacher" when reading through education articles or even looking at job descriptions, but I have yet to find a set definition. The following is an excerpt from an article titled *No Teacher Left Unqualified* in which a teacher expresses her thoughts on the term "highly qualified": "I feel like highly qualified doesn't mean much and they put a lot of emphasis on it and all it really means is that you have specific degrees and you passed a couple of tests, but it doesn't mean that you are a good teacher." The article then presents important aspects of teaching that current teachers believe are important if not more important than having highly qualified content knowledge. The aspects mentioned are having good pedagogical skills, exposure to professional development, and teaching experience (Karelitz et al., 2011). This suggests that current teachers tend to value pedagogical skills, which are taught in teaching credential programs, and experience, which is acquired over time. In regard to professional development, I believe credentialing programs and school districts can do more to offer professional development workshops. Most research finds a positive relationship between the number of years a teacher has spent in the classroom and his or her influence on student achievement – but the benefit of that experience appears to plateau after the third to fifth year; an increase in professional development workshops might prevent teachers from reaching that plateau (Winters, 2011). Professional development workshops will expose teachers to innovative scholarly research, which will then improve teachers' skills in critical thinking and problem solving, re-ignite their intellectual curiosity, and cultivate excitement about their disciplines (Manak & Young, 2014).

The task of expanding a prospective teacher or current teachers content knowledge does not solely depend on the credentialing program or school district in which a teacher works. The Geological Society of America encourages K-12 educators to get involved in professional organizations such as GSA, NAGT, NSTA, and NESTA; attend their meetings and participate in workshops and field trips that they sponsor; Partner with geoscience faculty at local colleges and universities, and learn about their research and the tools they use (GSA, 2011). I became educated on many of these organizations while completing an assignment for Introduction to Teaching Reading Single Subject. The assignment required that I research a professional organization in my field of study. This assignment proved to be very insightful because I was able to read the organizations position statements on current changes in education and become exposed to variety of resources that are available for teachers in the field.

The Geological Society of America states that highly qualified Earth Science teachers must receive training at the college level (GSA, 2011). The National Science Teacher Association released a position statement on *The Role of Research on Science Teaching and Learning* stating that research suggests educators are not preparing all students to achieve high levels of science performance (USDOE, 2011); teachers are failing to graduate enough students with the skills needed to fill the growing number of jobs in science, technology, engineering, and mathematics (STEM) (NRC, 2010). Therefore, a degree does not necessary equate to a deep understanding in a given field of study. These findings open way to the discussion on content knowledge.

Common content knowledge is defined by its shared use in common across adult pursuits other than just teaching (Phelps et al., 2014). Horizon content knowledge is defined by knowledge of how different content ideas are connected across the content domain, often with more elementary or basic ideas connected to more complex or advanced ideas (Phelps et al., 2014). Specialized content knowledge includes types of content knowledge that are only used in teaching (Phelps et al., 2014). Content knowledge is a long-established basic prerequisite for teaching a subject, and it is an essential requirement for teacher certification (Hill, 2007). However, scholars have argued that teachers need to develop forms of content knowledge that go beyond basic content proficiency to be effective in the classroom (Phelps et al., 2014). This appears to be especially true with the introduction of the new common core and next generation science standards. The Geological Society of America encourages the inclusion of undergraduate and/or graduate geoscience courses in all teacher candidate preparation for those seeking elementary and middle childhood licensures (GSA, 2011). Such requirements would insure that teachers develop skills that go beyond basic content proficiency. Teacher educators should begin to build programs that promote, or even require, expertise within the disciplines our teacher candidates aspire to teach. They must create teacher-preparation curricula that are based on the practice that students construct knowledge of a discipline by engaging in the habits and practices that are valued and used by experts in the field (Johnson et al., 2011). Teacher educators and teacher candidates would be well served to use the tools, work at the construction site, and be apprenticed to journeymen who understand the field and its tools (Johnson et al., 2011).

The National Science Teacher Association released a position statement on the adoption and implementation of The Next Generation Science Standards (NGSS); stating that the standards will provide students with the skills and knowledge they need to be well-informed citizens, will prepare them for higher education and future careers, and will deepen their understanding of the science community. I am in favor of the redirected focus the NGSS have created. The new standards aim towards producing a deeper understanding of content as well as exposing students to application of content by focusing on a smaller, more teachable number of disciplinary core ideas. The standards also stray from the traditional separation of content and time restraints set on students, which I believe will prove to be beneficial. The NSTA suggests that for the Next Generation Science Standards to be implemented successfully, long-term systemic efforts must be made. The efforts described include changes in instruction, curriculum, assessment, teacher preparation and professional development, accompanied by extensive financial, administrative, and public support. Because of my past experiences, I like that the Next Generation Science Standards were developed to help all students develop science proficiency by requiring instruction that provides them with opportunities for a range of scientific investigations and thinking, including – but not limited to – inquiry and investigation, collection and analysis of evidence, logical reasoning, and communication and application of information. The NGSS aim to spark student interest which is great because research shows that lack of interest in students' prior experience can affect their ability to use this prior experience as a foundation for their learning (Peters & Daly, 2013).

My past research experiences, involvement, and the years of courses I took in the field of Geology have prepared me to successfully implement the NGSS when in my own classroom. Courses in my credentialing program have thus far provided me with the pedagogical knowledge and teaching techniques that will contribute to my success as a teacher. My course, Learning Technology for Educators, provided me with knowledge on technological and online resources that will greatly benefit myself as a teacher and that will spark student interest and encourage student interaction. Diversity, Interaction and the Learning Process, taught me teaching strategies and classroom management techniques that have proven to be beneficial when substitute teaching; I am looking forward to trying these techniques in my own classroom. Theories and methods for Linguistically Diverse Learners, required that I read about English Language Learners. I picked up on useful strategies that enhance ELL experiences in the classroom and have witnessed the strategies being implemented in the classroom I am currently observing. The most beneficial classes I have taken thus far in my credentialing program have been Introduction to Teaching Reading Single Subject and Foundations and Introduction to Teaching Single Subject. The readings and assignments in both classes have expanded my knowledge in the field of education tremendously. I often find myself telling people that taking these two course together was my most stressful and demanding semester I've ever had in college, but I also note that the knowledge I have gained in such a short amount of time is unheard of. This is supported by Astin's theory of involvement (1984), which suggests that the amount of physical and psychological energy that students invest in educational activities is positively associated with student learning and personal development (Gayles & Ampaw, 2011).

If I were to offer advice to individuals contemplating entering a teaching credential program I would say, do it! It is a lot of work and often forces you to step out of your comfort zone, but I think it is necessary preparation if you want to succeed as a teacher. If you get use to stepping out of your comfort zone before entering a classroom and school environment, you will have one less obstacle to face during your first years as a teacher. For those who are already in a credentialing program I say, think less and do more. I say this in regard to workload. I myself am guilty of complaining and stressing about the amount of reading and work being assigned. The less we think about everything we have to do and just do it, the easier the tasks become and the faster we get through them. Teacher educators are pretty good at selecting books and articles that are interesting and relevant, making the assigned reading much more enjoyable. I look forward to upcoming courses and experiences in the credentialing program.

CHAPTER 10

Miquel: The Great Emancipator of Education

I am Miguel Santana and I am working on my credential to become a Social Science teacher. Becoming a teacher is no crusade for me. There is no big agenda like most people say when going into teaching.

While Miguel may say that there is no real agenda for him becoming a teacher as that was the case of why many teachers especially those teachers of color, but after having Miguel in class, he has the passion and the love of history that I, Cleveland Hayes II, wish many of the students had. In my mind it is not important why Miguel has decided to go in to teaching because his passion and the love of the subject and the love of making content accessible to students beyond must memorizing facts is the important part (Hayes, 2014).

Miguel's story in his own words: I want to become a high school teacher for many reasons: steady paycheck, benefits, schedule, hours, vacation, and being able to attend many school sporting events. Some of these reasons have to do with helping my family take care of my younger sister and also contributing financially. The recession hit my parents' jobs hard at the same time I was diagnosed with Crohns Disease. Becoming a teacher does a lot for my family. When thinking about the reason why I want to become a teacher I realize that it sounds incredibly selfish. Bibo (2015) states, I think we have to look deep within ourselves and recognize that not only does the world need great teachers, role models willing to give selflessly, but that we too have a need to play the role or inspirer, sage, and friend. Reading this made me feel less selfish.

My master teacher says my strength is my openness of my struggles with the students. Showing my humanity to the students broke down barriers and allowed them to more open. They were liberated from the thinking that they are the only ones struggling. I will become a teacher to help my family but I will be also helping my community. I will be a role model for the younger generation and through my selflessness, I will inspire students. Through my years in K-12, I never had a teacher that really opened up to students or that challenged me to think critically.

There is where the foundations course really but this together for me. One of the major assignments for this class was to design a Critical Pedagogy lesson. The Professor, requires that we ask our students what is going on in their lives, what is important to them, what conversations are they having outside of school. Then we are required to plan a content lesson based upon the conversation with students. However, based upon my own K-12 experience, it took me a while to think of questions like this on my own. When dealing with history, I was taught to memorize names, dates, and timeline of events and never to think on my own or to see other points of view. It wasn't until I attended Polytechnic State, where I was liberated from one way of thinking to a more critical based thinking (Duncan-Andrade & Morrell, 2008). After I received my Bachelor's degree in History, I realized that knowledge is easily obtained via World Wide Web, but the skills on how to interpret and understand the knowledge is vital to an individual's learning process. It is through my experience at Polytechnic State that I have adopted the same teaching motto, "learn by doing." Interactive and hands on learning, best serve students ability to obtain the types of skills that are necessary to think critically.

When thinking about critical thinking it is important to first define it because many people have different ideas on what it means to be a critical thinker. Wallerstein (1983) states that "critical thinking begins when people make the connections between their individual lives and social conditions" (p. 16). Critical thinking is about making connections with the content material that is being taught. This is not an easy process to learn on one's own. Students must have a teacher that has the ability to relate to students and that can identify the connections. If a teacher cannot relate to their students then students will fail to understand and even be less motivated about what they are learning. The goal is to develop active learners rather than obedient robots. Developing active learners will benefit students beyond the classroom and will carry on with them throughout their lifetime. Something that Dr. Hayes told us the first day of class, "teaching is not a "how to process," but a "how to think process."

The biggest trend during my years of education came during the No Child Left Behind (NCLB) era. In the article, Fuller, Wright, Gesicki, and Kang (2007), "the legislative crafters of NCLB assumed that proficiency meant a similar level of student performance across test and states" (p. 269). NCLB was a standard based education reform to track students' progress nationally. This lead to educators to teach to pass a test because these numbers determined how well teachers taught and the quality of the school. These tests did not take the student body into consideration. These test did not take into consideration the, the lived experiences and internal experiences that are important when teaching kids. There was no culturally responsive teaching being taught and the only funds of knowledge that was important was that determined by someone who didn't teach the kids in the school or in many cases that looked like or had the same lived experiences as the students (Gonzales, Moll, & Amanti, 2005; Ladson-Billings, 1994). Now that I am older, I look back and truly see the negative impact this has on students. For years, I thought I was not as smart as other students because I didn't do as well on the state testing. I would get an average and below average results. I now realize that grades and test scores do not define your intelligence. I was lucky to have parents to keep supporting. Many of my classmates however, were not so lucky and became so discouraged that they grew to hate school. Through further research, I learned that many states with high poverty and high population of minorities resisted the NCLB act the most (Shelly, 2008). This was due to the level of fairness. The states that resist do not see it being fair because with a high minority and poverty population, they are farther behind. I find that NCLB does not track progress accurately because a standardized test does not determine intelligence. Students don't have an adversity to learning they have an adversity to school. A student that can be taught to memorize information is not more intelligent (Duncan-Andrade & Morrell, 2008).

Another trend seen today is the Academic Performance Index (API), which was part of the Public Schools Accountability act in California. The NCLB act was passed at a federal level, which ultimately led states to create systems to follow the national trend. The API act was created to assess school performance and ranking for all public schools in the state (Tobias, 2004). This might seem like a great idea but I see many flaws in this type of accessing. First, is the same flaw of NCLB, scores doing not determine a student's intelligence. Second, the more important thing schools are not focusing is on scores. Schools are no longer interested in students learning. This puts pressure on teachers to quickly speed through material in order to prepare students for the test. I have seen this first hand with classes I have been in, primary and secondary level of education. Teachers speed through material, complete activities to help students memorize the content, without any concerns if students truly understand what they are being taught. The NCLB act and API system may have been passed with good intentions but I see it turned away from what is good for the students to a passing of a test.

Another system that came out of the NCLB act is the California Educator Credentialing Examinations, also known as the CSET. It was a struggle for me to get through these tests. These tests are another negative side of the NCLB trend. Again, we see the idea of test scores deciding an individual's intelligence. I had to take one of the test three times, missing the pass mark by 1 or 2 points. How does this test define my ability to teach my subject? I would think my degree in history, graduating with honors, and being a member of the history honor society, I would be considered highly qualified. Each test cost a $69 and I have just learned, that when you want to see past scores, the test taker must pay a $10 fee. This system seems less about being a qualified teacher and more of

California politics collecting more money. I meet many people who are cannot become teachers because they keep failing the test and are limited on money to keep paying the fee. The test is also only administered six times a year, which puts more pressure on people to pass due to time constraint.

The newest educational trend today is known as the Common Core Standards. The standards were created to ensure that all students graduate from high school with the skills and knowledge necessary to succeed in college, career, and life, regardless of where they live. The key word used is "skills" because this is a focus on the students' thinking process. The Common Core is geared towards getting the students to think critically. The strategies used in Common Core are designed to develop skills that students can take with them throughout life. During my observation hours, I see a tremendous difference in instruction from then and now. English classes have begun to work with more non-fiction material that is designed to have students in critical thinking on current topics in society. Math classes focused on cooperative learning and explanation. Obtaining the right answer is no longer the goal. Teachers want students to explain their answers and also be able to teach others their process. Common Core is still early in its development to tell if it will make a big impact on our students. The success of Common Core will rely on the teachers that execute the strategies. If executed correctly, I believe that Common Core will be a success.

The teaching credential program at the University of La Verne (ULV) is focused on developing future teachers who will be able to execute in the classroom. I am currently still at the beginning of the program, but the classes I have taken are going to come in handy when I teach. One of the first classes I had taken focused on classroom management. In the book, *The Classroom Management Book*, the author states, classroom management is all about effective teacher instruction, not about discipline (Wong, 2014). This is very important to know because if all you do is discipline, then you are simply a babysitter and not an educator. Knowing the difference between management and discipline will be vital to surviving the first year of teaching. It is important to have the students learn classroom procedures and always come in having a plan. The students will exploit any sign that a teacher is not organized. The ULV credential program prepares future teachers to face challenges like this so they will be effective teachers. You cannot be an effective teacher if you do not have control of the class.

The ULV credential program is also teaching how to integrate technology into our classrooms. Many teachers today, fight against technology and say it's nothing more than a distraction. Their mind set is based on, if we learned without technology then so can our students. Not only does integrating technology make class enjoyable for students but it also gives them hands on skills with technology. With technology advancing, our students need to be able to use technology so they have experience going out into the real world. In the book, *Retool your school: The educator's essential guide to Google's free power apps*, the authors state that, you need the skills, the tools, and you also need the approach. Just the tools alone without the approach aren't going to work. And the tools without the skills aren't going to work (Lerman & Hicks, 2010). This statement explains that simply having technology isn't enough; teachers need to be educated on how to use this technology in the classroom. Teachers need to know technology so they may teach it to their students. Teachers have to understand that we are preparing students with skills to jobs that may not exist yet. Teachers need to keep up with the times so their students could keep up as well. Having a technology for educators' class is essential to developing future teachers on how to properly integrate technology.

The credential program at ULV has also been helping in learning on how to instruct English Learners (EL). With the growing number of ELs coming to the United States, teachers from K-12 need to have the skills to make content material comprehensible. About 79 percent of English Learners in the United States speak Spanish as their native language (Calderon, Salvin, & Sanchez, 2011). In the ULV credential program, students are being taught on how to instruct in many different ways. For example, students are learning how to teach direct instruction, cooperation learning, and inquiry lessons. When learning each of these types of lessons we are also being taught on how to adapt the lesson to ELs' needs. The ULV program has done a good job of instilling ways to adapt to an EL that students now find it second nature in teaching. In the book, *Making Content Comprehensible for English Learners: The SIOP Model*, it gives many strategies on how to instruct ELs. The book was assigned to one of my classes, and found important because it stresses the importance on building a strong foundation of vocabulary. Building background has been a common theme I have seen throughout the classes I have taken at ULV. It is important to have students build a strong foundation so you may build off of. The strategies and techniques for ELs being taught at ULV have been useful. Building background proved useful in my fieldwork this year when I was beginning a new chapter. I focused in the beginning with getting students familiar with the vocabulary which set the foundation for the rest of the lesson.

Besides teaching how to instruct ELs, the credential program has been teaching on how to adapt to students with disabilities; orthopedic impairment, vision impairment, and autism. In my fieldwork, I have two students with orthopedic impairment which is a physical disability that affects a child's educational performance. I have learned that there are ways to alter a lesson to help the needs for these types of students. The student can have a variety of types of orthopedic impairments. The student in my class had to use a walker for his severe limp. I noticed that the student would come to class everyday exhausted. I altered my lessons to less copying of material and focused on more partner interaction. As long as I kept him busy with discussing what we were learning, I saw that his focused improved which showed in his work.

The ULV credential program is teaching future teachers how to adapt to different types of students, but also, teaching us to be critical during uncritical times. Being a critical thinker is a democratic learning process that frees an individual of one way of thinking. The uncritical of times is the environment we are going into. School is not a democratic instruction. Students are told when to eat, to use the restroom, and to go to another class. Most schools still have the old trends of NCLB still lingering. I will be entering the teaching force during a transitional period between NCLB and the Common Core Standards. The ULV program is preparing students to build a democratic classroom community, which will help us during the transitional period to the future.

In the book, *To Teach*, William Ayers (2010) states that in school, there is no privacy and there is little individuality. In order for educators to be critical in uncritical times, we need to create a democratic environment. This means to build relationships with the students, liberate the curriculum, and create a safe learning environment. This means; familiarizing with the community, identify any extracurricular, and learn about their interests. During my fieldwork, I took the time to go see a student in my class at her basketball game. Just by showing up and showing interest, the student had a positive attitude in class. With just a little effort to get to know students, they begin to open up and feel more comfortable in participating. Liberating the curriculum is also a way to think critical during uncritical times. As public school teachers, we are restricted by the content standards on what we can teach. However, Ayers (2010) proposes that teachers can break down barriers, unpack preconceptions, and create worthwhile experiences. Meaning that teachers should be able to make connections to content material with real life. The idea is to have students understand why what is being taught important, and how they will use it after the class. Most people believe that most things they learn in school is not applicable in the real world. It is the teachers' job to get the students to think critically on how they would use what they are learning in the real world. Building bridges and liberating curriculum both contribute to building a safe environment. But instead of thinking of it as environment, think of it as a democratic community. In a democratic community, everyone participates and helps one another out. A teacher should expand the community outside the classroom and in some cases outside the school. I find that the more dedicated you are to your students, the more dedicated they are in learning.

Anyone going in to teaching must realize that a professor cannot teach you everything there is to know. They best way to learn is through experiences and with hands on situations. It is one thing to tell you what you will experience in the classroom and another to actually experience. Many issues that students have going into teaching is that they do not have enough hours spent in a classroom (Stoddart, 1990). It is for this reason why certain school districts allow for internship teachers. This allows for teachers to gain experience in the classroom with students. The ULV credential program is great with require fieldwork hours that allows for students to gain experience. My words of wisdom for anyone wanting to be a teacher is to gain experience not just in the classroom but with working with others as well. Any experience in managing or coaching will be beneficial to you in the classroom. Many school districts favor coaching experience when hiring a teacher. Coaches tend to have skills that allow them to be facilitators and guides for students. Coaches usually are able to adapt to different types of students and alter instruction that they would better understand (Udesky, 2015). I use the words "tend" and "usually" because this is not a perfect way to hire someone. I know many people who are coaches yet lack managing skills. The best thing for anyone going into teaching is to gain experience.

As I write this, my viewpoints are all a result from my lived experiences in life. Lived experiences will influence the way you teach. We as teachers are going to want to fix the wrongs we see in the classrooms. Growing up, I had lots of teachers run the classroom through fear. Fear of getting the answer wrong, fear of being called on, and fear of being embarrassed in front of your peers and personally I do not want students to have the fear I endured as a kid. It created a sense of stress and panic that I still carry today. Now with my medical issues with Crohns disease, when I get stressed, I shut down mentally and physically. In the class I am at for my fieldwork, there is a student with a similar disease who I see struggle every day because of the stress brought by teachers. I share with him and others on my ways to fight stress. I like to think that my lived experiences can be turned into positive influence for students. I don't think everyone has this way of thinking however, because I know some student teachers who loved the idea of popcorn reading and do not see the negative affect it has on students, but since they had done well with it, they believe their students will have the same results.

It is through my own experience that I developed my own teaching philosophy over time. When I first entered the program, I merely just copied Polytechnic State's motto, "learn by doing," because it has taught me a lot in my four years as an undergrad. I have grown to be a more proactive educator. I believe is that a teacher should be a student as well by actively learning and engaging with students. Keeping up with academic trends as well as social trends: as examples. Instead of trying just to better my classroom, I want to interact with the entire school and build a community of active students. I ultimately want students to see my humanity that I to was once in their shoes. Break down the hierarchy of system and create a democratic environment where students can actively engage in learning under my management.

I like to say that I am a fool, not because of my intelligence because it is how I have initially been perceived. In my youth, I was judged according to my last name and placed into an EL class in elementary, even though the only language I speak is English. I was also judged on my test scores as I was placed in an English linguistics class in middle school for getting below average on my state test. In high school, I was told that the only way I will enter college is if I received an athletic scholarship. Life has being filled with barriers, challenges, and people telling me what I can and can't do. They thought I was a fool when I told them I would do better, and I did. I now find myself entering a profession that is field with many older generation people. Most of whom are content on keeping the imaginary meritocracy system active. Completing my field work at my old high school, I see that many teachers do not have hope for the kids. There is no belief that students can do better and now see me as fool thinking otherwise. I want to prove these teachers wrong and liberate them from this way of thinking. I want to liberate the students from the notion that there is a ceiling on their limits. People back then thought Abraham Lincoln to be a fool for freeing the slaves and breaking barriers and I can only hope that after this program at ULV that I will be the great emancipator of education.

CHAPTER 11

Owen: Is Math that Terrible?

My name is Owen Patrick, and my content area is mathematics. Before starting this credential program, I only wanted to teach high school mathematics. Now, after just slightly over a year working at a middle school, I would be willing to work at any level of secondary mathematics. I chose this title because I believe that mathematics is beautiful, artistic, relatable, and all around essential to everyone's life. People do not like mathematics, "nearly a third of Americans (30%) say they would rather clean the bathroom than solve a math problem" (Change, 2015, p. 2). I believe that the reason people do not like mathematics is because they do not understand it. "Three in ten Americans (29%) report that they are not good at math., women are significantly more likely than men to say that they are not good at math (37% vs. 21%) and younger Americans are the most likely to believe that they are not good at math (18–24 years old, 39%; 25–34 years old, 36%)" (Change, 2015, p. 1). The reason people do not understand math is because of the terrible math teachers they have had. "Nine in ten Americans (90%) report that the lack of emphasis on developing good math skills will have a negative impact on the future of our economy" (Change, 2015, p. 2). Math is the language of the universe and a way for us to understand what is going on in our universe. Also, on a much smaller scale, math is integrated in our everyday lives. The future of our nation, our students, need to be able to understand this language to deal with their individual lives and the lives of everyone they come in contact with. Students have gone through teachers that have gone through the math books and shown their students the concepts and vocabulary terms. I want to be a teacher that makes math come alive by making it understandable to my students.

I have a lot of personal experiences that have informed my teaching beliefs. Going through middle and high school, the majority of those experiences were terrible teachers and their profession of how not to teach. An example of this would be during my junior year when I ended up teaching the class the material because the teacher gave up on teaching us but did not give up on giving us tests and worksheets. However, the terrible experiences did not falter my desire to learn more mathematics, and actually led me to becoming a teacher. I enjoyed math but most of my classmates did not because they did not understand it. I believed, and still believe, that if I could get people to understand the material, I can get people to enjoy mathematics. In order to help people understand the material I believe I must "be sure the content is meaningful and connected to their lives, the classroom, or both" (Burant, 2010, p. 180). In fact, the purpose of this paper is to reflect on my past experiences, reflect on different aspects of the teaching profession, reflect on my experiences in this program, and relate it all back to the big question: how do I, and other math teachers, get students interested in learning about mathematics?

Ever since I was young, my parents pushed me to always try my hardest in school. It was because of this support from my parents that my grades never lowered, and I became valedictorian of my senior class. However, for most classes, my grades never lowered because of my determination and work effort. I played three sports throughout high school which left little time for homework. I needed determination to achieve in these sports and my classes, and this determination has carried over into my college career, and will continue to carry over into my career as an educator. The few classes that came more natural for me was all of my math classes. For as far back as doing first grade multiplication times tables, math was my easiest and favorite subject. I accelerated through different courses which landed me in two math classes my senior year, calculus and statistics. At a school my size it was quite the load, but for me it was fun. As you can imagine, I entered college as a mathematics major, and eventually earned a Bachelor's of Science in Mathematics. I selected mathematics as my subject area because of my deep understanding and natural inclination for mathematics. My capability and interest in mathematics kept me in the math classroom, and will keep me in the math classroom.

There are many other reasons to become a teacher. For example, I have always wanted to become a teacher, I just did not know it when I was younger. I had "an early and murky notion that [I] would like to work with children [and it] became a more clear and near-at-hand goal through college" (Schutz, 2001, p. 5). Another reason I want to become a teacher is to give the students a chance to have a male teacher. "Teaching has long attracted substantial numbers of women." In fact this trend has "coincided with a public perception that teaching is low in status, not well paid and is essentially work more suited to women." This results in schools experiencing "serious problems in recruiting male teachers and thus providing a gender balance of teachers working with children in primary classrooms" which is important for the children to have growing up (Richardson, 2005, p. 1). Another reason I wanted to become a teacher was because I wanted to make a difference in people's lives. I believe that "teachers get incredible joy in seeing the difference they make as students gain new insights, become more interested in a subject, and learn about themselves" (UNC, 2008, p. 1). It is because of all these reasons that I can look past the hardships and low pay. "We can [all] collectively bemoan the well-established low correlation between academic ability and earnings among teachers," because we all know that teachers do not get paid well at all (Leonard, 1987, p. 23). However, the benefits of teaching, and the reasons of why I want to teach, outweigh the negatives. The infinite benefits of teaching that goes well beyond anything money can buy, and that benefit is how teachers can positively guide their students on the right path. As Henry Adams says "a teacher affects eternity: he can never tell where his influence stops." I will not stop until I become a teacher.

This simple question of why a person wants to become a teacher is very important for other teacher candidates and those preparing teachers. The reason it is important is because of the honest answer a person gives to this question will differentiate whether they are a teacher for one year or twenty. Teaching is not an easy profession to get into which is what some teacher candidates might believe. Those candidates might have reasons of becoming a teacher like the summer and holiday breaks, getting paid a full year for working nine months, teaching is easy a bunch of old ladies can do it. However, those candidates are wrong, their reasons are wrong, and they will not be in this profession for long. This profession should be viewed with more respect, and I believe that anyone joining this position for the wrong reasons might as well leave now because they will not last.

The respectful profession changes constantly. A few years ago it was all about No Child Left Behind. No Child Left Behind (NCLB) was put into law in 2001. "Under NCLB, federal education funds were made contingent upon a variety of accountability and reporting standards, creating new administrative costs and challenges for local school districts" (Neely, 2015, p. 1). It is because of these challenges, and many more challenges, that education has shifted gears away from NCLB. Now the trend is Common Core. However, not all states are completely happy with Common Core and the nation might move onto a new trend soon. There are arguments for and against Common Core. Those arguing for Common Core state that "the common core state standards (CCSS) provide a framework for higher level skill development than has been the case with earlier state standards" and that "the CCSS focus on the use of instructional techniques that are more open-ended and higher level" (VanTassel-Baska, 2015, p. 1). Those arguing against state that "the new assessments are too difficult, do not focus on important content, and require the use of technology in which students are not proficient" and that "there is real concern that teachers and schools lack the capacity to implement these new standards effectively" (VanTassel-Baska, 2015, p. 2). At the end of all of this arguing, "the CCSS in ELA and mathematics present a daunting challenge to our schools at a time when they may be least prepared to take it on, especially given lack of funding for teacher salaries, declining morale, and competing agendas. Yet, it also offers the best hope for coherent high-level schooling for American students" (VanTassel-Baska, 2015, p. 3). I just hope educators give it a chance before jumping to the next trend.

Straying away from the trends in education and looking at the credential program itself, I first want to start by sharing my philosophy prior to this program, how it has changed, and how other educators can use this information. My philosophy can be summed up by being about helping the students, and that has not changed. There are many reasons people become teachers and many might say it is because they want the best for their students, but I truly want the best for my students. They are the future of our nation, and in a larger sense our world, and these young individuals need to be guided in a positive direction. I believe that teaching means more than making sure the students understand math concepts, I believe it is teaching them to become better people all around. This philosophy, this way I can help the students, will not ever change. However, my philosophy has changed in other aspects because of one of my current class's emphasis on being critical. My Foundations Course, asked me to reflect on the following statement within this paper: *Being Critical in Uncritical Times*. This statement has changed my teaching philosophy because it has made me want to give the students more critical about their surroundings. There are many activities or projects that I can give students that will give them a chance to think critically, and make a difference in their community. These activities "can be used individually or as a series of building modules in almost any class – psychology or beyond – that has critical thinking as one of its goals" (Kraus, 2013, p. 9). Also, I want my curriculum to challenge my students to think more critically by having them answer questions that require more thought than multiple choice questions do. To be able to make my students think more critically will make them more rounded and better prepared for the real world. "We, [as teachers], can encourage a generation of students who know how to think for themselves and do not simply believe whatever they read or see on the Internet" (Kraus, 2013, p. 9).

I have had many misconceptions about the teaching profession, and this has changed my overall understanding of becoming a teacher. I quickly learned that teachers deal with a variety of differences and difficulties with students at any level of education. I also learned that there are many different ways to teach the students the information that are not the traditional whiteboard lecture way. I learned that students have different reasons for not doing the assignments like: disinterested, not understood, no time or place at home to do it, and many more. I learned how much work and effort goes into each lesson planned by the teacher, and it was way more than I previously believed.

One final example of how my philosophy has changed is how a teacher can successfully integrate technology and cellphones into their classrooms. My previous philosophy on technology, based on my personal experiences, was that technology, especially cellphones, should be banned in the classroom. However, I have learned of fun and educational ways of using cellphones and other technology in the classroom to make mathematics more interesting for the students. Overall my main philosophy of becoming a teacher to help the students has stayed the same, the details that come along with that philosophy have been adapted and changed for the better.

I believe that other educators can use this information to see how philosophies shift before and during a candidates' experience in a credential program. If this is a good shift in philosophies, which I believe it is, then teacher educators can use it to help give their candidates their own philosophy shift in the right direction. Also, teacher candidates can use this information as an example of something they might expect as they go through their own credential program. Either way I believe it is good information that help better teacher educators and teacher candidates.

Speaking of the credential program, the credential program has given me even more experiences that has informed and shaped my teaching beliefs. For example, the fieldwork I have done at Blanco Middle School has been greatly beneficial towards my personal teaching style, and has shaped the way I want to run my classroom. Blanco incorporates Common Core standards, collaborative projects, and alternate forms of assessments, which are all new aspects of teaching to me. I have also seen more traditional teaching at Blanco with lectures, tests, quizzes, and daily homework. The experiences have, and continue to, shape and inform my teaching beliefs. I have observed and helped math teachers at Blanco that have shown to me how to get some students interested in mathematics through different activities and projects. However, they still have days where the students are greatly disinterested with the concepts being discussed. So this experience has helped me greatly in learning ways on how to get students interested in learning about math, but I still need to research more.

All of the content learned thus far in the credential program has been useful, but there is one certain part of the content that I have found the most useful. The most useful content was learning about the different teaching strategies and activities that can be done in the classroom. I have utilized these activities in my lessons, and learned which activities work better than others. The activities that I have learned have also given me many different ways to assess my students, rather than repeatedly giving them tests. Alternative forms of assessment are important for students because it has an important purpose. However, "this purpose may not be achieved without more attention to reducing the paperwork burden and providing teachers with more models of how to address state standards in meaningful ways for students" (Flowers, 2005, p. 11). Another reason why the strategies and activities learned have been most useful to me is because they have shown me various ways of introducing the new material. Some examples of activities that introduce new material include: anticipation/reaction, people hunt, guess before you read, go to the corner, and your opinion counts, just to name a few. Giving the students new and different introductions to the material makes it more relatable which is good because they learn differently than the students of the past. In order to better get my students interested in learning math, I must "create a better match between new student learning styles and [my] instruction approaches [which] often means switching to a more active mode of teaching and learning" (Schroeder, 1993, p. 5). Clearly all these strategies have their benefits, and they all relate to the purpose of this paper. Each activity, strategy, and alternative form of assessment that I have learned will be used and, depending on the response of the class, repeatedly used to keep my students interested in learning about mathematics.

Even though the content taught in the program has been useful, it is only recently that the program has taught me to be more of a critical teacher. In fact if it was not for the Foundations and Introduction to Teaching course, I would not be having conversations about being a critical teacher. "Critical thinking is the systemic approach of skillfully evaluating the information to achieve the most reasonable solution" (Shah, 2010, p. 66). In order for people to reach the most reasonable solution they must think critically, and people will begin to think more critically if they are taught to think more critically. There are more ways to have the teacher candidates begin to think critically earlier in the credential program. For example, a project that requires the candidates to reflect on their own upbringing and how it differs from other candidates would be a good way to start the candidates to think critically. It is easier to reflect on yourself and your own personal experiences. Another example of having the candidates think more critically earlier in the program is to have them utilize a classroom activity, which was not taught in the program, in one of their lessons for their fieldwork. This way the teacher candidates can learn by trial and error which activities work in their future teaching content. This will help us teachers develop a style that "might allow us to embrace the insights of constructivism without losing the substance of the social critics' arguments" (Davis, 1997, p. 1). I truly believe that the earlier teacher candidates can start giving lessons in their fieldwork, the better off those teacher candidates will be. "Time and experience provide more opportunities to identify areas in need of growth and development and to hone skills the novice teacher identifies as lacking" (Spooner, 2008, p. 6). An example of something that can be taken away from the credential program is the TPA. To me the TPA is simply another hoop for us candidates to jump through. The TPA contains questions that we have already answered in our classes, so it is just a repeat assessment of things we have already learned. Also, the TPA's are not always graded correctly. "The overall or modal score given on 16.5% of all the tests taken were incorrectly scored by the initial assessor" (Riggs, 2009, p. 10). I believe there is better stuff for us to do with our time that is spent on the TPA. I can parallel my experience with the credential program and make my curriculum for my future students more critical by adding meaningful material, and taking away material that wastes time by having the students repeat information.

I believe that I have made true progress through the challenges I have been faced with during this credential program. As previously mentioned, I have learned about many different strategies, activities, and assessments to have in my arsenal as I teach. I have also learned how to integrate technology into the classrooms, and I have learned about the current trends that our nation's education is going through at the moment. A challenge not previously mentioned that I have faced is the challenge of teaching all learners. By all learners I mean English Learners, Talented and Gifted students, Special Needs students, students at urban schools, low income students, students from foster homes, and many more. I have learned about teaching English Learners from the very beginning of this program when I learned about BICS and CALP. BICS and CALP can be most easily summarized by the iceberg metaphor. In this metaphor there is an "above-the-surface language (Basic Interpersonal Communication Skills, BICS) and the vastness of the underlying proficiency below the surface that is referred to as Cognitive Academic Language Proficiency (CALP). Like an iceberg, BICS may represent only about 10% of the overall proficiency of an academically competent learner" (Roessingh, 2006, p. 92). There are many different strategies and activities that can be used to help those students better understand the lesson.

Only recently have I fully began learning about how to teach students with special needs, including the incredibly talented and gifted students. There are also many different strategies that can be used to help these students, and they actually are useful for all classes. It is important not to single these students out from the rest of the class, but instead make sure they feel included with the rest of the class. In fact, "inclusion of [all] learners in ordinary classrooms with their peers has become the single most important issue for some advocates" (Hallahan, 2014, p. 11).

Also only very recently, I have been learning about how to teach students at urban schools, low income students, and students from foster homes. Learning about these types of students has been a special challenge for me because I have not lived in their shoes and have no experience that can match theirs. Granted I have not lived a rich and luxurious life, I was not raised in an urban area, I was not raised in a low income home, and I was not a foster home child. Therefore, this challenge opened a brand new world to me and it was very interesting to learn about these students. I feel like there are many other incoming teachers with a similar detachment to these types of students. Teaching becomes much more difficult when the teacher is detached from the students and, as difficult as it may be, I believe it is essential for teachers to come from this lifestyle so they can better reach those students. These students have not had the equal playing field that I believed the schooling system was, and it has become even more difficult for these students to be successful as the opportunity gap widens. A teacher can relate much easier to their students if they understand their students' life, and the best way for a person to understand a certain lifestyle is to have lived it themselves. "Poor students are assigned disproportionately to the most inadequately funded schools with the largest class sizes and lowest paid teachers" (Gorski, 2013, p. 1). Learning about all of these different types of students has broadened my horizons in teaching and shows, to me, how much I have progressed through this credential program. It will also help me in my overall purpose which is to make ALL of my future students interested in learning mathematics.

Through all of my life experiences, my experiences in the credential program, and my evolved teaching philosophy has given me a new perspective on the credential program. I wish I could have written myself a letter explaining all of the changes that I have gone through since the beginning of the program. Since I cannot do that, I will share my words of wisdom with any teacher candidates reading this paper who are working on their own credential. My first word of wisdom is more congratulatory than anything. Before I started the credential program in the fall semester, I attempted and passed the CBEST and all of the CSET tests that are required for teacher candidates. This was a right move because it put me ahead of nearly all of my fellow candidates, and helped me focus on the workload of that first semester. Another congratulatory word of wisdom was becoming eligible to substitute teach at the local district. My ability to sub for the teachers I was observing in my fieldwork was valuable for me because I gained more experience teaching and got paid for that experience.

Now not all of my wisdom is congratulatory. A word of wisdom I wish I had before starting this program was an emphasis on staying on top of the workload. Too many times I have procrastinated and the work has piled up to nearly unconquerable heights. Procrastination is a real problem for college students, "More than 70% of college students frequently procrastinate, and this procrastination is an ongoing problem for more than half of the students" (Moore, 2008, p. 1). My word of wisdom is to not procrastinate. Also, be prepared for the amount of essays, reflections, journals, blogs, and other random ways teachers can gain your feedback. This is especially related to math majors, or other majors that do not require their students to write a good deal of papers. I have had to write more papers in this year of the credential program than was required of me in all of my mathematics classes. It is a different style of teaching than the strict teaching style that college math is about, and those people need to be prepared for it.

Another word of wisdom is related to the TPA's. I wish someone would have emphasized the ridiculousness of the TPA's from the beginning. However, the TPA's have been here for a while, and have been in effect since 1998 (Riggs, 2009, p. 1). Also, they are not going anywhere so here are words of wisdom to help deal with them. No matter how much it appears you are repeating information from one box to the next, add the information. The more information you place in the TPA the better the graders will view your answer, and the higher grade you will receive. Also, do not wait until the night before the TPA is due to turn it in. The TPA is not an assignment that can be done the night before, start on it well before the due date. Lastly, review the answers you put in the TPA boxes. I mean more than a simple spellcheck, really read it out loud to make sure that it makes sense. If a person does all of this they should have no problem passing the TPA's.

A final word of wisdom, which I wish I listened to more, is to enter and go through the credential program with open eyes. At the beginning of this program I was thinking of just getting through the classes, getting my credentials, and getting my teaching job. Little did I know that there was so much to learn about this teaching profession. My word of wisdom is to be willing to learn new activities, strategies, and teaching styles. Do not shut out certain aspects of the credential program because there is something to be learned from it all. "Lifelong learning is something which one does for oneself that no one else can do for one: it is a public and personal activity, rather than private or individualistic" (Crick, 2005, p. 1). The importance of learning should not have any limits in general, so there should not be any limits put on the learning that can be done in the credential program.

With that being said, having open eyes does not mean to accept everything that the credential teachers say. It is perfectly alright to have your own opinion on different aspects of teaching. If one would want to voice that opinion, then they better be prepared to back up that opinion with research because that is exactly what the teachers will use to back their own opinions. However, there are many aspects of teaching that changes all the time, and there are many ways to teach students the content that you need to cover within a year. There are many wrong ways to do so, but there are many right ways so do not let any teacher tell you there is only one way to teach. I have learned many different ways on how to make mathematics more exciting for my students, and I will use everything I have learned during my credential to make my future students more interested in learning about mathematics. Be open to everything the credential program has to offer and you will graduate from that program more qualified, better prepared, and more ready to teach the youth of this nation.

CHAPTER 12

Vijay: Education and the Pursuit of Happiness

American author Elbert Hubbard said, "The teacher is the one who gets the most out of the lessons, and the true teacher is the learner" (www.brainyquotes.com). After graduating from the University of La Verne, with a Bachelors degree in Business Administration, I began to explore my options in Corporate America. At this juncture, I had been coaching high school basketball for eight years, beginning directly out of high school. I have been working with young people for a very long time and while my degree choices led me in one direction my time working with young people had led me to teaching. Before making the decision to teaching, I had made my mind up that this would be my last year coaching and I was planning to move forward in a different environment.

The very last day the basketball season I sat in the weight room with my team. Their heads tilted down, eyes watery, and body language-screaming *despair*. We had just lost our final game of the season, and although we won an impressive seventy percent of our games, the dissatisfaction of a bad performance left too much of a negative impact. Most of my players knew that this would be my final game as their high school coach, and they felt disappointed that I was about to walk out of the door with a loss. I began to speak to them as a team, looking into their eyes as they fought back tears. Within moments, I found myself having a flashback of the past six years I had spent being a high school basketball coach. The relationships I had built with my players, the challenges and obstacles we had overcome together, the triumphs, the losses, and everything in between. It was in that moment, as I began to speak about our season, I realized that I could never walk away from this. I knew in that very moment that I was put on this planet to be a guiding light in the lives of those who needed it – it is something bigger than myself.

One thing, I think teacher educators and teacher candidates can get from Vijay's introduction to his experiences is how important connecting to students is in their development. As teacher educators, one thing we hear often and this statement would be, "why do I have to worry about being culturally responsive"? I just want to teach math, yes I am sensitive to the culture of other students but does it really matter. Our response to those students in yes it does matter and its more than being culturally sensitive and or being culturally responsive. We make the argument that teacher education program should be very methodical about teaching candidates how to make these connections and saying that its embedded means its taught on a superficial level. That if students in the classes are more concerned with passing exams than they are making connections to students in very meaningful ways then the teacher education program is missing the mark on this one.

This epiphany led me to my next job opportunity as a varsity high school basketball coach at Poder High School in Poder, California. I have always had a profound interest in the social sciences, more specifically, world history. I had observed countless classrooms during my years coaching and have always had a profound respect for the profession. My biggest challenge as an educator will also be my biggest asset. As a business major, I have not been exposed to history material since my first year of college. This will be a challenge for me to learn fact-based course material in order for me to teach from a foundation of knowledge. However, my background in business has provided me with great communication skills, critical analysis ability, ethical awareness, and situational adaptive skills. I believe that these aforementioned qualities will result in my successful ability to communicate content material, remain an adaptive teacher, and advocate for the success of my students.

Poder High School has been in a very difficult position for the past decade in terms of academic achievement and athletics. The school's poor performance has led to it being declared a "Program Improvement" school under the No Child Left Behind Act. According to the Regional Educational Laboratory, under the NCLB Act each state must operate a two-level education accountability system, with one level focused on school performance and the other on district performance. The high school's difficulty meeting performance standards has led to major implications for the student body, faculty, and educational environment as a whole. Adequate yearly progress (AYP) is the measure by which schools, districts, and states are held accountable for student performance under Title I of the No Child Left Behind Act of 2001 (NCLB), the current version of the Elementary and Secondary Education Act (Editorial Projects in Education Research Center, 2011). Poder High School has not meet standards under No Child Left Behind for two years and as a result school district allowed all students the opportunity to transfer to the other high schools in the district, in our instance East Poder High School, with district paid transportation and no athletic transfer restriction. This has established the unfair reputation for Poder High School as being labeled as a 'failing school.' The school's staff and administration has been working tirelessly to help change this misconception and remove the Program Improvement Title. However, years of little district support in terms of the establishment of assistance programs, college preparatory workshops, standardized testing preparation, and other areas has led to a yield of little to no change.

The classification of Program Improvement and its resulting challenges has negatively impacted the student body and faculty at Poder High School.

The effect of school culture on school improvement efforts is significant. The attitudes and beliefs of persons in the school shape that culture (The School Culture, 1992). The questions we must consider are, "What needs to be done in order for the school to remove its Program Improvement title?" "How can we, as educators, and community members assist in changing the culture a school may face after its classification as a Program Improvement school?" "What is my role as a teacher in helping the school and its students meet the AYP requirements mandated by the state of California? "What challenges may I face as an educator at a Program Improvement school or district?" "Does an AYP score truly measure the progress and success of schools? Are the resulting consequences fair and supportive to assist a school to remove the Program Improvement title?"

My experience at the University of La Verne teacher credential program has been positive and has prepared me for the challenges described above as a coach at Poder High School, a high school considered low performing by the state of California. I will talk more about this is my story, but one thing that my foundations course taught me and that is a number does not define a "good" school. There are some great kids at Poder High with all of their challenges and because of these challenges the teachers really have to be innovative to get the kids to buy what we are selling.

I cannot stand up in front of my students and lecture for 50 minutes and talk history with kids who are reading history in ways that they cannot connect with. I have to connect history to the kids lived experiences and not assume that they are empty slates that need to be filled. This is the beauty of foundation courses in teacher preparation programs and teacher education programs need to have them and keep them (Hayes & Fasching-Varner, 2015).

There are four classes that have been impactful in my development as a teacher. The first course, Theories and Methods of Education for Linguistically Diverse Students (TMELDS) have been one of these impactful courses. This course provides a basic introduction of first and second language acquisition theory and research. In addition, the course provided an overview of teaching approaches for English Language Learners (EL's), and covered specific strategies for teaching content and developing language. This course provides future educators with various strategies we can utilize in our classrooms to engage students in content-specific learning. These approaches provide methods to integrate students who are still in the language-acquisition phase to become acclimated with classroom dynamics and culture. Teaching in an inclusive classroom is vital to the success of students. Active learning is central to problem solving and inquiry. In addition, it also promotes the development of students' communication skills. Today's inclusive classrooms provide both challenges and rich learning opportunities for teachers and students (Jarrett, 1999). The strategies acquired in TMELDS provide the necessary foundation to build confidence and develop language skills in students who are acquiring a foundation with the English language. I was able to understand the critical aspect of teaching content to students, however necessary, in order to ensure that the material is learned. "SDAIE is the primary methodology used by content teachers. Their expertise and knowledge in a specific field of study allows them to have the flexibility to develop ways to concretize their lessons in ways, which makes them comprehensible to ELLs. The grade-level content standards and curriculum is the focus of the classes (Schwartz, 2010). TMELDS class objective of assisting future educators to learn the rigors of teaching content to those who are developing English, as a second language is critical in our society today.

In today's educational environment, there has been a major shift toward the implementation of literacy standards throughout every content area. Content is *what* we teach, but there is also the *how*, and this is where literacy instruction is important comes in. There are an endless number of engaging, effective strategies to get students to think about, write about, read about, and talk about the content you teach. The ultimate goal of literacy instruction is to build a student's comprehension, writing skills, and overall skills in communication (Alber, 2010). Literacy Instruction in the Disciplines (LID) covers the philosophy, methods, and materials to teach content area literacy skills. The strategies discussed in LID prepare teacher candidates to conceptualize the importance of instituting literacy development throughout each discipline. In order for students to be successful in understanding and applying information, they must be able to think like a professional in the given field. Reading, writing, and speaking using content-specific vocabulary and key words encourage thought development and material retainment by students. I have been able to make connections from the theories learned in LID and the classroom where I am a student teacher. I have been able to encourage literacy in many forms in the classroom and the motivation I have seen with the students has greatly increased. While there are many who think taking a reading course for secondary candidates, the change I have seen in my students makes the course worthwhile. I have seen become eager to practice literacy where they talk together about books, share their writing, and discuss homework (Wilkinson & Silliman, 2001). The skills I have acquired in this course provide me with the ability to promote learning while creating an invigorating classroom experience.

The University of La Verne is very fortunate that it has a class known as Foundations and Introduction to Teaching (FIT). This course has allowed me to examine principles, issues, and policies, which influence educational curriculum. The most beneficial quality of the Foundations Course (FIT) has been the emphasis on culturally responsive teaching and becoming a social justice advocate. This class comes to late in the credential program. I will talk more about the later but this should be the major focus of the diversity course and then the foundation course should teach us how to apply those concepts.

A major problem with the credential program at the University of La Verne is the lack of emphasis placed on preparing future educators to teach in urban areas. "Too many teachers are inadequately prepared to teach ethnically diverse students. Some professional programs still equivocate about including multi-cultural education despite the growing numbers of and disproportionately poor performance of students of color. Other programs are trying to decide what is the most appropriate place and "face" for it. A few are embracing multicultural education enthusiastically" (Gay, 2002, p. 106). This course follows an urban school point of view – something that is very close to my teaching location and desires.

Poder High School where I have done all of my coaching is an urban school, and the Foundations Course (FIT) provides opportunities to utilize the theories and perspectives attained and utilize them in the classroom. Many courses in academia are geared toward "following the rubric," or "following the instructions." However, in Foundations (FIT) I have been able to take a personal approach to every assignment – growing as a learner with every experience I have. Being open to self-reflection and honest critique is hard. Spending years to develop it sounds punishing (Flanagan, 2014). My ability to go from theory to application has never been as great from any other class in the Credential Program.

"In addition to acquiring a knowledge base about ethnic and cultural diversity, teachers need to learn how to convert it into culturally responsive curriculum designs and instructional strategies" (Gay, 2002, p. 108). The assignments, critical pedagogy unit and others, have taught me the importance of leaning on the input and advice of others in the field, such as my classmates, building a network to receive productive feedback, and more importantly, getting to know my students; their motivations, experiences, and direction. These qualities are undeniably beneficial in an urban school setting. "Teachers need to know how to use cultural scaffolding in teaching these students – that is, using their own cultures and experiences to expand their intellectual horizons and academic achievement. This begins by demonstrating culturally sensitive caring and building culturally responsive learning communities" (Gay, 2001, p. 109). Bringing students' interests into the curriculum through discussion and relation to content material creates a learning environment in which there is a personal stake in the learning experience.

Using the argument put forth by Hayes and Juarez (2012), what this foundation course has taught me is that teacher education programs need to understand the role that experiential knowledge plays in the discourses of kids of color. They also argue that it is important teacher education programs to recognize the knowledge of students of color as legitimate, appropriate, and critical to the way they navigate in a society grounded in racial subordination, and when they do not do this, teacher education programs deny the humanity of and thus silence and constrain these students, regardless of their democratic intentions.

Since I have enrolled in the credential program at the University of La Verne, I have not had a more useful resources course than Learning Technology for Educators (LET). LET's primary function is to provide teaching candidates with the training and knowledge of utilizing technology in today's educational environment. The course's focus on developing digitally literate educators is essential to build engagement from students in a digitally literate world. Learning through projects while equipped with technology tools allows students to be intellectually challenged while providing them with a realistic snapshot of what the modern office looks like. Through projects, students acquire and refine their analysis and problem-solving skills as they work individually and in teams to find, process, and synthesize information they've found online (Why Integrate Technology into the Curriculum, 2008). It is critical to provide students opportunities and experiences to challenge themselves academically and personally. With the use of technology, students have the opportunity to work collaboratively and efficiently. Their learned experiences and applications will benefit them greatly as they step out of the classroom and into a modernly digital world. The second added benefit of teaching with the use of technology is the access provided to teachers. Technology also changes the way teachers teach, offering educators effective ways to reach different types of learners and assess student understanding through multiple means. It also enhances the relationship between teacher and student (Why Integrate Technology into the Curriculum, 2008). Building engagement from our students is a crucial step in being a successful educator. Technology can assist in building a bridge between educator and student; allowing for creative development at the same time. LET provides allowed students to create a interactive video describing the function of a digital education tool of our choice. This video required that we describe the function of the tool and its application in a modern classroom. This assignment was very beneficial to me as a teaching credential student, as I learned about a handful of useful tools that can assist in building student engagement and classroom efficiency in any school setting.

The attainment of beneficial resources, discussion and thought has placed me in a position to be confident as I continue on my path as an educator. However, there have been courses and course assignments within the credential program at La Verne that provided little to no benefit for me as a future educator. These particular courses must be evaluated to provide a more stimulating and knowledge-based experience for teaching credential candidates. Diversity, Interaction, and the Learning Process, there is a major emphasis in creating lesson plans and viewing videos in class. Although I do believe in the importance of lesson planning and organization, I do not feel that an entire course dedicated to its perfection is necessary. In addition, this course failed to provide real application of course content to the real environment. Instead, we learned of theories and discussed our interpretation of their various approaches. It is one of the toughest teaching assignments, putting a novice into an urban classroom full of students who have various problems, are at all different ability levels and who are unwilling to learn and cooperate. (Urban Education: Teacher Certification). I believe it is critical for each student candidate to not only learn the rigors of curriculum planning, but to also learn the pitfalls and alternatives during the application phase.

This is diversity course without any diversity. What I see with the diversity course at La Verne is very similar with that in many U.S. teacher education programs. In the U.S. teacher preparation programs have never been set up to prepare future teachers for social justice in education. Hence, the failure and obstruction of cultural responsive teaching in U.S. teacher preparation programs are system successes, not unreasonable, unexpected, accidental, or surprising institutional disappointments or aberrations. Barriers and obstacles are deliberately set to derail and sabotage educational social justice – *too much schooling, too little education* (Shujaa, 1993).

Yet, and importantly, the obstruction of culturally responsive teaching/social justice in teacher education requires no racial conspiracy of Whites against racial minorities (Ladson-Billings, 2005; Leonardo, 2005; Liston & Zeichner, 1991; Martin, 1995, 2001). The daily business of teacher preparation and schooling is, rather, already set up to perpetuate the systemic privileging of Whiteness in U.S. society (Bell, 2002; Britzman, 1991; Schick, 2000). The perpetuation of Whiteness in U.S. society and its educational institutions requires only business as usual (Marable, 1993; Moreno, 1999; Smith, 2004; Spring, 2001).

How do teacher educators not see and avoid seeing the conditions of racial apartheid in education and the current state of race-based educational emergency that are obviously visible around them? Our emphasis on the daily workings of Whiteness as knowledge practice in teacher education is particularly pertinent at present because teachers in contemporary classrooms play a central role in perpetuating inequities in education (Darling Hammond, 2004; Hayes & Juarez, 2012).

Earlier in this chapter, I praised Theories and Methods of Education for Linguistically Diverse Students (TMELD) for preparing us to teach language diversity. However, this course is also problematic. For example, there are these dyad projects. Dyads have many advantages as a functional unit for collaborative learning. The likelihood of participation by all students is increased when there are only two individuals involved (O'Donnell, 2012). Although there are benefits in terms of collaborative learning, the dyad assignments we were given were very unrealistic. These assignments were clearly geared toward a suburban school setting, providing little to no insight on application to a urban school environment. I believe that it is critical that future educators be prepared for teaching in any environment, to ensure the success of their students. "The equivocation is inconsistent with preparing for culturally responsive teaching, which argues that explicit knowledge about cultural diversity is imperative to meeting the educational needs of ethnically diverse students" (Gay, 2002, pp. 106–107). Coursework in our teaching credential program should always be multiple-perspective faceted, even if it does create more work for us teaching candidates. In preparing us to teach in a culturally diverse classroom and handle the rigors associated with that setting, we are much more prone to be successful in the future in terms of our impact on students. Poder High School, for example, is one of many schools in an urban environments which require teachers who are able to not only be culturally responsive, but prepared to use "outside the box" methods to ensure student's academic success. Utilizing suburban school theories and tools will have little to no success in many classrooms at this particular school.

As Hayes and Juarez (2012) argue, social justice and culturally responsive teaching in teacher education are not spoken here when programs proudly point to traditions of inclusion and democratic education in our university, college, and department while the syllabi, teaching practices, and curricula of our programs are indicative of education that is by, for, and about White people. Importantly, democratic education is most often education that is democratic for people historically identified as White and violent, both symbolically and physically, for everyone else. As Don Lee (1963/1974) explains, "My teacher's wisdom forever grows, he taught me things every [student] will know; how to steal, appeal, and accept things against my will. All these acts take as facts, the mistake was made in teaching me how not to be BLACK" (p. 201; emphasis in the original).

Technology in today's digitally literate world is an essential tool to ensure success in nearly any career avenue. However, in urban school settings, it must be acknowledged that a lack of resources, access, or functionality is a reality for many students. A national count of computers in public schools shows a ratio of 3.8-to-1 for the number of students sharing an "instructional computer" with

Internet access – but the data makes no distinctions between computers in the class-rooms and those in school technology labs (Technology in Schools: The Ongoing Challenge of Access, Adequacy and Equity, 2008). Although I benefited greatly from the LET course, I feel that there was little to no alternatives and theories presented on how to handle situations where technology is needed but an obstacle is standing in the educator's path. Educators in urban and rural schools are much less likely than suburban educators to feel adequately trained (Technology in Schools: The Ongoing Challenge of Access, Adequacy and Equity, 2008). Preparing future educators to handle the rigors of an environment in which technology is lacking or limited would be beneficial in terms of developing future educators, which are adaptive to their respective environment.

Dr. Martin Luther King Jr. (1947) said, "The function of education is to teach one to think intensively and to think critically. Intelligence plus character – that is the goal of true education" (p. 1). Future educators who hope to enter the field of primary or secondary education must be very reflective in terms of their goals and motivations. They must ask themselves questions such as, Why do I want to be an educator?" "What are the benefits of the career choice?" "You're there to inspire kids. You are there to understand them, reach them, and help them be the best they can possibly be (Venosdale, 2010).

I advise every individual who is considering entering the teaching profession to understand that this career is not about them. It is not about making money, and it is not about accolades or awards. Teaching primary or secondary school can often be a low-paying job. In addition, in many areas of the country the hiring of new teachers has slowed significantly, making it difficult for education majors to find jobs in their field. Average mid-career salaries for this major are $51,400 (Stockwell, 2014). Teaching is not a financially lucrative career and teaching candidates must be prepared to accept that reality. What it is, however, is intrinsically motivating as we make such a positive impact on the lives of our students. Beverly Hardcastle Stanford, a professor emeritus at Azusa Pacific University claims, "they [teacher candidates] should never base their decision to pursue, or not to pursue a job in education on the money. You need a better reason, like because you love kids and you want to make a difference in their lives. Those who work doing something they find meaningful get much more satisfaction than those who work for money. Teachers can change lives and it can be extremely rewarding (as cited in Smith, 2013). To enter this profession and be truly successful, a future educator's primary motivation should be to make an impact on the lives of their students and nothing less.

Teaching candidates must be prepared to be adaptive to their environment. Experts call it differentiated instruction – in essence, adapting lessons for kids of different abilities within a classroom (Chandler, 2012). Remaining adaptive in lesson planning and gearing content material and its presentation to assist students from each end of the spectrum is necessary to be successful as an educator. Many of us face challenges early on: during the teaching credential program with course work and state requirements, or later as we enter the career and endure the rigors and obstacles in our paths. Needless to say, it is of utmost importance to always remain flexible and ready to adapt to any situation – especially at the benefit of our students.

When I first walked into the offices on "D Street," I could not contain my excitement as I walked into the door of the main office of Educational Leadership. I dropped my manila folder with all of my program requirement documents scattering in different directions. I came into the program with the goal to become a respected, hard working, and proactive educator – fighting as an advocate for my student's success. This goal has not wavered or changed for me as I have continued through the La Verne's Teaching Credential Program. It has, in fact, only been strengthened as I have seen my progression as a future educator. My philosophy has always been to work toward understanding my students and helping them understand me. As we establish this, my focus turns to adapting as much as possible to remain relevant in the battle to help my students derive the educational experience the each deserve. The only change I have made to my philosophy is that I must remain open to nearly any possibility. I had the mindset I would run one-hundred miles per an hour and do things "my way."

However, it is realistic to realize that things will not be that easy. I am going to have to deal with bureaucratic obstacles, resource obstacles, and other unforeseen challenges. In addition, I have accepted that I must figuratively label myself as "play dough," ready to be molded and susceptible to change at a moment's notice given the situation. With this mindset, I have absolutely no doubt in my mind that I will be successful as and educator and make the lasting impact that I so strongly believe in.

The game of basketball has opened so many doors for me throughout my life. When I entered the world of coaching, I knew that there would always be something about the draw and experience, which would never let me go. That passion and drive opened the door of secondary teaching for me. The very same passion I have had as a basketball coach has directly spilled into my drive to be an impactful social science teacher. The experience I have had at Poder High School over the past nine months has left such a powerful impact on my life. I see myself as being at "home" – in an urban schooling environment in which students need dedicated and flexible teachers who have student achievement at the center of their hearts. As I move into this next stage of my life, I go forth with all of my heart and focus – into a world where I will always be a lifelong learner a student's teacher and a student's student.

CHAPTER 13

Wade: A Teacher's Last Step before Game Time

Why teach? Why teach social studies? Most people consider history to be boring, not relevant to their life, or not relevant because history pertains to the past. A quote from a George Bernard Shaw play entitled *Man and Superman* captures a certain perception in education that humors me, "He who can, does. He who cannot teaches" (Shaw, 1903). That might have been true over one hundred years ago, however, it could not be farther from the truth in the twenty-first century. Being a teacher is not easy and it requires a certain skill, passion, will, patience, resilience and calling that not everyone has (Maring & Koblinsky, 2013). Education is one of the most powerful weapons in the world, as the Latin principle states, "Knowledge is Power."

In the eighteenth century, Thomas Jefferson argued that a democracy needed an educated and informed citizenry in order to function correctly (Wagoner, 2004). In the twentieth century, philosopher and educational reformer John Dewey continued that argument (Dewey, 1967). More so than any other discipline, it is the job of a social studies teacher to educate our students on how to be effective, active and most importantly informed citizens (Crowe, 2006). The National Council for Social Studies defines social studies as, the primary purpose of social studies is to help young people make informed and reasoned decisions for the public good as citizens of a culturally diverse, democratic society in an interdependent world (NCSS, 1994). With the amount of technology and information available it is therefore of the utmost importance that social studies teachers educate students with the skills of how to properly "source the source" in order to enable them to be powerful American citizens.

The credentialing program at the University of La Verne brings people together from different experiences, ethnicities, economic backgrounds, disciplines, schedules and places from around the area. However, we all have one thing in common; does not matter if our shared desire is a recent revelation or a passion for decades, we all want to become educators. The teacher-credentialing program is just the beginning, the first step or 'the pregame,' to our life long careers in education. I do not look at the program as the finish line, nor is it the start line. It is the practice, the early morning runs, the weight room sessions, and most importantly, the pregame warm ups. The tedious tasks such as the TPAs, CSETs and annoying 'busy work' assignments are the curve balls, the injuries, the bad coach and the screaming parents. The program prepares a new teacher with the tools and abilities to be prepared for that first day of school. That is the tip off, the kick off, the opening whistle, or the starter's gun.

This story begins in Mr. Clayton's fourth grade history class where a nine-year-old boy decided he wanted to be a teacher, unless the NFL or Dodgers came calling. I was never particularly motivated to excel in school until I had Mr. Clayton; that was also when I realized my passion for history. In California, fourth grade is the year we focus on California history. We visited a local Mission, went gold mining, and one thing that resonated with me was my teacher's idea to bring in real artifacts. All of a sudden history was something I could literally wrap my hands around. From that point on I decided I would be a teacher, just like Mr. Clayton. My interest in history and teaching continued until it peaked during my junior year of high school in my United States history class. It was during this class that my desire to be a teacher was solidified. From that point on I knew I was going to teach history and coach football and baseball.

It wasn't until my world got flipped upside down during a semester studying abroad in Barcelona, that I witnessed social studies first hand. Even though I went to college across the country, this was the first time I really got outside of my comfort zone and truly learned what I was made of. I took classes on Spanish, European and even Catalan history, politics and culture. It opened my eyes to a new world and forced me to rethink the way I thought and the way I had always learned. In Barcelona, and its state of Catalunya, its citizens live in Spain. Yet they don't call themselves Spaniards, they call themselves Catalan. They speak their own language, have their own culture and lived under a dictator that tried to repress every single aspect of their culture for more than thirty-five years (Conxita, 2008). The conversations, debates and questions I engaged in with my Spanish, or Catalan, contemporaries deeply impacted my outlook on social studies. That debate is something that continued to drive me to the present day. The best part of social studies is that there is a debate, provided that one can present evidence to legitimize their claims, there is no right or wrong answer. Historians argue opposite sides of history, but they use the same primary sources (Gilderhus, 2007). Social studies isn't defined by "the facts," it is defined by one's ability to provide evidence for one's opinion. During my time in Spain, my experience of learning inside, but mostly outside of the classroom, instilled a passion in me of understanding history and social studies in a different way. This way was never taught to me until higher level history classes in college. A way of being able to determine, on my own, what was fact and what was fiction. It is those same skills and desire that we need to impart on our students, the ability to determine, on their own, what the truth is and the aptitude to act on it.

I encourage other future teachers to recognize the moments and experiences in their life that forced them to rethink the way they think and challenged what they believed to be true. We all have experiences that have molded us into the person and educator we are today. Let those lived experiences guide you through the credentialing process and into your own classroom. Share your experiences with your students and show them how each experience changed your thought process from point A to point B.

I teach because it comes naturally to me and I cannot envision myself doing anything else. I couldn't agree more with the statement, "Teaching is at the core of my being and always has been" (Gabbard, 2011, p. 279). I also enjoy teaching because I not only have the knowledge, but experiences, that I think would have a positive effect on students. I also love learning, and no matter how much I think I know, teaching enables me to continue to learn. An aspect of teaching Rita Culross discovered as she began her teaching career stating, "it afforded [Culross the opportunity] to continue learning to approach the same basic questions, but through an evolving lens of knowledge" (Culross, 2004, p. 63). The social interaction that teachers have with their students enables both students and teachers to learn from each other. I have worked in an office setting and I noticed very quickly that it was not what I was meant to do. Carol Lefevre (1965) would call me a rebel stating, "For some teachers, rebellion against authority and the adult world may be an important reason for teaching" (p. 122).

Lefevre (1965) brings up an interesting point of rebellion; in education there are controversial topics that teachers can teach or those that should not be talked about. It is difficult to "rebel" in education with principals, superintendents and parents constantly looking over a teacher's shoulder. However, it is important that teachers understand where, when and how they can rebel. Whether that's teaching about "touchy" or "taboo" topics such as race, historical injustices or abandoning a lesson because there's a situation in the community, or country that needs to be discussed. It is important that these topics be discussed because young people need to be aware of the nature of controversy and be able to see how arguments are constructed to sway our opinions (Oulton, Day, Dillon, & Grace, 2004). Teachers need to prepare themselves to have these conversations by choosing their terminology carefully while crafting and framing questions and statements to enable students to have open discussions with their classmates. In order to present this type of situation for students a teacher must, have a high degree of scholarship in order to analyze and interpret the issue and to formulate an acceptable conclusion (Cline, 1953). Substituting information or statistics for the teacher's opinion should never take place; it's important for students to lead the discussion and come to their own conclusions through the use of the scientific method (Cline, 1953). Explain to the students why the subject is being discussed as opposed to jumping right in. Teachers can remain impartial by teaching through an epistemic criterion, which best fits the students' needs because it requires that views be judged by the evidence or arguments where two or more conflicting views are presented with equal evidence and credibility (Hand, 2008). A teacher can use a case based lesson which centers around narratives about a significant event that leads to a dilemma designed to stimulate shared inquiry, reflection, critical thinking, and problem solving (Muth, Polizzi, & Glynn, 2007). An example case study would be the Minutemen in Arizona, who are citizens who notify Border Patrol Agents of people trying to cross the border illegally. It is important for teacher candidates to learn how each of us can navigate through these situations and not ignore teachable moments.

A study was conducted interviewing principals and teachers in West Virginia, Maryland and Virginia to determine the expectations of newly credentialed students. The study found that cooperating teachers and principals hold high expectations for new teachers, and share a desire for a motivated, honest, collaborative, interactive teacher candidate who is academically prepared for the challenges of today's classroom (Bigham, Hively, & Toole, 2014). I believe the University of La Verne education department does prepare us for those challenges in today's classroom.

As credential candidates at the University of La Verne, students are to take a wide variety of classes before receiving their teaching credential. The credential program at La Verne requires teachers to take classes in how to teach linguistically diverse students, exceptional individuals and their families, literacy, strategies, and specifically how to teach one's content area (University of La Verne, 2014). Some classes were better than others to prepare us for when we have a classroom of our own. One class that I am glad we are required to take is the Special Education class entitled "Introduction to Exceptional Individuals and their Families." Of the classes I have taken so far, this has been one where I learned the most. We forget that we will teach different types of students with different abilities and learning styles (Hallahan, Kauffman, & Pullen, 2015). This class has not only taught us strategies for teaching learning disabled students, but it has also given us strategies that we can use with our general education students as well. The ability to not only pinpoints exceptionality but, more importantly, to know how to effectively teach that student is becoming more important for teachers than ever before (Baldwin, Omdal, & Pereles, 2015). All students have different needs and this class has given us the skills and awareness to be able to address those needs. The class has been taught very well through a combination of about 80 percent lecture and instruction with 20 percent of our own interaction and implementation of the strategies. The most valuable aspect of the class has been combining the instruction and theory with practical use in the classroom and relation to real life situations.

Although I'm far into the teacher-credentialing program at University of La Verne, I have come across one class in particular that I did not find to be practical. I do not believe the material of the class was impractical. This class has very important material that focuses on how to teach English Learners in public schools. Here in Southern California, we are almost guaranteed of having an EL student in our classroom and having the knowledge of how to teach that student is vitally important. The University of La Verne course catalog describes the goal of the class as Provides candidates with specific understandings and skills related to classroom teaching with emphasis on ELD and SDAIE (ULV, 2014). Essentially the class is focused around how to teach students who are English Learners or have varying levels of English competency. The importance of the class is confirmed by Baker and his colleagues (2014), as English learners face the double demands of building knowledge of a second language while learning complex grade-level content, teachers must find effective ways to make challenging content comprehensible for students. Despite the importance of the class, the structure of the class was extremely disorganized and unprepared. The professor never went over assigned reading and accountability was limited for both the professor and the students. In reflecting on how to better structure the class, I believe a change of professor would do the trick. The instruction involved being told, rather than being taught, through a 5–10 minute PowerPoint that followed with the students physically performing the strategy or activity for the next hour or more. I'm in favor of actively learning the material and using it practically, however, for the reason that we received such little instruction I didn't learn anything from the class.

The complete lack of use of the assigned text during the class was inappropriate. The class never once discussed the assigned reading, and there was no accountability by the teacher to confirm if the students did the work. The only accountability for the teacher was through class evaluations. Because there was no accountability, no one did the homework. Brophy and Good (2003) argue that homework is an important extension of in-school opportunities to learn, which is especially true for a class that meets once a week. Another example would come from a study conducted by Grodner and Rupp (2013) where they randomly assigned homework to homework-required and not-required groups. They found that "students in the homework-required group have higher retention rates, higher test scores, more good grades, and lower failure rates.

The class focused a lot on how to write lesson plans as opposed to preparing us how to teach English Learners. I could argue that the class was taught this way to enable us to pass the TPA1, rather than to learn strategies that we can actually use in our classrooms. It was a very disappointing start to the credential process at La Verne and leads me to feel extremely underprepared to teach English Learners.

This class could be improved by simply teaching the material on the syllabus instead of having us participate in meaningless activities each week. We are graduate students; we can listen to a lecture for two hours. I believe this class was simply taught poorly by the professor, as opposed to the class being structured poorly by the university. I believe holding the professor accountable would be the solution to this problem. At the University of La Verne, professors can see which students fill out the online class evaluation, they don't know who said what, but they know who responded. Our classes are small and by not making evaluations mandatory, one takes a risk that the professor could determine what one particular student said about them. The University does not create a secure environment which would allow students to honestly and critically evaluate their teachers and which defeats the purpose of the evaluations. If University of La Verne continues to use student evaluations of teachers as their way of holding teachers accountable, the University needs to make changes to its rules. Don't allow professors to see who does an evaluation, make them mandatory and provide the students with questions that enable them to accurately display their opinion of the professor and the class.

There is some disconnect between the theories and strategies that we learn in our classes at University of La Verne and the practical information of how to execute them in the classroom. Some professors do a better job than others of displaying and teaching us how to use specific strategies in our classroom. However, I would like to see all professors tell us what strategies they used in their classrooms, what things worked, which didn't, and most importantly how they handled certain situations. They have significantly more experience than we do but sometimes they focus so much on teaching the theory rather than how we can apply it. I'm most interested in learning how they handled the everyday struggles of teaching. For example, how they reacted to a student sleeping during class, what interactions or events lead to trips to the principal's office or simply how to deal with a crazy parent. I found that they are willing to tell us these things, but one must ask, rather than assume they'll impart their wisdom on us. Obviously the answers to these questions vary and significantly depend on one's school; however I would greatly enjoy hearing more personal input and expertise from our professors in their every day lesson plans.

Some things we learn in class transition seamlessly to our experiences. I can see that in some of my lesson planning and even subconsciously while I'm at the front of the class. A study conducted by Allsopp, Alvarez-McHatton, and DeMarie (2006) found that, the majority of teacher candidates (94%) responded that noticeable linkages existed between courses and practica. Some aspects of what we learn transition smoothly and quickly to our field experiences, but others do not. Those other aspects I would like to see more examples from our professors.

University of La Verne is instituting a new program of co-teaching in teacher education classes that I greatly benefited from. Classes are taught by a doctorate professor as well as a teacher in field, whether that be an elementary, middle or high school teacher. The second point of view and voice from someone currently teaching in urban schools was beyond beneficial for me. Every class that was co-taught for me was taught seamlessly by both teachers and the insight they both provided was enormous for my growth in the class. I believe this is how La Verne is trying to bridge that gap between what teacher candidates learn in classes at La Verne with the practice of their field work classes.

The theme of bridging the gap between what's learned in class and being able to use that knowledge outside of the classroom is not only the focus of La Verne with its teacher candidates, but also is a countrywide discussion with the Common Core standards. The new Common Core standards, for Social Studies, greatly focuses on the need of the individual student to come to his own conclusion based on interpretation of primary and secondary source information. Most of that study focuses on helping students to become independent thinkers where they drive their own learning. Not only is it encouraged that students come to their own conclusions but also that they are able to cite evidence. I came to this same conclusion after graduating from college as I began substitute teaching.

As an undergraduate history student, one learns that history is not defined by facts or events but how we interpret those events and connect them to other aspects of history or study. An undergraduate history student spends countless hours reading secondary sources where authors debate events, using the same primary sources yet they argue different characteristics of the story (Gilderhus, 2007). When I was an undergraduate student I was infatuated with these different debates historians would have with themselves. In my research papers, I loved to study the historiography of a particular subject. I'd find the hole in that historiography and that's where I would position my argument. Once I graduated from college and returned to my high school, I began substitute teaching. It was then, that I found another hole in our education system. I had just spent hours and years in the library reading and understanding that history is based on one's ability to argue differentiating opinions of the same events. When I stepped back into a high school United States history class, I found that disconnect. I thought to myself, "Why aren't we teaching our students the same way? Why are we teaching them history based on a timeline of facts? That's not what history is." When I wasn't substitute teaching, I observed a United States history class and I worked with a former teacher to develop a lesson plan in which we combined secondary sources to teach Manifest Destiny. I greatly enjoyed the process because it enabled me to do what I love: research. I found two secondary sources that argued different aspects of the same event which then forced the students to come to their own conclusion on the matter, rather than to tell them "this happened and this is why."

Now that I am a credential candidate and have spent hours in the classroom I am seeing the change that comes from using these types of documents to enable students to come to their own conclusion about what happened and which side they position themselves. I don't really believe this shift in focus would have affected the way I teach or would have taught if we were still using the No Child Left Behind standards. If anything, they reassured my confidence and provided me with more freedom. That freedom enables me to let the students guide their learning and allows them to debate with their classmates. This enables the students to learn the skills that are necessary to have as an adult and functioning citizen of this country. Scott Roberts (2014) argues that these types of inquiry-based lessons are the future of social studies instruction and that it is the duty of social studies teachers to institute these changes in their lesson plans. I believe that is the current challenge in social studies, getting teachers to change the way they teach to this more student-based learning experience.

One thing that concerns me, in regards to the shift to the Common Core, is that testing is done on computers. If students don't own computers, or have technology at home, school districts will now be in charge of their students' literacy in technology as well. This could be a potential problem with schools that struggle to get funding for these expensive products, further widening a gap in achievement. I definitely agree that school districts should be responsible for students' technology literacy, and that it is absolutely a skill students need to have. However, in the world of ever-changing technology, students in urban school districts might be stuck using outdated technology. I am hopeful about the changes in education brought on by the Common Core Standards, however only time will tell whether those changes are the best for America's future.

Since beginning the credential process at University of La Verne, I don't believe my teaching philosophy has gone through any drastic changes. If anything, the most valuable thing I have learned while at La Verne is the importance of having a safe and comfortable classroom environment in which students feel at ease when sharing their opinions or thoughts. Bucholz and Sheffler (2009) argue the same, the type of classroom environment that a teacher creates and encourages can either increase or decrease a student's ability to learn and feel comfortable as a member of the class. The classroom environment should do as much to foster cooperation and acceptance as the teaching methods that the teacher uses. If a teacher expects students to participate, share opinions and generally make themselves feel vulnerable, that teacher needs to create an atmosphere that can foster that behavior. A study conducted by Patrick, Ryan, and Kaplan (2007) found that, when students feel a sense of emotional support from their teacher, academic support from their peers, and encouragement from their teacher to discuss their work, they are more likely to use self-regulatory strategies and engage in task-related interaction. This is an aspect that is of the utmost importance in a social studies classroom if one wants our students to voice their opinions, disagree and debate historical events.

For many students, motivation is more than half the battle. A study conducted by Richard Bowman (2011) found that exceptional educators provide students with the ability to engage in three overarching human needs. He defines them as, "autonomy, the freedom to make choices and determine one's future; mastery, the ability to learn and develop expertise; and purpose, the quest for meaning in one's life" (p. 265). But that's the challenge. How do we allow students to be autonomous, show themselves that they are mastering the material and help them find the purpose social studies can have in their lives? I believe the structure of the Common Core helps to achieve those three needs, but at the end of the day it is the responsibility of the teacher to structure the class in a way that achieves those three things. Many students might not get that motivation from their friends, family or community; therefore, it is the teacher's job to provide them with that environment.

The biggest change I have experienced during the credentialing process is the type of school where I would like to teach. For the longest time I always wanted to teach at a top tier public school, where a teacher can focus on teaching, doesn't necessarily experience many behavior issues and the vast majority of students are driven to go to good four year colleges. I went to one of the best public schools in the state and I always envisioned myself going back there to teach. I have realized now that I do not want to be at that type of school. I would like to be in an urban school that presents more and different challenges for me as a teacher and as an individual. I came to this conclusion through a couple of chance occurrences. A friend and roommate of mine from college grew up in a very poor community, graduated from college and was making a name for himself in his community. He eventually became a victim of his community when he was mercilessly shot after getting into an argument with an acquaintance. I intend to carry on his legacy by teaching in a community similar to his and hope I can have the same effect that he had on his own. I believe I can handle any type of student. I believe I can bring about positive change in students' lives. And I believe I have more to learn from my students than they from me.

At the same time as my friend's inexplicable tragedy, I was enrolled in the Foundations to Teaching course at University of La Verne. This course forced me to rethink a lot of what I thought I knew about teaching. Instruction of the class focused on aspects of teaching and education that are not usually talked about and were presented in ways that I had never experienced before. This saying is significantly over-used, however, the amount of critical thinking that took place in that class was off the charts. A couple things that stick out to me: we discussed the growing gap in education, how to make education equally accessible for all students, how and why we need to motivate our students and most importantly how we can navigate and affect aspects of education that are broken. Much of the focus was around preparing us to teach in urban schools and it came at a time in my life when I was attempting to determine where my path in education was leading. And I determined I can and will be a successful teacher in an urban school setting. Abdal Haqq (1998) argued that effective teachers in urban schools truly believe that all children can learn, create a positive learning environment and most importantly do not accept excuses for student failure. Being understanding of students' situations and environments but still holding them accountable is very important in my philosophy. Rebecca Bowers (2000) wrote a sentence that is my exact goal in education and I think would serve as a good mission statement for any teacher, "teachers who implement a pedagogy of success help young adolescents in urban middle school classrooms to become thinking, knowledgeable, responsible citizens with much to contribute to the world of the twenty-first century" (p. 235).

Similar to my ability to find a hole in a historiography in college, students are like that historiography. A teacher needs to study them, find what motivates them, how they learn most effectively, how they think, how they come to their conclusions, why they aren't doing their homework, why they're always getting into fights or why they're bored in class. Through my coursework at the University of La Verne I believe that I have the ability, skills and desire to answer those questions. Everyone from friends to professors always asks the question, "Why do you want to be a teacher?" For the longest time this question made me nervous; however, after going through the credential program at the University of La Verne, learning from my professors but most importantly my fellow classmates, I can answer that question. I want to be a teacher because I enjoy it, I enjoy the process of seeing students progress in their knowledge and abilities. I want to help foster an environment that may lead to a positive change in the life of that child or community. But now I know I want to be a teacher because I am good at it. I can handle the challenges. I can do the work that is necessary to be an effective teacher over the course of a career. Most importantly, I have the motivation to not allow myself to get complacent at the expense of my students. The credential program at the University of La Verne has helped equip me with the tools to state, with the utmost confidence in my ability, that I will be that teacher.

CHAPTER 14

Mary: The Bell Rings … The Journey Begins

The bell rings and anxiety sets in. It's third period and I'm in my Spanish III class. It's the day of oral presentations. An overwhelming fear takes over my body. I'm short of breath. What if I stutter? What if I use slang? What if I use the wrong *tiempo verbal?* Before I know it, the period is over. The bell rings again. Except this time, I am a teacher candidate. I hear the students' chatter. Announcements are on the speaker. My master teacher reluctantly introduces me to the class. What will the kids think of me? What will my master teacher be like? It's a weird sensation; I am still a learner, but also a teacher. With me, I bring a journal, a couple of pens, my lived experiences, some anticipation, and an open mind. Although the ringing of the bell still causes stress, it also brings to mind success. Each of my successes is marked by change. It is vital to realize that the job of an educator is to continue to learn; learning and teaching walk hand in hand, they are ever changing.

Similar to a caterpillar searching for the perfect place to embark on its transformative journey, I began the teacher education program. From intake to now, I have had to cry, defend, bend, flex, mold, and laugh throughout my experience. I feel profoundly passionate about teaching, but I have had to look at myself within the field of teaching under a microscope, which has been a rigorous process. However, this process is worth it. Through the camouflage and chameleon-like qualities that we must have to be educators, it can be extremely difficult, at times, to remember who you are and I've genuinely had to ask myself those hard questions: Who am I? Why am I here? What's my purpose? "Classrooms can be places of possibility and transformation for youngsters, certainly, but also for teachers" (Ayers, 2010, p. 20). As educators, we are the face of education *for* students, and it is our obligation to become students of our students. When we ask these difficult questions, we make advances towards transformation.

I aim to be an educator that opens worlds of knowledge to students in a positive way. Yet, the credential does not make the teacher. Research finds that "external teacher credentials tell next to nothing about how well a teacher will perform in the classroom" (Winters, 2011, p. 1). My teaching experience throughout my program will play a huge part in becoming the teacher that I want to be. I am pursuing a secondary education Spanish credential. I selected this content for many reasons. First and foremost, I am passionate about the subject. Growing up biracial was and is for me, an obstacle; my mother being from Ecuador and my father from Alabama. Race was a dividing factor in my family used to perpetuate hatred. My personal experiences and intimate connection with the language have made me a very enthusiastic and unique individual and teacher. "In response to experiences like these, researchers in a range of disciplines have focused on the need to be more welcoming and culturally responsive to communities of difference" (Oliva, 2013, p. 91). The fact that I come from such difference provides me with an amplified perspective of my content area. In this way, I believe that I did not choose my content area, but rather that it chose me.

Another reason why I am pursuing my single subject credential in this field has a lot to do with my belief in social justice. I strongly feel that the words *educator* and *social activist* are synonymous. Stenhouse (2012) reminds us that service learning "can give teachers courage and skills to counter unjust and ineffective educational practices. Potentially, a body of teachers prepared as effective change agents can transform the disempowering educational practices so prevalent in education today" (p. 74).

I believe that language builds bridges towards social change and empowers people to communicate. Language is an extremely powerful tool. We use language to express our deepest desires, fears, and emotions. In addition, learning a second language, like Spanish, is practical in today's world. Many Latinos are not represented in core curriculum, thus never showing students the amazing things our community does. In my Spanish classroom, I hope that all students, including Latino students, leave with pride and a better understanding of who they are. In Boston, Darder (1992) found that "the curriculum did not reflect significant inclusion of Latino cultural values, history, or realities of the Latino community" (p. 1). The growing Spanish-speaking populations in our country, among the rest of the world, urge us towards cooperation, as well as collaboration. Our first step in achieving these goals is via communication.

Communication begins with ourselves. Looking at ourselves and our teaching in a critical way is essential to becoming effective teachers and lifelong learners. In Allen's analysis of Freire's *Pedagogy of the Oppressed* he claims, "Freire offers a general theory for transforming a somewhat abstract oppressor, thus leaving it up to the reader to decide whether to be the oppressor or the oppressed" (2002, p. 1). It is this type of pedagogy that is needed in our schools; teachers asking, "Who does this benefit?," "What interests does this serve?," "What's my role in all of this: oppressor or oppressed?" After reflecting on myself and my education, I have come to develop a teaching philosophy. Although I have developed my own personal philosophy of teaching, I also understand that my philosophy and the way that I learn and teach will change over time. I must grow to accept these future changes and shifts throughout my career. At intake I expected to learn the style of teaching that I learned from in K-12, but I've learned that this "teacher-centered" education is not effective. The most effective style of teaching is learner-centered. "In contrast to traditional pedagogy, scholars suggest that student-centered, democratic, participatory, and activist forms of pedagogy provide meaningful learning experiences that are libratory and empowering" (Stenhouse, 2012, p. 51). What Stenhouse (2012), then, tells us is that meaningful learning experience make way for more authentic learning and thus, a more effective pedagogy. As a single subject credential teacher candidate, I want students to draw meaning from my content area. If I fail to do this, then I'm failing to provide and share with my students the very experience that called me to teaching.

For this reason, it is my teaching philosophy that student-centered education is the best way to reach and teach our students. Every student deserves a quality education, but how we define "quality" here is what brings upon so much controversy. "A good quality education is one that enables all learners to realize the capabilities they require to become economically productive, develop sustainable livelihoods, contribute to peaceful and democratic societies and enhance wellbeing" (Ganihar, 2015, p. 43). It is through democratic and equitable classrooms that we are capable of empowering our students to take an active role in the education that so profoundly affects their lives. In order to take on this challenge, it is fundamental that I make connections with my students by building bridges from their world to my world.

A good education is one that is liberating. It is centered around educating without barriers, educating without bias. When I was younger, I believed in a very radical, chaotic version of revolution. Combating imperialism and capitalism by joining guerrilla warfare was my naïve and let's just say it, ignorant, way of looking at revolution. Pedagogical research has coined a term referred to as "revolutionary pedagogy." "The aim of such a pedagogy is to encourage the development of critical consciousness among students and teachers in the interests of building working-class solidarity and opposition to global capitalism" (McLaren, 2001, p. 136). Since intake, I have been able to see revolution in different ways. I genuinely believe that it is through thinking globally and acting locally that we can effect change and combat exploitation. And that's what is truly at the heart of revolution: change. In order to make change, we must start with the core value of respect. "Students must experience tolerance in their own lives in order to teach respect. To do this, teachers must both model tolerance and respect and give students real opportunities" (Landorf, 2007, p. 41). For many students, we are the only positive role models that they may have. A ripple effect occurs when we demonstrate and model compassion and respect in our classrooms. Education can be revolutionary when educators embody these characteristics.

Although, teaching has many positive aspects, as teacher candidates and as new teachers, we face a variety of challenges. In this teacher education program, teaching is taught in a very technical and science-like manner, which can create many obstacles when it comes to dealing with human beings. Teacher education programs can stifle creativity in teacher candidates. Working and building one's own teaching ideals and teaching style is a challenge when a teacher candidate steps into another teacher's classroom. As a teacher candidate, I do not know if my master teacher's ideals align with mine or if she even wants me there. Teacher education programs can fix this by knowing their students (teacher candidates) as we are taught to do. It is a challenge to be myself, let alone expand my teaching style in my master teacher's classroom.

Observations in the master teacher's classroom are critical in developing one's own teaching philosophy. My master teacher relies heavily textbooks. It's been an uphill battle to find my own voice when my teacher feels that the textbook and teacher manuals are superior; for example, I had to teach a lesson about the Incan emperor, Atahualpa. The textbook, of course, only has an excerpt of the story, but as the teacher candidate implementing the lesson, I felt that this lesson held a lot of prejudice and knowledge gaps. The story takes place during colonial times when Spanish conquistadors "discover" the Americas (which is completely false). Education isn't only textbook material. The most revolutionary education is RE-Education. Arriving in Peru, the conquistadors take Atahualpa captive (one of the last Incan emperors remaining). The guards that would watch Atahualpa's cell would play chess every afternoon. During a heated chess match, Atahualpa advised one of the Spanish captains to make a move, which led to him winning the match. The guards were shocked to find that Atahualpa learned to play chess by just watching. The Spanish guards and captains took a vote and decided that Atahualpa would be condemned to death. Following this reading, I came to realize that the students knew nothing of the historical relationship or the everlasting effects of colonialism on Indigenous peoples. In my mind this is a profound knowledge gap and essential for student comprehension. "The cultural, religious, and economic agendas that colonial powers brought to the Americas still influence indigenous cultures" (Monaghan, 2002, p. 1). Not only was my point of view not taken into consideration, but I also had to teach the lesson in the way that she preferred. This then led to another challenge.

New teachers and pre-service teachers face the problem of feeling alone or isolated. In a case study about pre-service teachers, David Donahue (2000) recalls one of the participants in the study, "Her comment highlights the tremendous difficulty of forming mutual and reciprocal relationships and fostering thoughtful conversations with others, particularly in schools" (p. 443).

This can be especially difficult when we do not connect with our master teachers or fellow peers. Finding support is not only important as a first year teacher, but also just as important in the teacher education program. It's crucial to find like-minded individuals to bounce ideas off of, to vent to, and to simply just be there. Teaching can feel daunting at times without a support group. It is easy to feel burnt out, overworked, overwhelmed, and underpaid among all the other emotions that teaching takes us on.

What has helped me with a lot of these struggles is visualizing my future classroom and my future self within that classroom. Szente lists strategies that lead to achievement, "These strategies are: (a) realizing and changing negative thoughts about oneself, (b) creating positive affirmations, (c) goal setting/action plan, (d) visualization, and (e) celebrating successes" (2007, p. 451). I visualized typical stressful days with lots to do: lunch in the teachers' lounge, ornery students, grading ridiculous amounts of homework, parent teacher conferences. I also visualized what I categorize as "worth-it days": laughing with my students, aha moments, homework turned in and on time, students visiting my classroom during lunch or after school, solving problems together, and of course seeing my students walk on graduation day. I additionally celebrated my successes during my clinical teaching, which has helped me with self-esteem.

I struggle with finding the balance between idealism and reality. I went into teacher education with the naive idea that teaching K-12 would be simple in some way. I wanted to make a change in young people's lives and I thought that being a caring teacher would be enough. At intake interview, I thought that I would be one of those teachers that will revolutionize the profession. Many people go into the teaching profession with similar ideals. In a way, this can lead to disappointment if a realistic approach is not taken into account. "Most of us come out of college full of theory and hope. But then our lofty aims often bump up against the conservative cultures of our new schools, and students who often have been hardened by life and public schooling" (Burant, 2010, p. 22). The collision, or *choque*, of idealism and reality has been disheartening from intake until now. I have been courageous enough to face the *choque* of these two aspects of my philosophy, yet it still can cause an internal conflict.

Despite the conflict that I am continually facing, I now understand that teaching is infected by an array of factors. No one-day is the same; there is no such thing as a typical day in teaching. Students come from a million different walks of life. Students are more than just pupils, they are people who have different lived experiences and outside of school have different lives. Keeping this in mind, assumptions shouldn't be made about the people in my classroom. This is something that I suggest that teacher candidates challenge themselves to confront: our hopes and dreams of the teachers we want to be with the harsh realities of life that prevent these things from being fulfilled. Certainly, it is easier said than done to confront these issues. A powerful tool that I have been armed with in this program is critical pedagogy. "Both students & teachers are affected by learning & teaching, so critical pedagogy is concerned with both students & teachers & also their changes" (Ghaemi, 2014, p. 18). Ideally educators would love to see themselves as heroes in their students' lives, but realistically students prevailing through life's struggles is the closest that we will ever get to Superman (and this is something that I feel that as new teachers, we are not prepared for nor can any book teach). I implore you to find the hero, then, in your students.

Passion is a driving force and very easily makes teaching your life. It is important to remember that teaching isn't the only hat that we wear. Again, at the intake interview, I felt very passionate about my subject and my teaching. Since then, passion has become a question of, "Am I passionate about my subject or am I passionate about the kids?" The answer may very well be both, but in order to give my students an effective, caring teacher, I must stay balanced in my life.

Students and professors in teacher education programs, have a responsibility to future teacher candidates to make suggestions for the betterment of the teacher education program. My university promotes smaller class sizes allowing for a more personal experience. My preliminary thoughts of the program had much to do with my undergraduate experience at the same university. My undergraduate program always had professors that were available in many ways; for example, they made their own appointments, responded in a timely manner to emails, they were available in office to speak about literally, anything. I viewed the university as having more available professors because they had smaller class sizes and therefore got to know their students personally. Similar to a factory, teacher education programs are pumping out teachers. Plenty of times, I have reached out to professors for support, only to be treated like a number.

> Learning support in the traditional form of formal induction programs and mentoring were recognized as useful; however, collaborative informal, unplanned learning from colleagues and former peers was also reported as a most significant and valuable source of support. (Papatraianou, 2014, p. 102)

It is a human connection that is lacking in teacher induction programs as well as our public school system. How can our education be facilitated if professors and administrators do not see the value of informal processes of support?

My suggestion is for teacher education programs to actively and critically take a long, hard look at themselves as pedagogues. As educators and teacher educators, there were times I felt I was not receiving the personal experience that education promotes. The university can begin by implementing a more student-centered pedagogy. Get to know the students, hold meet and greats, ask what their personal goals/dreams are, and so on. In addition the university does not train the master teachers that act as mentors to teacher candidates. "Despite the important role that mentor teachers play in the development of the future generation of teachers, research has demonstrated that few teachers receive training or preparation for mentoring" (Ambrosetti, 2014, p. 30). Just because someone is a veteran teacher does not make someone capable of passing on effective, up-to-date, culturally responsive practices.

Also, the university's teacher education program is full of hypocrisy. We are encouraged to be critical thinkers and apply critical values especially when it comes to advocating for students. What I found was a program that fails to directly confront homophobia, racism, and other contemporary issues. "Moreover, with the recent gay, lesbian, bisexual, transgender, and questioning student suicides across the country, it is even more imperative to begin addressing homophobia in our schools and classrooms" (Jones, 2014, p. 154).

I did a presentation in fall semester on the LGBT community. This is a relevant and prominent issue found in current events today. Not only was the class unresponsive, but also the professor had nothing to say or comment in regards to my group's presentation. "In fact, a number of school leaders refuse to admit that homophobia is a problem in their schools" (Jones, 2014, p. 155). After my very impassioned presentation, I was able to take away something positive from the experience: If a classroom of my peers along with the professor will not confront these issues in teacher education programs, it is even more crucial that I advocate for my students and confront the issues affecting the LGBT community.

> Therefore, educators in schools of education should begin examining how hegemonic masculinity controls the ways that teachers construct knowledge about homophobia in schools. Teacher educators should devise methods that allow pre-service and in-service teachers to begin to conceptualize how hegemonic masculinity functions and pervades school environments. In doing so, this recognition may be a catalyst that begins disrupting the perpetuation of homophobia in schools and classrooms because teachers will be able to recognize how hegemony functions. This personal recognition may be a viable starting point in addressing homophobia. (Jones, 2014, p. 166)

Oddly enough, I have been a guest speaker for Safe Zone Training for my university. "To counter heterosexism, homophobia, and gender binaries' in higher education, "safe zone" or "ally" programs are efforts by American universities to create a welcoming environment for lesbian, gay, bisexual, transgender, queer or questioning (LGBTQ) members of the campus community" (Ballard, 2008, p. 3). The training opened dialogue for educators, presented skits with possible scenarios, and provided guest speakers to speak on their own experiences as LGBTQ members. If we don't dare ourselves to have these at times awkward, uncomfortable, or hard conversations in teacher education classrooms, how can we expect to look a student in the eye? We must dare ourselves, as teacher candidates, to ask hard questions without fear. We must put pressure on teacher education programs, teacher educators and administrators alike, to confront injustice of all kinds.

Despite some of the improvements that my program can make, I feel very competent to write lesson plans, objectives, and other technical aspects of teaching. "Lessons must draw from critical theory/pedagogy for effective practices" (Elsbree, 2014, p. 5). I am prepared with strategies for differentiation in my classroom. However, I do not feel prepared to be an "out" teacher, to handle complex issues, to have hard conversations, to find resources, or to teach socially just curriculum in an oppressive educational system. That last one was a big one! So again the question arises – how close am I to becoming the teaching I dream myself to be?

Throughout this process, I have asked questions and I have just begun to stir the pot. *Being critical in uncritical times* means asking these questions and searching for answers. It means to face adversity and learn to crawl, walk, and then run. It means to stand up for what we believe in and have the courage to do so. By being courageous, we are able to push the envelope and dare our fellow teacher candidates to do the same. "Offering authentic learning opportunities can encourage a critical, social justice orientation to teaching and may inspire future teachers to enact courage in their teaching practice" (Coffey, 2015, p. 9). The bell rings and anxiety sets in. I bring with me a teacher that can. I bring a multi-faceted, determined individual. I bring a different face to teaching.

CHAPTER 15

Kaitlyn: Three Things I Learned during My Student Teaching Experience

Ever since I decided that I wanted to be a teacher, which was when I was about six years old, I had a vision of what being a teacher was like. When I thought about "the perfect teacher," I envisioned someone who is cheerful, welcoming, knowledgeable, and willing to keep her classroom exciting. I always admired my teachers throughout my school experience and I knew that I wanted to be just like them when I became a teacher. My teachers were smart, put together, organized, creative, and energetic. It is safe to say that I set the bar extremely high for myself by comparing myself to my own teachers.

As I got older and became more serious about my career as a teacher, I was confronted with two very different responses when I declared my career path. One response that I was met with was a positive one and people seemed to admire my strong desire to educate. The other response was one of doubt and worry. Usually, the people that were worried about me were teachers. They would tell me that teachers do not get paid enough for the amount of work that is required and that they are very underappreciated. While I agree with both of these points, they have never discouraged me from pursuing my dream of being a teacher.

As dreamy as I thought teaching would be, it has certainly had its ups and downs. I thought that all of my lessons would go perfectly, my students would all be angels, and I would have the most engaging and exciting classroom that anyone has ever seen. This, unfortunately, was not the case. I encountered roadblocks on a daily basis and I found myself on the verge of tears at least once a week. I did not expect the stress of feeling like I was failing my kids if they were struggling, or conflicting classroom management goals between my mentor teacher and me.

On a positive note, I also never expected to feel so comfortable with the other second grade teachers and to feel like I have so many people to count on if I needed anything. I knew that my student teaching experience was going to be challenging and would present me with obstacles to overcome, but I was hopeful that my passion for teaching and inspiring children would provide me with the desire to push through the struggles. Over the course of the nine months I spent at Riverside Elementary, I learned three priceless lessons that I will carry with me on my journey as a classroom teacher.

Student Teaching Is Like Living with a Roommate

Before beginning my student teaching experience, I had a very positive outlook on what the upcoming year would be like. I could not wait to meet my new students, I was excited to begin my teaching journey, and I was thrilled at the idea of learning from so many great teachers, including my mentor. Throughout the summer before the school year began, I would imagine what a normal day at Riverside Elementary would be like. I imagined children entering the classroom with big smiles on their faces and ready to take on the day. I pictured the first day running smoothly and getting the opportunity to begin learning about my students and their different personalities. I was excited to implement some of the things that I had learned over the past four years into my new environment. Although this was my dream situation, I was optimistic that my student teaching experience would be an outstanding one.

When I came to Riverside Elementary before the school year began to help my mentor set up what she referred to as "our classroom," it was the first time I learned the lesson that student teaching is like living with a roommate. But this roommate situation was like moving into someone's home where they had been living for 20 years. My mentor's classroom had something in every corner and materials had accumulated from what looked like her first year of teaching. As I looked around, I tried to find any space that I could make my own. Then I spotted a wooden desk and a mounted whiteboard that my mentor said was all mine. It was not much, and I knew that I would not spend much time sitting at the desk, but it was the only area that I had control over and I was over the moon. Within the first week of school, I had personalized my area just the way I liked. Everything had a place and everything was in its place; which was a breath of fresh air from the semi-chaotic and organized mess that was my mentor's classroom. This experience certainly made me feel like a new roommate that took advantage of the small loft she had just moved into. Regardless of how small my area in the classroom was, I was nonetheless thankful that I had any area at all.

Over the next few weeks, I began to feel the pangs of living with a new roommate. My mentor and I used this time to feel each other out and to learn the everyday mannerisms that we both demonstrated. At times, I could feel my mentor becoming possessive and trying to mark her territory. As someone who has been teaching for over 20 years and now had to share her space with a co-teacher, I could certainly understand her feelings. Yet, I still felt that I needed to make my authority known to the students, while making my mentor feel like I was not stepping on her toes. After the first few weeks of school, I soon realized that this would be an uphill battle that I would fight for months to come.

Sharing a classroom with a mentor, much like living with a new roommate, is a very delicate dance that must be approached in the right manner. The initial tone must be set in a positive way if you want to have a successful and prosperous school year. At first, the nature of the classroom was upbeat, but a little chaotic. There was no rhyme or reason to classroom procedures, which made it difficult for both the students and myself to feel out the classroom environment. As the days and weeks went on and classroom procedures were not practiced and routines were not drilled, I found myself thinking back to my classroom management class that I took while I was an undergraduate. I was shocked that such an experienced teacher lacked a fundamental aspect of good classroom management. Yet, being the new roommate, I knew that I could not say or do anything to change it. This obstacle leads me to the next lesson that I learned through my year of student teaching: *you can either emulate or do the opposite of your mentor, but either way, you are learning how to be a successful teacher.*

Learn to Emulate or Do the Opposite of Your Mentor

When I was growing up, my mom always told me, "When you become an adult and are faced with all that life will give you, you will have two choices: you can emulate or do the exact opposite of what your dad and I have taught you by example." I learned a lot from my parents, both by emulating things that I like in them, and doing the opposite of some things that I am not so fond of. I have learned a lot over the past year from my mentor and moving forward, I know what I want to emulate and what I want to do the total opposite of.

The first thing that I learned from my mentor is to have an uncluttered and organized classroom. I have learned the importance of this due to the cluttered and unorganized nature of my mentor's classroom. I have seen the panic and stress that overcomes my mentor and myself when we cannot find extra materials or an important piece of paper because they do not have a specific place in the classroom. I have learned that it takes away a lot of instructional time from lessons when students' supplies are a jumbled mess in an oversized bucket, as opposed to neatly put away in more appropriate size containers. Having my own, organized classroom will hopefully alleviate the ear piercing, "Ms. Thomas, we do not have any [insert desperately needed material here] in our bucket!" I love my students dearly, but I cannot think of much else that drives me crazier than having a student interrupt or delay my lesson because of missing necessities.

The second thing that I learned from my mentor is to never talk poorly about a student in the presence of other students, especially not that specific student. Unfortunately, I learned this by having to do the opposite of what my mentor did at times. This situation usually came about during high stress times for my mentor, such as during tests or the days leading up to a formal observation. While students were taking tests, my mentor and I always walked around the classroom to monitor the students and to make sure that they were keeping a good pace throughout the test. When my mentor would see that a student was working a problem wrong, she would either walk up to me laughing and tell me to "check out what Johnny is doing," or come up to me speaking loudly about how a student was "clueless." These situations made me extremely uncomfortable and the only things that I could do was smile and try to keep moving around the classroom. When this would happen, I knew that other students could hear what she was saying and I recognized that it was bringing down their self-confidence. The first time my mentor made a comment to me about a student in front of the class, I made a promise to myself that I would never do that to my students.

The third thing that I learned from my mentor is that you should always greet your students in the morning with a smile and a friendly welcome. She was great at this and was always cheerful as the students entered the classroom. This was an awesome way to start the day and it was allowed the students to feel like they were entering a safe space. I loved starting the day by standing in the doorway and watching my students come down the hallway. If I was having a rough start to my day, seeing their smiling faces was a guaranteed way to turn it around. Greeting the students at the door was also a good way to start off the morning routine. Doing this allowed me to remind students that they should come in quietly, unpack their school bags, get their planners checked, copy their homework, and start on their morning work. Since this morning routine was not implemented in the best manner, I made it a point to be at the door every morning in order to remind the students of what they were supposed to do as they entered the classroom.

The fourth thing that I learned from my mentor is that unspoken expectations can break the mentor-intern relationship. When the school year began, I felt overloaded by the amount of information that my mentor teacher was sharing with me. Instead of sitting down with me before the school year began to lay out her expectations of me, she just began showing me how to access the online Gradebook and the reading curriculum database. I quickly became overwhelmed and wondered if she expected me to keep up with grade recording for her. When I first started teaching, I began by teaching a few reading classes at a time. Unaware that my mentor expected me to keep up with the students' scores, I simply taught the lessons and collected data. When I finished teaching my cycle, I went back to making student observations. Before I knew it, my mentor was asking me if I had entered all of their scores and set up the new lesson on our reading database. Reluctantly, I told her no and that I did not realize that was something she wanted me to do. And that's when I was introduced to her famous saying, "it'll be alright." It was her passive way of saying that it was not okay and shoving it under the rug. As passed, the expectations continued to go unspoken and would soon cause major tension between my mentor and me.

The Toughest Experiences Present You with the Greatest Learning Opportunities

Before starting my student teaching journey, I probably would have described myself as a passive person. In my high school psychology class, we learned about the two ways people handle stress: fight or flight. Some people fight stress head on and work to overcome it until it has been resolved. Others choose to avoid stress or stressful situations and hope that they go away on their own. Before I was a student teacher, I was a flier, not a fighter ... and so was my mentor. I discovered that we were both passive people within the first few months of being in her classroom. By October, I was starting to be able to pick up on signs of my mentor's passive behavior. October was a month of stress for my mentor and me. She had her formal observation looming over her head and I was beginning to feel the pressure of my workload. We began tiptoeing around each other, while also starting to step on each other's toes. I was trying to establish myself as another teacher in the classroom and balance my coursework, and she was trying to keep her head above water. Soon enough, we both reached our breaking point at coinciding times. Due to her passive nature, my mentor did not want to talk to me about her issues, so she went to our assistant principal instead.

The summer before student teaching began, one of our professors told us that there was a hierarchy when it came to handling conflict: we were to try to problem solve between ourselves and our mentor, if that did not work, we were to meet with our mentor, and supervisor, and if that did not work, we were to meet with our mentor, supervisor, and administrator, and if all of those options were exhausted and resolution was still not found, we were to all speak with the head professor. To put it lightly, I was extremely upset that she went to an administrator about our issues before addressing me about them. Per the assistant principal's advice, my mentor contacted my supervisor to see how to handle the situation, to which my supervisor told her to talk to me about her concerns.

When the time came for us to have a conversation about our concerns, it did not go as well as I think either of us had anticipated. We were both heated and stressed out about in school and out of school situations. Because neither of us had clear heads, we didn't come to the resolution that we were both desperate for. Instead of voicing our concerns and working towards a solution to our issues, it became the blame game and we were talking in circles. A short week later, after we continued dancing around each other, we had a true, genuine conversation that was free of judgment and angst. The time had come for us to not only be honest and straightforward with one another, but to come up with a plan and goals for the rest of the year. I was straightforward and asked my mentor exactly what she expected of me in all areas of the classroom. I also made clear what my classes demanded of me as a student. I wanted my mentor to know that I had many other responsibilities in addition to being her student teacher. Through this experience, I learned that I needed to not only find my voice, but I needed to use it and I needed to be heard.

Over the course of time that I spent with my mentor, I felt like I was viewed as her assistant rather than her student teacher, but I never spoke up about how I was feeling. One morning before school started, my mentor told me how great it would be if I would make her some coffee every morning. I could not believe what I was hearing. I was shocked that she had the audacity to ask me to do something like that when it is clearly something that should not be asked of a student teacher. But because I was so taken aback by her request, I could feel myself agreeing to her request. At our next class meeting, I told my professor what my mentor teacher asked me to do for her. Thankfully, my professor had the same feelings towards the demand as I did and told me that it was inappropriate for her to ask me to do that sort of thing. Since this occurrence was before our "big talk," I passively denied her request by simply never making her coffee. She never asked again, so I figured that she took the hint. If I could go back in time, I would have utilized that opportunity to clarify my role in the classroom as a student teacher.

What It Is All About

As I now sit here, reflecting on the nine months I spent as a student teacher, wondering if my words will impact anyone else's experience in the classroom, I cannot help but feel an overwhelming sense of accomplishment, growth, and thankfulness. I am eternally grateful for the hardships that I was presented with, because I came out on the other side stronger and wiser than I thought was possible. Before beginning my student experience, I had an idea of what it would be like. I tried to imagine the bonds that I would form with my students and how I would get along with the other teachers, and it is safe to say that my expectations were beyond exceeded. Through all of the tears, mental breakdowns, and many self-reflections, I have learned that the most important thing that you can do as a teacher is to be true to yourself. I learned that you have to be who you are and do not try to be something that you are not, because your students are smart and will see right through any act that you try to put on. They deserve you at your best, even if you are feeling your worst.

CHAPTER 16

Lauren and Patricia: An Elementary Prison

Throughout this year, our eyes have been opened to many of the negative and positive aspects of the education system. We thought we would just be teaching, but we have actually learned more than we could have ever anticipated. There were many highs and many lows, but through all of it, we have come to know so much more about our students and ourselves. Throughout the year and with everything we have learned, there has always been one overall theme that has stood out to us, which is motivation, or lack there of.

When we were in school, we were always built up by our parents and our teachers, so much so, that we subconsciously became self-motivated individuals. We noticed from day one that there was a major distinction between our elementary experiences and these students.' There seems to be a lack of motivation in many of the home lives of the students, and if this isn't bad enough, in many cases, the teachers contribute to this negative self-image. Instead of students coming to school excited and eager to learn, we witness students who are scared and discouraged by constant intimidation tactics. This is certainly not how we felt in our elementary schools and is definitely not the learning environment we wanted for our students. We've seen so many students who get trapped in this cycle, and it is very difficult for them to break out. It is almost as if they are in an elementary prison.

Our struggle has been to teach motivation to help liberate them from this prison and realize their true potential. The obstacle is how can you teach motivation when they are constantly being torn down by the people who are supposed to be building them up the most? That was our goal. We are going to be taking you on a journey through some of our experiences and sharing some personal stories to help you understand some of the struggles these children are facing and hopefully offer some solutions on how to break them out of this elementary prison.

"One small negative thought in the morning can ruin your day."

We have all had that morning. We wake up and try to get our day started. We may spill coffee on ourselves on the way to work, burn our waffle for breakfast, or get in a fight with a family member, and from that point on, our day is ruined. If we, as adults can quickly relate to this, let us take a look through the eyes of a child.

Angie was a bubbly, energetic, and lively young girl on a typical day in my second grade class. One morning when I was walking to the office after the school day started, Angie was getting dropped off (somewhat late). All I could hear from the car was Angie's mother yelling, and the look on Angie's face was pure devastation. After her mother told her to go to school, she stepped on campus where the first words she heard were completely negative. "Tuck your shirt in!," "Stand on the line!," "Walk to class! You're late!" When I came back to class, I noticed that Angie was completely off task during morning work and was not the same energetic girl as she normally way. She was acting out and distracting others as well, and I could tell simply by looking at her that this could be a very long day for Angie.

We, as teachers, cannot control how the child feels at home, but something we can control is how our students feel at school. If the teacher she first came into contact with had offered a helping hand, a smile, or reassurance that she was cared for, the beginning of the day could have turned out differently. Fortunately, because I knew how parts of her morning went, I was able to try to change her attitude. I bent down to her desk, smiled and said, "How are you doing?" She said she was fine and was just a little tired. I told her that her day could go two ways: 1. She could let her bad morning influence her whole day by thinking and dwelling on it or 2. She could shake it off, start over and end up having a great day. Guess which option Angie chose? Option two.

It made me quickly notice how little it takes to completely change someone's day. Throughout student teaching, I realized a simple element that can change the dynamic of the teacher-student relationship. It may seem very minute and obvious, but many teachers forget to incorporate this one very important element. This obvious element in the classroom is simply *conversation*. Teachers who talk to their students (like the real people they are) are likely to have much more control and enjoy the teaching more than others. On the other side, their students show up excited and energetic to absorb more and more knowledge each day. There were certainly many days where I was in a bad mood and did not want to talk to anyone, which is very difficult when you are a teacher. On these negative days, I noticed a much more disruptive classroom environment. It is very difficult to ignore all of our out-of-school stressors in the classroom, but for me, it is necessary to check your attitude at the door and put a smile on your face.

Children need positive influences and we can be just that for our students. We need to talk to our students in order for them to trust and respect us. Children need to know they are loved and cared for, and we can show them that they are. I would have never known Angie's horrible morning if I had not been walking to the office at that specific time. How many other negative situations have I been oblivious to? There is no way for teachers to know every single aspect of a students' day, but we can inspire them in our classrooms to have a positive day which hopefully leads to a positive life.

"One small positive thought in the morning can change your whole day."

"Don't compare yourself to other people. You will be disappointed."

Think about a goal you have tried to accomplish. We all have them, whether it is scoring well on a test, making the volleyball team, slimming down to the perfect spring break body, or any other ambition we strive for. Sometimes, even when we feel like we are doing so well, as soon as we look at the person next to us we are instantly reminded that we are not. If you scored a 95 on the test, they scored a 100. If you made the volleyball team, they became the captain. If you feel like your tummy is getting flatter, they have a six-pack. Your achievements that felt so great a minute ago suddenly seem like nothing in comparison to someone else.

This unfortunately is something we see in the classroom every day. It is natural for students to want to do keep up with their peers, but the trouble comes when teachers become the ones doing the comparing, and not in a positive way. If this seems hard to believe, listen to this story:

> *Robby was one of my third grade students this year. When he started the year we knew he was a little behind in his reading abilities, but since it was so early we did not know how behind he truly was. One day the students were instructed to read a passage and answer questions about it. Robby was trying his best, but it was one of the more difficult passages. His neighbor, Kristin, on the other hand was reading at a fourth grade level. This passage was a piece of cake to her, and she was quickly finished. All of a sudden I heard yelling coming from the area these students were sitting. The teacher was screaming at Robby. "What kind of answers are these! They don't even make sense, and how are you still on number three? Look at Kristin's paper. She's been done for almost five minutes now and her answers are perfect! Why can't you work as hard as Kristin?" After a few attempts at creating excuses, Robby tearfully muttered, "I just don't know how to read."*

The teacher's loud threats and accusations did not make Robby work any faster. They did not make him answer the questions better. They did not help him at all. The only purpose that harsh comparison served was to embarrass him in front of his peers and lower his self esteem. It turned out Robby was only on a first grade reading level, and needed extensive interventions throughout the year to help him increase his reading abilities. He was working just as hard as Kristin on this assignment, if not harder, but simply did not have the skills to produce the level of work that she could at that time.

Being a brand new student teacher and very unsure of myself, I did not know what to do at this point; but as my time in the school increased I learned how to build Robby and my other students up. I let them know that everyone moves at a different pace and that they determine their own success. I also tried to foster in my students a want to encourage their peers instead of envying their progress. I taught them that it is fine to use their classmates' successes as motivation to succeed themselves, as long as they have the understanding that their successes might not be the same as someone else's. Just because the end result does not look the same, does not mean it is not just as amazing.

"Don't compare your beginning to someone else's middle."

"You might think you are brave, you might think you are smart, but to many it will never be enough."

Many of us may have experienced another person talking "behind our back," and have felt the hurt that comes with it, especially when the person is supposed to care about us. This is easier to relate to, but have you ever overheard someone talking about you not "behind your back," and instead, right in front of you? Constructive criticism is sometimes difficult enough to hear, but think about someone blatantly criticizing you and having no regard for your feelings right in your face.

This was a common occurrence between teachers and students. As an adult, the negative comments directed towards us can be very difficult to hear, but picture yourself as a seven-year-old child. Imagine you are the seven-year-old-you listening to authority figures constantly talk about you right in front of you. Thankfully, my mentor teacher usually tried to lift students up rather than tear them down, but during lunchtime, I witnessed very different remarks from other educators.

> *Every day for lunch, the students file into the cafeteria with their trays, wait until everyone is seated, and begin to eat. Unlike many elementary schools, the students here must remain completely silent from the moment they enter the cafeteria to the moment the leave. Because of the painfully silent dining experience, the students are able to hear any and every conversation that the teachers have with one another. One day, the students were overwhelmed with difficult tests, and I could not believe the conversation I overheard. After one teacher asked a co-worker how her students were*

> *doing on the test, she replied, "Oh! They are failing almost every test, not paying attention, and distracting others. I mean ... some of the 'good ones' have passed, but as for the others [the bad ones] – they have all failed." I looked over to her class, and my heart broke into pieces for these children. The students looked dismayed, defeated, and in the simplest term, hurt.*

I could not believe what I had just heard. When the children heard this horrible news about only the "good ones" passing, they still had three other tests to take that day. Unfortunately, this was only one of many discouraging comments I heard from teachers during lunch.

Rather than putting the students down for constantly receiving failing grades, I try to encourage them and search for some sort of reason. If students are failing every test, the reflective practitioner within should think about ways to help rather than hurt. Seeing the faces of those hurt children taught me that each and every day we should offer support and encouragement, regardless of the past test scores and backgrounds of our students. This year, students have failed tests that covered material I explained, which is a horrible feeling. I had to think about the lessons and reflect on different ways I could have engaged the students. Some teachers feel the need to blame others (their students) for their possible lack of instruction. Additionally, I made an effort to smile at the students eating silently that knew their teacher was talking about them as the "others." Instead of students thinking they are unintelligent and will never succeed, we should give constant reminders that they are very capable of success.

> "You are braver than you believe, stronger than you seem, smarter than you think and more loved than you will ever know."

> "You can dream, but sometimes you just have to be realistic."

Think back to when you were a child. What did you want to be when you grew up? Was it a doctor, a famous astronaut, or maybe even a pop star? When I was younger I remember about 10 kids in my class claiming that they would each be the President of the United States. I guess some things never change, because there were several students in my third grade class who claimed that they too would be the President one day. Unfortunately, many teacher's response to this dream is "Well, you know only one person can be the President ... maybe you should pick a different career." I have never understood why people take such extraordinary dreams and equate them with impossibility. Worse than crushing a child's dream however, is when someone tells a child of the negative future they believe he or she will most likely have. This terminates a child's motivation and takes away one of the most essential qualities they have: hope. Unfortunately, I have seen such a scenario take place:

> *It was the end of the day on a Friday afternoon. My third grade students had no particular assignment so they were pretty much doing whatever they pleased. Some chose to read or draw, while others opted for talking to their classmates. Some of these conversers were getting a little rowdy, but I thought that could be expected during the last 20 minutes before the weekend. It did not seem like that big of a deal to me, but then again, I was just the student teacher. Before too long a faculty member walked in and started berating the class-the whole class. The yelling was pretty intense, but I thought it would end with a "Stop talking" or "Keep it down." It did not. Instead, it turned into a rant about how third graders do not know how to behave and how they never do the right thing. And it did not stop there. The students were told that if they keep this behavior up, they would end up in jail and to watch out because people can get arrested as young as ten years old.*

Did this make the students stop talking? Yes, but what other internal damage did these severe and unnecessarily cruel remarks do, especially to the students who were not even being disruptive? I was deeply affected by this incident, and ever since then I have been inspired to instill confidence and determination in my students so they know that they can reach their dreams. They should be lead towards these dreams and away from the failure and disappointment brought on by predetermined futures. I believe that a lot of what adults say to children, and especially what teachers say to them, leads to a self-fulfilling prophecy. If we tell them they cannot accomplish something they are less likely to believe that they can and will consequently not try as hard for it. Not trying leads to negative results, making the prophecy come true. On the other hand, if we foster their talents, nurture their abilities, and support their dreams, they are much more likely to achieve success. Resorting to negativity and painful threats is far less motivating then showing positivity and helping them reach their goals.

"Don't be pushed by your problems; be led by your dreams."

"You are likely to surround yourself with those who do not see any good within you."

Imagine being ordered to remain seated for eight straight hours. You do not get up to walk around. You do not talk to others. You do not accomplish anything throughout the day. You receive constant orders to do extremely difficult tasks, and you quickly give up.

> *Mrs. Wilson's class was directly across from my classroom and everyday she came into school extremely flustered. She was an "old-school" type of teacher, and her lessons did not include movement, discussions, or cooperative learning. Every grade level meeting included complaints from Mrs. Wilson regarding the following: low test scores, misbehaving students, and an all-around "horrible" class. At first, I felt bad for Mrs. Wilson because she was an older woman who lacked technology skills, but after the first week, I was not feeling sorry for Mrs. Wilson anymore. I was feeling sorry for her students. She was constantly screaming throughout the day, telling her students to "hush up" and sit down. By the end of the day, Mrs. Wilson and her students looked drained. Mrs. Wilson was drained from the constant yelling, and her students were drained from listening to it.*

Before student teaching, professors and family told me, "you will learn what to do, but you will learn more about what not to do." Mrs. Wilson showed me directly what I should not do as a future teacher. Her students were not "horrible" children. Many of them wanted to learn so badly, but there were not many avenues to acquire knowledge in that classroom. One particular day towards the beginning of the year, I was able to read with her students, trying to find their correct reading level. I was nervous because according to Mrs. Wilson, these students were basically not capable of anything. As I started asking them questions and reading with them, I saw immense potential in these students. I was excited to tell Mrs. Wilson that the majority of her class was meeting the reading level for second grade. After I told her different students' passing scores, she combatted the positivity with negativity. She would tell me that one boy may be on level, but cannot sit still or loves to talk to his peer. The months passed by and Mrs. Wilson's students were not living up to their full potential. It was so clear to me how well these students could have done if they were given different avenues to explore the material. It became very evident that I have to be flexible and accept change in order to become a better educator every year. As future teachers, we cannot surround these children with negativity. In some cases, we might be the only positive aspect of their life.

> "Surround yourself with those who are positive and see the greatness within you, even when you don't see it yourself."

"If others are telling you that your dreams are too big, adjust your dreams."

As adults, many of us have dreams to travel. I personally have always wanted to go to Italy. I am sure many people have their dream vacations planned as well and are working hard to earn and save enough money to turn these dreams into realities. But what if someone told you it would never happen? What if they said you had to spend your money on something else, or that you would probably never earn enough to get there in the first place? What would you do? Would you listen to them and put your passport away? Would you give up on your dream just because they said so? As independent individuals, we like to think that we would stand up for ourselves, but what if we were not fully independent individuals? What if that person was bigger than us, had more authority, and supposedly knew what was best?

This is the struggle so many students face as their teachers and parents try to suppress their dreams and goals, and without these, what motivation do they have to succeed? While their dreams might not include places like Italy, to a young student, going to recess can be just as grand, and the thought of not having it just as devastating.

> *Thomas was a rambunctious third grade boy. He was always talking out in class, getting conduct marks, and though not malicious, was labeled a serious troublemaker. Due to the amount of classroom disruptions he caused, recess was taken away from him almost every day. One day, Thomas decided that he would get recess. He stayed quiet in class, did all of his work, and did not get a single conduct mark. I was so proud of him and I could see in his eyes how excited he was when the bell rang for recess. As the students ran to the playground, Thomas looked like he was about to burst through the finish line of a race. His smile was a mile wide. Then, out of nowhere we heard his teacher's voice yelling "Thomas! Get on that fence!" He stopped dead in his tracks. Why would he not have recess? He had done everything right! I could not just stand by and let this happen. I reminded the teacher of his wonderful behavior today and waited for her to correct the mistake. All the while, Thomas is crying out "I wasn't bad! I was so good!" Instead, she calls out to him "Just consider this punishment for all the other times you've been bad this year."*

Instead of admitting to her error and fixing it, this teacher chose to punish Thomas to maintain a façade that teachers never make mistakes. She could have instead used this situation as an opportunity to relate to her student and talk to him on a more personal level. She could have told him how sorry she was for her mistake, how proud she was of his progress and hard work, and that none of his efforts went unnoticed. Students need to know that there is always a goal. There is always something to work towards that will make all of their efforts worth it. How will students maintain motivation to try for anything if they are punished regardless of what they do? What use is it to save money for your Italy trip if you know your boarding pass will be taken away at the airport? There has to be a message that hard work pays off, and that this hard work can help students achieve any dream, no matter how big or spectacular.

> "If you can imagine it, you can achieve it; if you can dream it, you can become it."

We realize there are some things about the education system that we cannot change completely, but we think that many of the struggles that administrators, teachers and students are facing can be severely reduced if motivation is present. Ultimately, we believe that children must feel like they are capable of achieving success in order to truly succeed. All children NEED someone to believe in them. We, as teachers should be those believers. As years go by, students are not going to remember specific lessons you taught, the clothes you wore, the words you said, or even all of your actions, but they are going to remember how you made them feel. You can be someone who held them captive in their elementary prison or someone who helped set them free. How do you want to be remembered?

CHAPTER 17

Jordan and Catherine: Realizations about Classroom Environment

> We cannot seek or attain health, wealth, learning, justice or kindness in general. Action is always specific, concrete, individualized, unique.
>
> J. DEWEY, *Democracy and education: An introduction to philosophy of education*, 1920

∴

Introduction

This quote describes our newfound understanding about the classroom environment that was developed during our student teaching. We think it is safe to say that many pre-service teachers feel that classroom management is on the top of their list when it comes to apprehensions about teaching. Many days were spent in our pre-service classes discussing pedagogy, curriculum standards, and our teaching ideals, but we were about to be faced with real world challenges, for which we could not be prepared.

During student teaching we were going to be responsible for a class full of students, and for the first time, we would have to manage behaviors and instruction. We learned the importance of planning effective, engaging lessons that would minimize unsavory behavior.

We spent the summer leading up to student teaching discussing the importance of setting clear expectations through the implementation of rituals and routines. But no matter the amount of knowledge we absorbed during classes, we could not help feeling apprehensive about the upcoming year.

Now that our student teaching is coming to a close, we understand what we lacked going into the experience, the value of the individual. Each student taught us a significant aspect about the classroom environment, and as Dewey expressed, the learning environment cannot be viewed through generalizations.

During student teaching we realized classroom management is just a portion of what contributes to a positive classroom environment. Though classroom management tools and techniques are necessary it is also important to understand the unique characteristics and behaviors of each student.

We came to these realizations upon reflection of various interactions with student. Though we taught in different grade levels and at different schools we both learned how individual students affect our teaching, and the importance of growing from these experiences to improve the classroom environment.

Stacy

If a teacher could have a class full of Stacy's [1], teaching would be a more desirable profession. She is a bright, attentive, hard worker that works well with most of her peers, and has an outgoing personality that is infectious. Now, you would think a childlike Stacy would not have taught me anything about classroom management, seeing that she is practically the ideal student, but she taught me the importance of consistency in classroom management. Our classroom uses a behavior system that gives marks for every behavioral rule broken, such as being disrespectful, talking without permission, and the usual behaviors that negatively impact their learning. Some students receive multiple marks a day, and most of the class receives at least one mark per week. Only two students have gone months without receiving any marks, and one of those students is Stacy. Like I (Jordan) said earlier, Stacy takes pride in her work and has no trouble with following the classroom expectations. So imagine how I felt when I had to give Stacy her first mark ever in third grade. During reading, our students have to answer and discuss questions that correspond to the book they read. This task usually results in many students receiving a mark for being disrespectful to their group members or not paying attention. During this time, my mentor teacher and I would walk around the room and guide the discussions if the students were having trouble. One day during discussion, I came to Stacy's group and all I could hear was arguing. They had already received a warning for their behavior, but they continued on. Because of the teams' behavior each student received a behavior mark, which reduced Stacy to tears, and made me feel awful.

After later reflection, I could not help but think about how badly giving Stacy a mark made me feel. She broke the same rule as everyone else in her group, but having the others mark their chart did not affect me as much. It made me think back to instances when I may have let her slide because I knew a mark would affect her emotionally. Had I given her more chances then I would have given some of the other students in class? Am I really being a fair teacher? I always thought of myself as a fair person, but I realized this was a moment that made me veer from my principles.

I learned there is a fine line between playing favorites, and addressing behaviors differently based on a student's personality. I would never want to cross the line and discipline a student based on my personal opinion of that child, but I do think it is important for new teachers to realize one size does not fit all when it comes to addressing behavior. Stacy, like her group members displayed inappropriate behavior during their group discussion, so they all received a mark, however, because of the kind student Stacy is, that mark was all she needed to remind her of our classroom expectations. For other students it may take more action than one mark, it may take multiple marks, conversations about their behavior, or even changing groups, for them to make better choices, and that is okay too.

Mark

Students are given expectations daily when they are in school. They are expected to get to school at a certain time, they are expected to pay attention during each subject, and they are even expected to sit in a desk for eight hours without fidgeting.

I (Catherine) believe one of the most important lessons I learned while student teaching is that giving students choices can greatly impact their learning and the way they look at their own education. In a world full of rules, the students greatly appreciate when they feel that they can make decisions about their own life.

I saw the importance of choice on a day that Mark was choosing to not complete an assignment. Mark was a very energetic boy that loved conversation and would rarely be found sitting in his seat.

During subjects that Mark liked, he would be excitedly bouncing in his seat with his hand raised, eager to ask any question or express any thought that popped into his head. During the subjects that he disliked, he would act the exact opposite. Mark would rather wander the classroom and think of any excuse to not complete his work or pay attention to the lesson. Because of this, he would often find himself in trouble and made frequent visits to the assistant principal's office. Earlier during this class period, Mark had received behavior marks for talking during instruction and quickly put his head down on his desk.

When the assignment was given out, Mark threw his papers on the ground and continued to sulk. Because of this, he got multiple behavior marks, which only ended up making his attitude worse.

After five minutes of watching Mark pout, I walked up to his desk. I told him that he had two choices: he could continue to sit and not do his work and earn a zero or he could start working and earn points. More importantly though, I told Mark that I could not make the choice for him and neither could my mentor teacher, he had to be the one to choose which type of behavior he was going to display that day.

After I said this, Mark stared at me for a minute. He then replied, "oh," and promptly got to work.

This brief moment taught me something that I need to remember each day as a teacher: *children need to feel that they have some control during the school day.* They might not be able to choose which teacher they have or what time they will go to lunch, but they do have the power to make small decisions during the day. Something as simple as letting a student choose the book they are going to read for a book report or whom to sit with during group work can make a world of a difference in a classroom.

Many of us choose to be teachers because we like control and many times have a hard time letting others make decisions, but giving up small amounts of control to your students will make them feel that they are part of a community.

John

"Do you like turtles? Where do alligators go during the winter? How old are you?" These are just a few questions that pop into John's head during any given lesson. If I (Jordan) called on John there was a 50/50 chance that his question would veer from the intended lesson.

Though John is easily distracted at times, he is also a student who shows genuine engagement in our daily lessons. During an indoor recess day, while everyone else in the class was coloring, I found John extending our earlier writing lesson and writing his own story about a turtle named Sammy (if you haven't realized yet, John is a huge fan of turtles).

With this healthy appetite for learning, comes a responsibility of the teacher to determine the appropriateness of student questions during each lesson. I struggled with managing off topic student questions. Should I find the answer immediately, scold him for going off topic, or brush the question off and say we'll discuss it later.

To put things into perspective, the school at which I student taught has scripted lessons for majority of the subjects taught, and did not always lend itself to veering from the script to address other matters the students may want to discuss. I rarely broke away from the given scripted lesson, as my mentor teacher never did, the students seemed to understand the material for the most part, and there wasn't enough time in the day to move at the pace the programs required with adjustments.

It wasn't until I started my special education portion of student teaching that I realized how important it is to address those random, or probing, questions. While working with the special education teacher, I was placed in the lower reading class. This class still used the same reading program as the higher students, and the teacher was supposed to implement each lesson with fidelity like the other classes, but this teacher did things her own way.

Before even entering her class she told me, "Our class is Las Vegas, what happens in Vegas stays in Vegas." This was the first teacher I saw who took the time to really think about, and answer, these often rabbit-hole questions.

At first, I thought the time dedicated to finding their answers could have been better spent on reading strategies. After working with this teacher for a few weeks, I realized how beneficial this was to her students.

A majority of the students come from a low socioeconomic background, and have limited background knowledge. I realized that this teacher took the time to present and discuss information that they would not have experienced outside of the classroom.

All of this newfound understanding of how important it is to build background knowledge brought me back to John, and his endless amount of questions. John has curiosity that sometimes goes with the lesson, and sometimes doesn't.

I learned that it is important to make time for these seemingly random questions, because like the curriculum based lessons we are trying to teach them, receiving answers to their questions continues to expand their knowledge of their world.

Jayden

When I (Catherine) began my student teaching experience, I had the thought that I would try and appreciate every child, even on the challenging days. What I did not anticipate was that within a class of 23 children, it was very hard to keep them all on the same page for any given subject. One child may be having a fantastic day on Monday and another might have been getting in trouble all day. I remember a day that really showed me how important patience was within a classroom.

I was teaching math to my homeroom students. I taught in the inclusion classroom, so I had students of all learning abilities and styles. During the teacher led instruction, Jayden actively participated. He knew the answers to every question that was asked and completed guided problems minutes before his peers. He excelled during this math lesson more than he had with any lesson in the past.

Everything was flowing smoothly until we transitioned to the independent practice. He completed one problem and then Rich, Jayden's alter ego, showed up. He would no longer answer to Jayden, but would only reply to Rich.

Normally, this type of behavior would warrant behavior marks and a visit from the assistant principle if it continued. But on this particular day, my mentor teacher and I decided to just go with the behavior and see where it would take us.

I sat down next to Jayden and helped him refocus on the math work. We completed one problem together and then I moved onto another student who was asking for assistance.

A few minutes went by before Rich showed up again, disrupting the class with a fake phone call to Jayden asking him to make him some macaroni as an after-school snack. My mentor teacher quickly was at Jayden's side, trying to get him back to work, but this just caused him to become more disruptive as he yelled that his name wasn't Jayden.

As the class period went on, my mentor teacher and I noticed that Jayden only became Rich when he came to a problem that led to frustration. Because he became frustrated, he decided that he would rather cause a disruption that would allow him to escape the classroom, and therefore his math work. When I came to this realization, I decided to devote the rest of the class period to helping "Rich" finish his math work.

Yes, I called him Rich, and yes he did talk about the macaroni that he was going to eat after school. But we finished the math problems and Jayden did most of the work, he really only needed guiding questions from me to help get him through the tough parts.

The rest of the day flew by without any more disruptions from Rich. The following day, my mentor and I were apprehensive about the reappearance of Jayden's other half, but he did not show.

This situation taught me how important it is to be patient with your children, especially when they get frustrated. At times it seems easier to just dismiss a child if they are causing disruptions to a classroom, but it is more important to take the time to figure out the cause behind the behavior than to send the child out, when they would just miss valuable time in the classroom.

Sean

Growing up I (Jordan) always looked up to my teachers. I was the kind of student who wanted them to like me just as much as I liked and admired them. Now the tables have turned, and I realize I want the same thing from the children in my classroom. It is human nature to want people to like you as a person, but for the first time, I was in an authoritative position, and I found being liked and being respected by my students to be a true balancing act. Sean, a first grade student, brought these challenging feelings to the surface during this experience.

Midway through the school year, I transitioned from third grade to first grade to work on my special education practicum. This was not just a change for me but a change for the students. I worked closely with two children, one of which was Sean.

Sean was a very independent first grade student; he preferred individual activities and put a lot of effort in his work. Before working with Sean, my mentor teacher informed me that he was a shy child, and can be perceived as aloof. She told me that it took weeks for him to respond openly to her and gain his trust. I realized that I would also have to go through this process with Sean as well.

When I began working with Sean every time I extended my hand to show him something on his paper he pulled his paper away and turned his head away from me. I praised his hard work and correct responses during class, but it didn't seem like it was enough. I tried being stern when this behavior occurred, I let him know that this is not acceptable behavior, but the more I corrected him, the more he would shutdown and refuse help. It was wearisome for me to watch my mentor teacher work with Sean, he was attentive and responded to her very well, and I struggled getting the same behavior from Sean.

As I continued working with Sean I learned to give him more space. When he felt independent while working, his confidence increased and shut downs decreased; it was best to not continually check in with Sean, but to intervene only when necessary. When I worked one-on-one with Sean I incorporated short games of I spy, his favorite game, during our activities, which allowed Sean to have a break from work and build a rapport.

Slowly, but surely, I noticed a change in Sean's behavior, he responded better to the instructions I gave, and I could see that I was earning his trust and respect. Working with Sean helped me understand that not all of your students may like you, and that is okay. For some students they need time to get to know you and your expectations. It is important to allow.

Marcy

Halfway through my student-teaching practicum, I (Catherine) moved to the special education portion. With this change came a new experience teaching in the resource room. In this type of instruction, there are no more than five or six students per teacher. Small group instruction allows for differentiated learning that the students do not receive in whole group instruction.

Smaller classes give students ample time to discuss their thinking and clarify any confusion they may have during the lesson. Instruction is more explicit. It gives the students more examples and individualized feedback. During this time, I observed noticeable, rapid growth with one of my students, Marcy.

This student had just been placed in small group instruction for math. When I worked with her in the whole group setting, Marcy was quiet and struggled with her math work daily. She did not always complete her homework and her math grade began to drop.

Because of her stagnating progress, my mentor teacher and I discussed moving Marcy into small group math instruction. When I started working with this group, I expected Marcy to perform in the same manner, but what I saw surprised me.

Marcy demonstrated a change in behavior. She frequently raised her hand when questions were asked, was extremely motivated each and every day, and always completed her homework. Marcy's grades began to increase and were eventually the highest of the small group.

This experience made me realize how important it is to take the time to accommodate each child. Each student will learn at a different pace and will need different materials to succeed. We as teachers need to recognize the different learning styles and incorporate different methods of teaching that will best fit each student.

Conclusion

During this experience we learned that there is not a perfect plan that will work with every child and every classroom. Children are individuals and it will take a classroom teacher much time to understand the inner workings that make each child tick.

What an inexperienced teacher needs to understand is that day to day planning and scheduling revolves around the actions of the students. We have come to realize that each student behaves in a different way and requires a different type of management; no two children are going to behave in exactly the same way.

Each child comes from a different background, a different home life, and a different set of experiences. Looking back at the words from John Dewey, we have realized it is important to use individualized and unique student moments to better our teaching. Once you understand the student as an individual, those needs translate to the classroom as a whole.

CHAPTER 18

Through the Fire: A Critical Race Perspective toward Preparing Critical Educators

An Introduction

For classroom teachers to successfully teach all students, regardless of social background and cultural or ethnic differences, they must have the knowledge and skills to effectively implement a culturally responsive pedagogy grounded in being a critical educator (Gay, 2000; Ladson-Billings, 1999). Unfortunately, the teaching force in the U.S. remains predominantly White and female and the student making up of the two credential programs that are the subjects of this book are no different (National Summit on Diversity in the Teaching Force, 2002; Sleeter, 2001).

At the same time, most teachers continue to exit their preparation programs with little to no knowledge of themselves as racial beings or of social groups outside of their own and unprepared and unable to identify, implement critical learning strategies aimed a being more culturally responsive teaching (Bell, 2002; Cochran-Smith, Davis, & Fries, 2004; Cross, 2005; Juarez, Smith, & Hayes, 2008). The student's voices while varied appear to have several threads of commonality one being and/or becoming a critical educator.

This last chapter is geared towards who are planning to teach as well as those who prepare teacher educators. In this last chapter, while there are many possible, we look at two conceptual orientations we believe will help teachers and teacher educators push forward on becoming critical educators. These two concepts grounded in Critical Race Theory are, first, unhooking from Whiteness, and second, disrupting the school to prison pipeline. Finally, the primary goal of this volume as well as this chapter is make the argument that critical teacher education should be the foundation of any teacher preparation program (Gollnick, 1995; Hayes & Fasching-Varner, 2015; Juarez & Hayes, 2010).

Through the Fire with Critical Race Theory

Like Knaus (2009), we apply Critical Race Theory for the purpose of developing the need for critical educators both teacher educators and pre-service teachers. As a framework, we use the narratives of the student's in the earlier chapters of the book to put this final chapter together. One of the many things we were looking for in this volume from the students is their abilities and openness to become critical educators. Critical educators with the wherewithal as well as the skill set to challenge the systems that keep some students from reaching their full potential.

Tate (1997) asks the question, "Pivotal in understanding CRT as a methodology, what role should experiential knowledge of race, class and gender play in educational discourse?" (p. 235). Ladson-Billings (1998) states that CRT focuses on the role of "voice in bringing additional power and experiential knowledge that people of color speak regarding the fact that our society is deeply structured by racism" (p. 13). Solórzano and Yosso (2001) define CRT as "an attempt to understand the oppressive aspects of society in order to generate societal and individual transformation and are important for educators to understand that CRT is different from any other theoretical framework because it centers race" (pp. 471–472).

CRT scholars have developed the following tenets to guide CRT research; all of these tenets are utilized within the design and analysis of this study (Kohli, 2009):

1. *Centrality of race and racism.* All CRT research within education must centralize race and racism, as well as acknowledge the intersection of race with other forms of subordination (Kohli, 2009; Sleeter & Delgado Bernal, 2002).
2. *Valuing experiential knowledge.* Solorzano and Yosso (2001) argue that CRT in educational research recognizes that the experiential knowledge of students of color is legitimate, appropriate, and critical to understanding, analyzing, and teaching about racial subordination in the field of education. Life stories tend to be accurate according to the perceived realities of subjects' lives. They are used to elicit structured stories and detailed lives of the individuals involved (Delgado, 1989; McCray, Sindelar, Kilgore, & Neal, 2002).
3. *Challenging the dominant perspective.* CRT research works to challenge dominant narratives, often referred to as majoritarian stories. CRT scholar Harris (1995) describes the "valorization of Whiteness as treasured property in a society structured on racial caste" (p. 277). Harris (1995) also argues that Whiteness conferred tangible and economically valuable benefits, and it was jealously guarded as a valued possession. This thematic strand of Whiteness as property in the United States is not confined to the nation's early history (Frankenberg, 1993; Ladson-Billings, 1998).
4. *Commitment to social justice.* Social justice must always be a motivation behind CRT research. Part of this social justice commitment must include a critique of liberalism, claims of neutrality, objectivity, color blindness and meritocracy as a camouflage for the self-interest of powerful entities

of society (Tate, 1997). Only aggressive, color conscious efforts to change the way things are done will do much to ameliorate misery (Delgado & Stefancic, 2001; Tate, 1997).

5. *Being interdisciplinary*. According to Tate (1997), CRT crosses epistemological boundaries. It borrows from several traditions, including liberalism, feminism, and Marxism to include a more complete analysis of "raced" people.

Critical Race Theory has emerged as a theoretical and methodological instrument that has been useful to centering education research on race and racism. CRT scholars center the experiential knowledge of peoples of color to expose everyday forms of racial violence, placing these experiences within a collective historical context (Elenes & Delgado Bernal, 2010; Fernandez, 2002; Zarate & Conchas, 2010).

Pointedly, the legitimacy of CRT in education has already been established (Ladson-Billings, 1998). According to Ladson-Billings (1998), CRT in education names one's own reality as a way to link form and substance in scholarship. CRT in education allows for the use of parables, chronicles, stories, *testimonios*, and counterstories to illustrate the false necessity and irony of much of the current civil rights doctrine: we really have not gone as far as we think we have.

Adopting CRT as a framework for educational equity means that our aim is to expose racism in education and propose radical solutions for addressing it. CRT in education makes sense when we consider that the classroom is where knowledge is constructed and distributed; hence, it becomes a central site for the construction of social and racial power (Fernandez, 2002; Ladson-Billing, 1998).

Becoming Critical by Unhooking: A Start

This chapter has many purposes as we move towards the development of critical educators. In this section of the chapter, we are making the argument that one of the ways of becoming a critical educator involves unhooking from Whiteness. We argue, first, that McIntosh's oft-used metaphor of "unpacking the invisible knapsack" doesn't do enough to challenge racism or other forms of oppression, and second, that people of color who consider themselves antiracists, like Whites, must also "unhook from Whiteness." Importantly, the process of unhooking from whiteness is different for Whites as compared to individuals and groups historically marked as racially not White and given the pervasive and durable history of White supremacy.

As we understand it, "unhooking from whiteness" is a process of breaking up what Stacy Lee (1996) calls the "hegemonic device." Lee defines *hegemonic device* as the strategy used by Whites to maintain the racial hierarchy and that also sets the standard for how minorities should behave.

Breaking the hegemonic device disrupts the dominance of whites in the racial hierarchy by redirecting the "causes" of racial inequities back to their root causes. This transformative resistance – a process we call *unhooking from whiteness* – forces persons and groups racialized as White and Other than White to see themselves as not racially neutral. We suggest that White dominance is created and maintained in large part by White people individually and collectively and at times with the support and assistance of people and groups identified as racial minorities through processes of White racial domination through the decisions, actions, and interactions of individuals and groups that further the historical privileging of Whiteness in terms of Whites' collective interests, histories, beliefs, values, accomplishments, and histories.

The process of unhooking from whiteness allows all, from their specific, albeit differently valued subject locations within society and in relation to the historical privileging of Whiteness, to be held accountable for participation in decision-making and practices that combine to result in the patterned exclusion of those marked as racially other than White. Toward this goal of rendering visible for examination the process of unhooking from whiteness, our hope is that by exposing the moments in which liberals is deployed as a weapon to maintain and sustain White dominance, we can also highlight moments in which it becomes possible to work against and challenge these very same tenets of liberalism (Delgado Bernal & Solorzano, 2001; Fasching-Varner, 2009; Lee, 1996).

Following Juarez and colleagues (Juarez & Hayes, 2010; Juarez, Smith, & Hayes, 2008), we posit that the multicultural paradox of US teacher education both carries and reflects the irony of modernity, with its pretensions of universal ideals and its racialized realities of daily life and lived practices, and thus is a paradox of liberalism (Goldberg, 1993). We define modernity as "the general period emerging from the sixteenth century in the historical formation of what only relatively recently has come to be called 'The West'" (Goldberg, 1993). "As modernity's definitive doctrine of self and society, [and] of morality and politics" (Goldberg, 1993, p. 1), in turn, liberalism refers to a core set of ideas regarding matters of equality, progress, individualism, and universalism, which are taken simultaneously both as basic assumptions, and as ideals to strive toward; the project of liberalism is to transcend social differences to unite persons on the grounds of equal moral worth (Mills, 1997).

We seek to better understand, and then work with others, to implode and recreate the ways that equality and other democratic ideals in US teacher education are regularly enacted to realize inequitable outcomes of White racial exclusivity and dominance. Specifically, we consider how the liberal paradox embedded within US teacher education helps to perpetuate society's existing racial hierarchies characterized by White supremacy. The supremacy of Whites in US society is readily visible across education, healthcare, employment, the media, and most key social domains.

At the same time, very significantly, White supremacy is never fully secured and must be continually re-established. Defined "as a racialized social system that upholds, reifies, and reinforces the superiority of whites" (Leonardo, 2009, p. 127), White supremacy is daily, perhaps hourly, remade through processes of race-based domination as individuals and groups on their own and collectively draw on institutional authority to justify and make decisions, act, and interact with others in ways further the historical privileging of characteristics, values, histories, accomplishments, and more associated with Whites (Bonilla-Silva, 2003; Gillborn, 2005). Striving toward an inclusive, integrated community blind to race-, class-, gender-, sexuality-, or creed-based differences, teacher educators individually and collectively tend to approach their work guided by universal, difference-neutral democratic, egalitarian-based ideals that, unfortunately, typically result in the buttressing of US teacher education's Whiteness and continued White racial dominance.

Critical Education without Critical Educators

Most teacher preparation programs self-evaluate themselves as successful in effectively preparing future teachers for today's classrooms. Yet, as we and many researchers have documented (Cochran-Smith, Davis, & Fries, 2004; Cross, 2005; Hayes & Juarez, 2012; Juarez & Hayes, 2014), critical education and critical preparation of teachers in teacher education are typically nowhere to be found in practice. Teacher education programs proudly point to traditions of inclusion and democratic education while their curricula and practices in their programs are indicative of education that is by, for, and about White people. Importantly, democratic education is most often education that is democratic for people historically identified as White and violent, both symbolically and physically, for everyone else (Juarez, Smith, & Hayes, 2008).

Critical educators and critical education are no where to be found when teacher education programs forcefully tell the faculty that diversity is the way we are going, like it or not, and then briskly skim over and casually dismiss questions about why we have no courses on the history of Black, American Indian, or Latino education, for example, given the demographics of surrounding communities. Pointedly, to be culturally illiterate does not mean that you do not know how to be nice, or at least tolerantly polite, to those with phenotypical features different from your own. At the same time, few things in the world are *more dangerous than sincere ignorance and conscientious stupidity*, to paraphrase Dr. Martin Luther King, Jr. (see Cone, 2004).

Critical educators and critical education are likewise nowhere to be found when teacher education programs continue to put together diversity hiring committees and then ask us if we know any potential applicants of color who teach *just science* or *just literacy methods*, but not all that political business because you get tired of W*hite people bashing*. Yes, you "want very much to have *a* Black person in [your] department as long as that person thinks and acts like [you], shares [your] values and beliefs, [and] is in no way different" (hooks, 1989, p. 113; emphasis in the original). Nothing new here, Whites have been deciding for the past 500 years what kind and how much "diversity" they will tolerate.

Critical educators and critical education are nowhere to be found when White teacher education faculty members and White students are offended, saying we are moving too fast in bringing a scholar from another university to talk about White racism and on being Black in historically White institutions. Certainly, White people are regularly offended – as demonstrated by *an appalling oppressive and bloody history known all over the world* (Baldwin, 1963/1985). After 244 years of slavery, 100 years of lynching, and 40 odd years of formal civil rights, we are moving too fast for whom, exactly? And, why is it White people who always decide how fast we should be going?

White people and everyone else need to engage these questions about the pervasiveness of Whiteness as the normative standard in education and every other important domain in US society. Until we all do so, in terms of identifying and questioning systems of White racial domination, we will not be able to consider how to begin working together to disrupt the ways that the historical privileging of Whites' collective interests, accomplishments, histories, and values continue to structure the everyday lives and opportunities of all of us albeit to the inequitable and often deadly detriment of some of us racialized as not White, and to the inequitable and often life-saving benefit of others racialized as White.

Critical Teachers Develop Critical Scholars: Disrupting the School to Prison Pipeline

Given the lack of critical educator and critical education in teacher education despite broad claims of well-established criticality in teacher preparation and credentialing processes. In this section of the chapter, we explore the increasingly symbiotic relationship between U.S. public schools and the nation's criminal justice system (Kim, 2010; Meiners & Winn, 2010; Sander, 2010; Tuzzolo & Hewitt, 2006) and the role teacher's play and can play to disrupt this symbiotic relationship. More specifically, /we examine the space between public schools and the U.S. penal system and both identify and analyze ways that institutional factors such as the school curriculum, discipline policies, and testing practices are consistently enacted in public schools to push groups of students out of classrooms and toward prisons in a type of school-to-prison pipeline despite the good intentions of educators and others. Following Smith (2009), we define the school to prison pipeline as the combination of school disciplinary and other official and unofficial policies, practices, decisions, interactions and perspectives enacted, put into place, or used to authorize the positioning of students, students of color in particular, on trajectories that move them toward their participation in the U.S. penal system.

Meiners and Winn (2010) use the term prison industrial complex (PIC) to explain this concept. They argue that the PIC encompasses the expanding economic and political contexts of the detention and corrections industry in the United States. We interpret this as schools provide a readily supply for the growing demand for prisons in the United States. Scholarly put, the PIC is an expanding economy: between 2000 and 2005, a new prison was built in the United States every 12 days and the term *million dollar blocks* was coined to name the massive disinvestment in targeted communities of color; so many residents from one urban city block are in prison (Gonnerman, 2004; Meiners & Winn, 2010; Stephan, 2008).

It is our contention in this chapter and a call to respond to teachers what the relationship between U.S. public schools and the nation's penal system or its negative impact on youth of color in particular. We suggest that because many educators, many who consider themselves critical, do not understand how the school to prison pipeline daily operates to uphold the existing racial hierarchy in the U.S., they may and frequently do participate, albeit perhaps unwittingly, in helping to perpetuate race-based practices and policies that regularly work to ensure that male students of color are more likely to spend time in prison than in college. It is our hope with this section in particular and this chapter specifically begins a critical conversation about a very important critical topic.

Whatever their intentions are, as individuals make decisions and choices, act, and interact with others in ways that perpetuate the existing racial hierarchy, they do indeed participate in helping to push students out of classrooms and into the penal system. It is our hope that by better understanding how connections between schools and prisons are built up there may be more possibilities opened up for learning how to begin interrupting oppressive relations and spaces and reorganizing them in more democratic and inclusive ways.

In the U.S., public schools are often on the front line in terms of prevention and intervention for many populations of youth and providing them with opportunities to realize full membership in society. Many researchers call for increased intervention programs to meet the needs of youth from communities of color and other communities traditionally underserved in U.S. public schools. At the same time, many contemporary public school and school districts do not have the funding to hire additional staff or the critical understanding of diverse populations to work with students who struggle in school. It is our contention that schools of education give their candidates this critical understanding and it's more than just knowing how to write a behavior.

In this chapter, we posit that the solution to the increased rates of students' arrests in public schools does not lie with adding additional programs to existing curricular and other programmatic offerings in classrooms. We suggest instead that schools and those within them must learn to daily recognize, and work toward interrupting and reorganizing the symbiotic relationship between schools and the U.S. penal system beginning with the oftentimes implied assumptions of the moral, academic and other forms of inferiority regularly attributed to Black and other Americans of color.

Black, Brown and Male and Trouble in Schools: Where Are the Critical Educators?

Why is it, then, that young Black and Latino males in particular are not on the college prep track and instead find themselves caught in the school to prison pipeline? The educational tribulations of African American males in U.S. public schools are well documented (Douglas Horsford, 2010; King, Houston, & Middleton, 2001; hooks, 2004, 1995; Noguera, 2008; O'Connor, 2006). Schools in the United States are racially structured such that Black males and Latino students tend to experience them in more negative ways.

Noguera (2000) argues that schools reproduce the very inequalities that they should break down. Black males and Latinos, especially those from urban areas, receive an education designed to make them compliant, obey official requirements, and take orders from superiors. Put bluntly, schools with their micro-sorting contributes to the pipeline by disproportionately placing minority students into underachieving classes that stimulate anti-social behavior and entail disparate push-out and incarceration rates (Smith, 2009).

There are several factors – the curriculum and patterns in tracking, standardized testing, and discipline – that together contribute to the disengagement and alienation that many young Black males experience and feel in school, thus leading to failure in the classroom, and all grounded in Whiteness as the normative standard against which students are evaluated and then managed. The Whiteness of public schools means that educators and others view Black males and other students of color from a perspective that privileges the interests, values, beliefs, and more of Whites. The privileging of Whiteness necessarily infers to the devaluing of anything that is not White.

Accordingly, patterns of interacting, speech, and other culturally-based ways of knowing and being that are not based on Whiteness are regularly interpreted by those with institutional authority as deviant and misguided. Behaviors of "acting out" in schools by boys who are White, for example, are often seen as precocious and signs of originality and creativity while the same behaviors by Black males are more likely to be seen as inappropriate, potentially dangerous, and even violent requiring disciplinary action.

Educational Slavery Today

In public schools serving communities of color from working class and poor economic backgrounds, it is regularly the case that classrooms are places of holding, not learning. Classrooms serve as a type of holding pen to keep and control and contain Black and Latino children's bodies, but not to teach them. Adults put in charge of children in school often interact with students in ways that would not be considered appropriate in other economic and racial settings. As educators and having taught in public schools designated as urban and Title 1, we have respectively and regularly witnessed the types of disrespectful interactions of adults with students of color in classrooms as documented in the educational literature (Juarez & Hayes, 2015).

Then, responding to the indignities and injustices they are subjected to daily, students act out in ways that are not viewed as appropriate by the faculty and staff. Police are called and students are suspended. These stories all share one thing in common – the students' disruptive behavior is the symptom of not being taught. The children are responding to the conditions of educational slavery they are subjected to on a daily basis.

And thus the vicious cycle proceeds largely uninterrupted. Black and other students of color who come from poor neighborhoods and do not fare well in school end up staying in these same poor neighborhoods where their valued resources remains limited at best. Their children are then born and a new generation of students grows up to face the dangers of *learning while Black and Brown*.

Curriculum, Tracking, and Testing: Practices of Whiteness

Why is it that adult interactions that would not be considered appropriate in some contexts are often excused and indeed usually seen as necessary and appropriate in settings inhabited by students of color from economically poor backgrounds? The answer lies within the notions of White superiority and Black and Latino inferiority. Pointedly, we are not referring to the belief systems of extremist race-based groups such as the Ku Klux Klan or others. Rather, by assumptions of White superiority, we follow Feagin (2006) in noting that there are race-based patterns of thinking that characterize the ways Whites as a group tend to make sense of the world around them.

In terms of notions of White superiority, these race-based patterns of thinking typically include assumptions that, first, it is appropriate that Whites are generally in charge or control of most of society's institutions. Second, assumptions of White superiority suggest that Whites as a group tend to have a superior culture and morality which then both explains and justifies why Whites are typically in charge of most institutions in U.S. society and retain the largest percentage of wealth and society's other valued resources. Pointedly, assumptions of White superiority necessarily infer assumptions of the moral and cultural inferiority of people of color as respective groups.

While individuals of color may often be seen as exceptions to the rule of the moral and cultural inferiority of people of color, for the most part, Whites as a group tend to think about groups of color as having and being characterized by a lesser level or degree of culture and morality within them as individuals and groups. It is not uncommon, for example, for Whites individually and collectively to attribute the over-representation of Whites in high status positions of employment as evidence that Whites individually and collectively have worked harder and therefore are more deserving of society's rewards than people of color. It is likewise not unusual for White people individually and collectively to presume that the over-representation of African Americans in U.S. prisons to be the result of [increased] Black criminality, especially as compared to a lesser degree of criminality among Whites as presumably evidenced by fewer numbers of incarcerated Whites. "Yes, there are more Blacks in prison because they commit more of the crimes," is a common quote that we hear often even though as stated earlier Black Americans only make up about 12 percent of the U.S. population.

These assumptions of White superiority and Black and Brown inferiority in behavior and potential to learn are deeply embedded within the daily practices of U.S. public schools. No one aspect of schooling practice is as highly visible and loudly debated as intersections between school curriculum and the experiences of Black and Latino males. Generally, curriculum can be understood narrowly as that knowledge which is taught in the classroom or it can be more broadly defined as all the things students learn as a result of attending school. Importantly, from our perspective, curriculum presented to young Black and Latino males is too often knowledge that directs them away from working to acquire official knowledge required for college prep tracks in school (Fowler, 2011; Love, 2004; Tullman & Weck; 2009; Zamudio et al., 2011).

The Whiteness of the curriculum in schools is underscored by calls to infuse multiculturalism into it. Importantly, the curriculum is organized and distributed in ways that are influenced by matters of race in public schools. Black and Latino students in particular are regularly excluded from access to high status advanced level math classes. Student placement in high status academic tracks is an important factor informing who does and does not have access to certain valued and unequally distributed knowledge. Students' racial background plays a factor in the selection of those deemed qualified to participate in gifted and talented (GATE) and advanced placement classes. Not surprisingly, GATE students are more likely to get accepted into prestigious colleges and universities than are students who do not attend curriculum programs or academic tracks designated as gifted and talented (Hughes & Bonner, 2006; Zamudio et al., 2011).

Importantly, students are frequently placed in high status academic tracks for those designated as gifted and talented based on teachers' recommendations and thus teacher perceptions of students. Teachers have been found to be more likely to nominate White students for high status academic level tracks as compared to Black and Latino students. This practice of race-based distribution of access to high status knowledge produces in U.S. public schools [and higher education] what Delgado Bernal and Villalpando (2002) have termed an apartheid of knowledge. Young Black men and other students of color are not acquiring the curricular knowledge in U.S. public schools needed to receive a high school diploma let alone to consider pursuing the rigors of post-secondary education in some cases they do not have the skills needed to pass the military entrance exam. In 2011, with the downsizing of the US Armed Forces, all of the military branches with the exception of the Army require a high school diploma. GEDs are not welcomed here. The military has for generations provided an out for many males of color from urban areas. Any encounter with the prison pipeline, however, ensures that young men of color will not have the option to consider a career in the military (Hargrove & Seay, 2011).

Black and Latino males proceed through the education pipeline learning how to underachieve, learning to devalue schools and academics, and learning to reject school as a place to develop their sense of identity and, particularly, their sense of self-worth and self-efficacy. The mission of a school, officially, is to prepare children for the sociocultural and political realities of society. The reality in education, however, is that U.S. public schools are creating generation after generation of Black and Latino males who often accept, even if unwillingly, their position in society as second-class citizens – albeit not always willingly.

In the classroom, by way of summary, Black and Latinos males have three main problems and these problems are not self-induced: (1) They are not permitted to learn, (2) They are not thought to be able to learn, (3) They are forced to learn survival lessons that many of their White counterparts are not required to learn (Pierce, 1975). The result of the learning problems put on Black and Latino male students in schools is that of gate-keeping. Students of color are turned away from the gate of access to high status knowledge in U.S. public schools because of curriculum-based, tracking-based, and testing-based problems put on them in classrooms, usually by well meaning people of goodwill who do not intentionally promote Whiteness at the expense of students of color. The gate-keeping mechanism called standardized testing is regularly used to authorize the exclusion of young Black and Latino males from considering opportunities to pursue well paying careers instead many are pushed out and leave undereducated (Fowler, 2011; Sander, 2010; Smith, 2008).

In some instances students are removed from classes they enjoy and forced to take additional math and language classes for a majority of the school day. The outcome may result in higher test scores, but the cost is great because these additional test prep classes do not allow students to take classes that may expose them and even prepare them for additional careers. In schools, that have vocation education and there is an honor for many Black and Brown students to have a career as a tradesman or electrician. But what happens is they are removed from theses classes, the vocational classes that could lead to high paying blue color jobs if not provide pre-requisite training for a military career and placed in hours and hours of remediation all in the name of high test scores (Hughes & Bonner, 2006).

Schools with low-test scores then become subjected to remedial types of teaching and learning that are not very engaging, and oftentimes perceived as insulting to students. And thus the cycle of school-created learning failure continues. Tedious and disconnected curriculum causes the kids check out. The teacher then blames the students for not learning the irrelevant material. He/she may then administer a test to show that, indeed, the students do not know the material. Students are then treated according to the level of test score they achieve and put into a lower status academic track that is headed toward prison, not higher education. Significantly, even if they manage to stay through 12 years of school and graduate, these young men frequently do not have the prerequisite skills to thrive in an undergraduate 4-year program.

Douglass Horsford (2010) states that schooling practices such as tracking, social promotion, and out of school suspensions contribute to the discouragement and disengagement experienced by many poor children and children of color. Instead of preparing the next generation of doctors, nurses, pharmacists, and dentists, American schools continue to perpetuate and even increase academic and other forms of inequality. Black and Latino males in particular stay poor, poorly educated, and unskilled as a result of the Whiteness in education.

hooks (2004) describes instances where teachers constantly remind Black men of their perceived intellectual deficiencies. She states, "time and time again, Black boys tell their life stories of being punished for daring to think and question" (p. 36). However, conversely, when schools give Black men the chance to prove themselves in academically rigorous courses, such as honors and advanced placement, these boys have had to "prove" they belong in such classes. And once they "prove" they belong in honors, these Black students have to be obedient and keep their mouth closed. Smart, young, Black and Latino males who want to be heard, often find themselves cast out, deemed troublemakers (hooks, 2004; Noguera, 2008; Pierce, 1975).

Developing Black and Brown Scholars

As we have argued in this chapter, Black and Latino males represent student groups that have been frequently overlooked and excluded, not with benign consequences. Whiting (2006) argues that to fix the under representation of Black and Latino males in gifted education, public schools must start helping students of color in developing a scholar identity instead of reinforcing and supporting society's emphasis on them developing anti-social identities that are not open to school learning. A scholar identity refers to a sense of self that allows Black and Latino males to see themselves as academicians, as studiously competent and capable, and as intelligent or talented in school settings.

Unfortunately, rather than scholar identities being developed, what we are seeing in schools are instances of race-based domination that presume Black and Latino males are incapable of developing themselves as academicians. Schools are more inclined to develop the physical aspects of Black and Latino males in order to later exploit their abilities on the football field or basketball court (hooks, 2005). The failure of schools to develop a scholar identity rests on assumptions of Black inferiority and White superiority with the actions and characteristics of Whites privileged at the expense of those of people of color. Until the Whiteness of education is interrupted, we will not see an increase in Black and Latino males in higher education or high paying "blue color" professions because they will continue to be tracked toward prison instead of higher education.

Educators can and must play an active role in promoting the development of a scholar identity in young Black and Latino males. Initiatives that schools must implement should focus on helping Black and Latino males to develop attitudes, behaviors, and values necessary to function at optimal levels at school and in the world. To support the process of image building among gifted Black and Latino males, educators must recognize the importance of how having a scholar identity can improve the motivation, achievement, and aspirations of these students.

Whiting (2006) argues that this scholar identity must be developed early if we have any chances of increasing Black and Latino males in the higher education to healthcare pipeline and keeping them out of the school to prison pipeline. Early access to rigorous and engaging curriculum is one of the best predictors of high school graduation and college admission (Hughes & Bonner, 2006). The earlier schools focus on developing the scholarly identities of Black and Latino males, therefore, the more likely we are to prevent further generations of Black and Brown men from becoming part of the prison system via the US education system. We put a road block on where the two intersect: the American Justice System and American school system.

The Good News

Fortunately, the story of harsh discipline is not the only story to be told in schools across the United States. What we are seeing are schools that are trying to get students off the prison pipeline often times facing isolation and reprimands for fighting the systems that continues the social reproduction (Hayes, Juarez, & Cross, 2011; Juarez & Hayes, 2010).

Following Beauboeuf-Lafontant (1999, 2002), we refer to these amazing teachers as warm demander teachers. Teachers who are warm demanders teach in the same schools and classrooms with the same so-called disruptive Black students that end up in the principal's office with their first office referral. This first office referral in most cases starts the process of getting onboard the school to prison express (Fowler, 2011; Kim, 2009; Smith, 2009; Tulman & Weck, 2009). The important thing to note is that these warm demander teachers are actually teaching students where other teachers continue to fail and often times get these students off the school to prison express (Sander, 2010).

Warm demander teachers are faced with the same behaviors and attitudes that other teachers are faced with in terms of students texting, cursing, and more in class. Yet, these teachers do not use a lens of Whiteness to interpret their students' behavior and potential. These warm demander teachers are warm and caring with students while simultaneously demanding excellence in behavior and academic performance. Failure in academic and behavioral performance is not tolerated by these teachers and what we then see is the develop of scholar identities in these young males.

Having had the opportunity to sit in the classrooms of these warm demander teachers, we have seen that students in these classes will be "model" students in their classroom and then exit to go to their next class wherein their behavior and demeanor changes dramatically in response to the tone set by the next teacher. Students live up to the expectations their teachers set for them. Whereas warm demander teachers do not allow bad behavior or poor academic performance, other teachers expect this of students.

Moreover, since there are teachers that can and do interrupt the schools to prison pipeline, the good news is that its role in the social causation of school to prison pipeline can likewise be interrupted. The weight of educational slavery can and must be broken to interrupt the intersection of the American Justice System and the American Education System. As we tell our own students who will one day soon be teachers themselves, I don't care if your students' parents are stealing cars or selling drugs – your job is not to monitor parents; your job is to teach students and to teach them well." The schools to prison pipeline will not be interrupted until today's version of educational slavery is interrupted and scholar identities are developed and assumptions of Black and Brown inferiority no longer carry any currency in schools or society.

Fostering Critical Conversations in Teacher Education
Using the tenets of CRT to consider (Aguirre, 2000; Dixon & Rousseau, 2006), we identify several lessons that we feel are critical in fostering critical conversations in teacher preparation programs. First, in order for a critical conversation to be had in teacher education programs there must be an understanding that racism is an endemic part of American society. The problem with the racial power of Whiteness is the ability to deny issues of race and racism and the consistent practice of refusing to consider the everyday realities of race and racism. To recognize racism's pervasiveness requires Whites to face their own racist behavior and to name the contours of racism (Bergerson, 2003; Dei, Karumanchery, & Karumanchery-Luik; 2007; Gillborn, 2005).

Second, in order for a critical conversation to be had in teacher education programs there can be no practice or conversation about colorblindness; in fact, colorblindness is not an appropriate ideal for social justice or in the development of critical educators. According to Bergerson (2003) Whites attribute negative stereotypes to racial minorities while at the same time espousing their opposition to blatant racism. Only in a racist society would it be a good thing not to see what you do see. Furthermore, when White liberals fail to understand how they can and/or do embody White supremacist values even though they themselves may not embrace racism through this lack of awareness they support the racist domination they wish to eradicate (Gillborn, 2005; hooks, 1989).

Third, in order for a critical conversation to be had in teacher education programs with aspirations to prepare critical educators there has to be an understanding that merit is problematic in the United States. It is not enough to say that anyone who works hard can achieve success. Students of color are systematically excluded from education and educational opportunities despite their hard work. The hard work of some pays off more than the hard work of others. Merit operates under the burden of racism; racism thus limits the applicability of merit to people of color (Bergerson, 2003).

Fourth, in order for a critical conversation to be had in teacher education programs with aspirations to prepare critical educators critical educators there has to be an understanding of the role that experiential knowledge plays in the discourses of people of color. When teacher education programs are unwilling to recognize the knowledge of students of color as legitimate, appropriate, and critical to the way they navigate in a society grounded in racial subordination, they deny the humanity of and thus silence and constrain these students, regardless of their democratic intentions. This posturing toward democratic inclusion is what Hytten and Warren (2003) call *appeals to authenticity*. In their model, when White faculty cites their own experiences to counter or contradict non-White voices, this serves as a means to undermine the experiences of people of color as less valid and useful.

Lastly, in order for a critical conversation to be had in teacher education programs with aspirations to prepare critical educators there has to be an understanding of Whiteness as property (Harris, 1995). Whiteness was invented and continues to be maintained to serve as the dominant and normal status against which racial Others are measured in classrooms and elsewhere (Juarez, 2008, 2013). Whiteness serves to make these racially marked Others less privileged, less powerful, and less legitimate. Until the racial power of Whiteness is not only recognized but also explicitly addressed in U.S. teacher education programs, it is highly unlikely that the democratic intentions of educational equity and social justice will be realized in the classroom.

Critical Educators: There Is Hope

Throughout this chapter, we have been making the argument for the need to develop critical educators if we are to begin to address some of the school inequities. The participants in the book were selected because of their promise to be critical educators in one form or the other. In this chapter we propose two ways that teachers and teacher educators can be more critical with the goal of increase academic success, beyond test scores, for those students who are in some cases traumatized by schooling in the United States.

We propose that critical educators can improve the education experience by unhooking from Whiteness and disrupting the school the prison pipeline. We argue that there is an urgent need for racial, in this case Black and White, coalitional politics (Aoki, 2010). In other words, given the enduring divides between Whites and those marked as not White produced by White supremacy, it is incumbent that African Americans and White Americans form sociopolitical coalitions to fight for racial justice. Implications for such politics are shared. Through coalition building forces Whiteness to realize that racism is not only about having prejudicial feelings about people of color, using each other as pawns in this game, but about the systems that are in place to keep one group of people at odds with each other to prevent the structures that are in place to maintain White privilege do not come tumbling down (hooks, 1989; Kim, 1998; Leonardo, 2009).

Coalition work is not easy for anyone let alone requiring in addition a coming to the coalition table having unhooked from Whiteness. If a person just works hard, then the phenotype of the person does not matter – so goes the limited storyline of liberalism which we have worked to demonstrate as central to the maintenance of Whiteness. Yet, despite the difficulties inherent to both coalition building and unhooking from Whiteness, we argue that working across the lines created by White supremacy can and must be crossed. Kim (1998) argues that coalition building should not be viewed as a site for comfort and refuge, but as a site for struggle and at times, yes, even a site for pain.

Fortunately, the story of harsh discipline is not the only story to be told in schools across the United States. What we are seeing are schools that are trying to get students off the prison pipeline often times facing isolation and reprimands for fighting the systems that continues the social reproduction (Hayes, Juarez, & Cross, 2011, Juarez & Hayes, 2010).

Following Beauboeuf-Lafontant (1999, 2002), we refer to these amazing teachers as warm demander teachers. Teachers who are warm demanders teach in the same schools and classrooms with the same so-called disruptive Black students that end up in the principal's office with their first office referral. This first office referral in most cases starts the process of getting onboard the school to prison express (Fowler, 2011; Kim, 2009; Smith, 2009; Tulman & Weck, 2009). The important thing to note is that these warm demander teachers are actually teaching students where other teachers continue to fail and often times get these students off the school to prison express (Sander, 2010).

Warm demander teachers are faced with the same behaviors and attitudes that other teachers are faced with in terms of students texting, cursing, and more in class. Yet, these teachers do not use a lens of Whiteness to interpret their students' behavior and potential. These warm demander teachers are warm and caring with students while simultaneously demanding excellence in behavior and academic performance. Failure in academic and behavioral performance is not tolerated by these teachers and what we then see is the develop of scholar identities in these young males.

Having had the opportunity to sit in the classrooms of these warm demander teachers, we have seen that students in these classes will be "model" students in their classroom and then exit to go to their next class wherein their behavior and demeanor changes dramatically in response to the tone set by the next teacher. Students live up to the expectations their teachers set for them. Whereas warm demander teachers do not allow bad behavior or poor academic performance, other teachers expect this of students.

Moreover, since there are teachers that can and do interrupt the schools to prison pipeline, the good news is that its role in the social causation of school to prison pipeline can likewise be interrupted. The weight of educational slavery can and must be broken to interrupt the intersection of the American Justice System and the American Education System. As we tell our own students who will one day soon be teachers themselves, I don't care if your students' parents are stealing cars or selling drugs – your job is not to monitor parents; your job is to teach students and to teach them well." The schools to prison pipeline will not be interrupted until today's version of educational slavery is interrupted and scholar identities are developed and assumptions of Black and Brown inferiority no longer carry any currency in schools or society.

Sometimes unhooking from whiteness will cause a person to lose advantage(s). This can be seen in the notion of "academic lynching." Before we "unhooked" we both bought into the idea that a meritocracy existed. Believing that if we worked hard we could achieve our lot was our defense mechanism, or our strategy to defend against racism, if you will. Sadly, though, acquiescence is like "colorblindness," it fails to recognize and analyze power. By acquiescing to racism, we in turn became disempowered and "defined" by racism, rather than definers of our own lives. Thus, acquiescing causes nonwhites to lose power. Unhooking from whiteness also might cause someone to lose power, but they maintain the power to define themselves. Back to the miner's canary, we suggest that it is in the interests of all of us to reconsider the ways we define ourselves individually and collectively as well as the advantages we have and presume to have earned.

Afterword

Kerri Tobin

One thread that runs through these varied and illuminating chapters – sometimes explicitly, other times implied – is the importance of education in the pursuit of social justice. Many argue that education and social justice are inextricable entwined. But what is social justice, exactly, and why do others believe it does not belong in education at all? This question has plagued our field for decades, most obviously since the National Council of the Accreditation of Teacher Education made the explicit decision to drop the words "social justice" from its standards in 2006. Lauded by the conservative right as a move away from a "radical political agenda" (Johnson & Johnson, 2007), this exclusion of social justice from the evaluation of teacher education programs proved problematic to many educators. As many contributors to this volume note, pre-service teacher education is often notable missing elements that help candidates understand how to enact critical pedagogy and truly culturally responsive teaching in their future classrooms. Since so many of us would include these practices in a definition of social justice education, why was this idea too radical for NCATE merely a decade ago?

And so it behooves us to ask, as we reflect on these chapters that help us see what is missing in teacher education, what is meant by *social justice*. Heybach (2009) urges us to consider the following: "why did these two words become a threat to so many policy makers? What do these words mean to those who acted to remove them?" NCATE's explanation at the time was that *social justice* was too vague a term and one with "political overtones" (Alsup & Miller, 2009). It was replaced with language about *diversity* and *tolerance*, milquetoast concepts requiring little to no critical thinking and even less questioning of existing social structures. By reducing its standards to these politically acceptable terms, NCATE made space for new teachers to be trained to teach without really understanding their role in education, without understanding how to honor and privilege students' own knowledge and ways of knowing (Alsup & Miller, 2010). In this sense, however, the NCATE decision may have been more a reflection of the state of teacher education than a driver of it. As the chapters in this volume make clear, the idea is still missing from many programs of teacher education, leaving many teachers on their own to figure out how their teaching fits into existing structures of inequality in US society.

When the decision was made, Johnson and Johnson (2007) expressed the thoughts of many educators when they reflected thus:

> Maybe it wouldn't bother us if we hadn't picked up tiny rotten teeth from our classroom floors in a toothfairyless neighborhood. Maybe it wouldn't seem as offensive if we hadn't watched our pupils gobble down free breakfasts and lunches – for some, their only meals five days a week ... if we had had a school library or hot water or some playground equipment ... if we hadn't watched our pupils cry and vomit on high-stakes test days when they intuitively knew they couldn't pass a test because of their limited vocabularies and lack of prior knowledge – consequences of poverty and societal neglect ... NCATE did not stand up for [our] children. (p. 1)

If *social justice* implies a political agenda, in what way could wanting children to have hot water and enough to eat be considered too "radical" for a "neutral" organization (Heybach, 2009) that certifies teacher education programs? How does wanting children's home knowledge to be celebrated and used a bridge to broaden and enrich their understandings, rather than criticized and evaluated in high-stakes ways by outsiders, comprise "indoctrination" or a biased "ideology" (Heybach, 2009)? As we have seen in this volume, however, teacher education programs continue to shy away from embracing these and presenting them to candidates as essential to the practice of teaching "other people's children" (Delpit, 1988). But we know they are essential. And we know that social justice orientation is critical. We know that education is best when it "promotes agency and simultaneously strives to disrupt current practices that reproduce social, cultural, moral, economic, gendered, intellectual, and physical injustices" (Alsup & Miller, 2010). And we also know whose interests are threatened by an education that might disrupt the current social order.

Although at present, NCATE has become CAEP and *social justice* has been added back in as a dispositional indicator for teacher candidates, it seems that the most important questions a social justice-oriented teacher education program should encourage pre-service teachers to ask – "Education for what? Education for whom? Education toward what kind of social order?" (Ayers, 2008) – are still not being foregrounded. It is incumbent upon all educators, but especially those who interact with new or aspiring teachers, then, to ask these questions ourselves, and to encourage ourselves to grapple with them and help our colleagues do the same. We cannot wait while teacher education programs to catch up, or even expect that they will do so at all, without great effort from us. We are responsible for our own and our colleagues' journey toward the "wide-awakeness" (Greene, 1977) that helps us make education transformative and empowering for all our students.

References

Alsup, J., & Miller, S. J. (2014). Reclaiming English education: Rooting social justice in dispositions. *English Education, 46*(3), 195–215.

Ayers, W. (2010). *To teach: The journey of a teacher.* New York, NY: Teachers College Press.

Delpit, L. (1988). The silenced dialogue: Power and pedagogy in education other people's children. *Harvard Educational Review, 58*(3), 280–298.

Greene, M. (1977). Toward wide-awakeness: An argument for the arts and humanities in education. *Teachers College Record, 79*(1), 119–125.

Heybach, J. (2009). Rescuing social justice in education: A critique of the NCATE controversy. *Philosophical Studies in Education, 40*, 234–245.

Johnson, B., & Johnson, D. (2007). An analysis of NCATE's decision to drop "social justice." *Journal of Educational Controversy, 2*(2), 1–9.

References

Abdal Haqq, I. (1998). *Professional development schools: Weighing the evidence.* Thousand Oaks, CA: Corwin Press.

Aguilar, E. (2013, November 4). *Why do you teach? What sustains us in our work.* Retrieved April 19, 2016, from http://www.edutopia.org/blog/sustaining-passion-reasons-teaching-elena-aguilar

Alber, R. (2010, August 4). *How important is teaching literacy in all content areas?* Retrieved April 8, 2015, from http://www.edutopia.org/blog/literacy-instruction-across-curriculum-importance

Alexander, M. (2010). *The new Jim Crow: Mass incarceration in the age of colorblindness.* New York, NY: The New Press.

Allen, R. L. (2002). *Pedagogy of the oppressor: What was Freire's theory for transforming the privileged and powerful?* Paper presented at American Educational Research Association, New Orleans, LA.

Allsopp, D. H., DeMarie, D., Alvarez-McHatton, P., & Doone, E. (2006). Bridging the gap between theory and practice: Connecting courses with field experiences. *Teacher Education Quarterly, 33*(1), 19–35.

Alsup, J., & Miller, S. J. (2014, April). Reclaiming English education: Rooting social justice in dispositions. *English Education, 46*(3), 195–215.

Ambrosetti, A. (2014). Are you ready to be a mentor? Preparing teachers for mentoring pre-service teachers. *Australian Journal of Teacher Education, 39*(6), 35–47.

Aminy, M., & Karathanos, K. (2011). Benefitting the educator and student alike: Effective strategies for supporting the academic language development of EL teacher candidates. *Issues in Teacher Education, 20*(2), 95–109.

Andrade, H., Hefferen, J. H., & Palma, M. (2014). Formative assessment in the visual arts. *Art Education, 67*(1), 34–40.

Aoki, A. L. (2010). Coalition politics. In E. W. Chen & G. J. Yoo (Eds.), *Encyclopedia of Asian American issues today* (Vol. 2, pp. 707–712). Santa Barabara, CA: Greenwood Press.

Archer, D. N. (2009). Introduction: Challenging the school-to-prison pipeline. *New York Law School Law Review, 54*(4), 867.

Ayers, R., & Ayers, W. (2011). *Teaching the taboo: Courage and imagination in the classroom.* New York, NY: Teachers College Press.

Ayers, W. (2010). *To teach: The journey of a teacher.* New York, NY: Teachers College Press.

Ayers, W. (2017). *Social justice and teaching.* Retrieved from http://billayers.wordpress.com/2008/05/07/social-justice-and-teaching

Baig-Ali, U. (2012). A young teacher's view of the profession. *Education Review, 21*(4), 25–40.

Baker, S., Lesaux, N., Jayanthi, M., Dimino, J., Proctor, C. P., Morris, J., Gersten, R., Haymond, K., Kieffer, M. J., Linan-Thompson, S., & Newman-Gonchar, R. (2014). *Teaching academic content and literacy to English learners in elementary and middle school* (NCEE 2014–4012). Washington, DC: National Center for Education Evaluation and Regional Assistance, Institute of Education Sciences, U.S. Department of Education.

Baldwin, J. (1963/1985). A talk to teachers. In J. Baldwin (Ed.), *The price of a ticket: Collected nonfiction 1948–1985* (pp. 326–332). New York, NY: St. Martin's Press.

Baldwin, L., Omdal, S. N., & Pereles, D. (2015). Beyond stereotypes: Understanding, recognizing, and working with twice-exceptional learners. *Teaching Exceptional Children, 47*(4), 216–225.

Ball, A. F., & Tyson, C. A. (Eds.). (2011). *Studying diversity in teacher education*. New York, NY: Roman & Littlefield Publishers.

Ball, S. J., & Goodson, I. F. (Eds.). (1985). *Teacher's lives and careers*. London: Falmer Press.

Ballard, S. L., Bartle, E., & Masequesmay, G. (2008). *Finding queer allies: The impact of ally training and safe zone stickers on campus climate*. Retrieved October 30, 2015, from http://www.eric.ed.gov/contentdelivery/servlet/ERICServlet?accno=ED517219

Banks, J. (1991). Teaching multicultural literacy to teachers. *Teaching Education, 4*(1), 133–142.

Banks, J. (1995). Multicultural education: Historical development, dimensions, and practice. In J. A. Banks & C. A. M. Banks (Eds.), *Handbook of research on multicultural education*. New York, NY: Macmillan.

Banks, T. (2014). Teacher education reform in urban educator preparation programs. *Journal of Education and Learning, 4*(1), 60–71.

Beare, P., Marshall, J., Torgerson, C., Tracz, S., & Chiero, R. (2012). Toward a culture of evidence: Factors affecting survey assessment of teacher preparation. *Teacher Education Quarterly, 39*(1), 159–173.

Beghetto, R. A., Kaufman, J. C., & Baer, J. (2014). *Teaching for creativity in the common core classroom*. New York, NY: Teachers College Press.

Bell, L. A. (2002). Sincere fictions: The pedagogical challenges of preparing White teachers for multicultural classrooms. *Equity & Excellence in Education, 35*(3), 236–244.

Benesch, S. (1993). Critical thinking: A learning process for democracy. *TESOL Quarterly, 27*(3), 545–548.

Bennett, L. (1964). Tea and sympathy: Liberals and other White hopes. In L. Bennett (Ed.), *The Negro mood and other essays* (pp. 75–104). Chicago, IL: Johnson Publishing Company.

Bergerson, A. A. (2003). Critical race theory and White racism: Is there room for White scholars in fighting racism in education? *Qualitative Studies in Education, 16*(1), 51–63.

Bibo, K. (2015). *Why teach? A teacher's prospective*. Retrieved from http://teaching.monster.com/education/articles/1794-why-teach-a-teachers-prospective#comment_form

Bigham, S. G., Hively, D. E., & Toole, G. H. (2014). Principals' and cooperating teachers' expectations of teacher candidates. *Education, 135*(2), 211–229.

Blanchett, W. J. (2006). Disproportionate representation of African Americans in special education: Acknowledging the role of White privilege and racism. *Educational Researcher, 35*(6), 24–28.

Bonilla-Silva, E. (2003). *Racism without racists: Colorblind racism and the persistence of racial inequality in the United States*. Boulder, CO: Rowman & Littlefield Publishers.

Bonner, E. P. (2009). Achieving success with African American learners: A framework for culturally responsive mathematics teaching. *Childhood Education, 86*(1), 2–6.

Boslaugh, S. (2014). Common core state standards initiative. *Salem Press Encyclopedia Research Starters*.

Bowers, R. S. (2000). A pedagogy of success: Meeting the challenges of urban middle schools. *The Clearing House: A Journal of Educational Strategies, Issues and Ideas, 73*(4), 235–238.

Bowman, R. (2011). Rethinking what motivates and inspires students. *The Clearing House: A Journal of Educational Strategies, Issues and Ideas, 84*(6), 264–269.

Britzman, D. P. (1991). *Practice makes practice: A critical study of learning to teach*. New York, NY: State University of New York Press.

Brophy, J., & Good, T. (2003). *Looking in classrooms*. Boston, MA: Allyn & Bacon.

Bucholz, J. L., & Sheffler, J. L. (2009). Creating a warm and inclusive classroom environment: Planning for all children to fell welcome. *Electronic Journal for Inclusive Education, 2*(4). Retrieved from http://corescholar.libraries.wright.edu/cgi/viewcontent.cgi?article=1102&context=ejie

Burant, T. (2010). *The new teacher book*. Milwaukee, WI: Rethinking Schools.

Burant, T., Christensen, K., Salas, D., & Walters, S. (2010). *The new teacher book*. Milwaukee, WI: Rethinking Schools.

Burstein, N. (2009). Providing adequate teachers for urban schools: The effectiveness of the accelerated collaborative teacher preparation program in recruiting, preparing, and retaining teachers. *Action in Teacher Education, 31*(2), 20–35.

Caditz, J. (1977). Coping with the American dilemma: Dissonance reduction among White liberals. *The Pacific Sociological Review, 20*(1), 21–42.

Calderon, M., Slavin, R., & Sanchez, M. (2011). Effective instruction for English learners. *The Future of Children, 21*, 103–127.

California Commission on Teacher Credentialing. (2015). Retrieved from http://www.ctc.ca.gov/educator-prep/intern/

California State Board of Education. (2015). *Content standards*. Retrieved from http://www.cde.ca.gov/be/st/ss/

Camper, C. (1994). To White feminists. *Canadian Woman Studies, 14*(2), 40.

Chandler, M. (2012, May 15). *Teaching for all levels – in one class*. Retrieved April 8, 2015, from http://www.washingtonpost.com/local/education/teaching-for-all-levels--in-one-Class/2012/05/15/gIQAv1lUSU_story.html

Chen, G. (2015, March 3). *10 major challenges facing public schools*. Retrieved March 30, 2015, from http://www.publicschoolreview.com/blog/10-major-challenges-facing-public-schools

Chesley, G. M., & Jordan, J. (2012). What's missing from teacher prep. *Educational Leadership, 69*(8), 41–45.

Christle, C. A., Jolivette, K., & Nelson, C. (2005). Breaking the school to prison pipeline: Identifying school risk and protective factors for youth delinquency. *Exceptionality, 13*(2), 69–88.

Cline, W. C. (1953). Teaching controversial issues. *Peabody Journal of Education, 30*(6), 336–338.

Cochran-Smith, M., Davis, D., & Fries, K. (2004). Multicultural teacher education: Research, practice and policy. In J. A. Banks & C. A. M. Banks (Eds.), *Handbook on research in multicultural education* (pp. 931–975). San Francisco, CA: Jossey-Bass.

Cody, J., & Roller, R. (2011, April 13). *Budget cuts to hit public education in California*. Retrieved March 18, 2015, from http://www.wsws.org/en/articles/2011/04/cali-a13.html

Coffey, H., Fitchett, P. G., & Farinde, A. A. (2015). It takes courage: Fostering the development of critical, social justice-oriented teachers using museum and project-based instruction. *Action in Teacher Education, 37*(1), 9–22.

Cole, H. A., & Heilig, J. (2011). Developing a school-based youth court: A potential alternative to the school to prison pipeline. *Journal of Law & Education, 40*(2), 305–321.

Common Core States Standards Initiative. (2015). *Myths vs. facts*. Retrieved from http://www.corestandards.org/about-the-standards/myths-vs-facts/

Cone, J. H. (2004). *Martin and Malcolm and America: A dream or a nightmare*. Maryknoll, NY: Orbis Books.

Conxita, M. (2008). The Francoist repression in the Catalan countries. *Catalan Historical Review, 1*, 133–147.

Crane, E. W., Huang, C.-W., Derby, K., Makkonen, R., & Goel, A. M. (2008). *Characteristics of California school districts in program improvement*. Washington, DC: U.S. Department of Education, Institute of Education Sciences, National Center for Education Evaluation and Regional Assistance, Regional Educational Laboratory West. Retrieved from http://ies.ed.gov/ncee/edlabs

Crick, R., & Wilson, K. (2005). Being a learner: A virtue for the 21st century. *British Journal of Educational Studies, 53*(3), 359–374.

Cross, B. E. (2005). New racism, reformed teacher education and the same ole' oppression. *Educational Studies, 38*(3), 263–274.

Culross, R. R. (2004). Why I teach. *College Teaching, 52*(2), 63–80.

Daniels, E. (2010). Letter to a young teacher: Go forth and teach. *California English, 15*(5), 22–32.

Darling-Hammond, L. (2000). Teacher quality and student achievement: A review of state policy evidence. *Education Policy Analysis Archives, 8*(1), 1–14.

Darling-Hammond, L. (2004). Inequality and the right to learn: Access to qualified teachers in California's public schools. *Teachers College Record, 106*(10), 1936–1966.

Darts, D. (2004). Visual culture jam: Art pedagogy, and creative resistance. *Studies in Art Education, 45*(4), 313–327.

Davis, B. (1997). Listening for differences: An evolving conception of mathematics teaching. *Journal for Research in Mathematics Education, 28*(3), 355–376.

Dei, G. J. S., Karumanchery, L. L., & Karumanchery-Luik, N. (2007). *Playing the race card: Exposing White power and privilege.* New York, NY: Peter Lang.

Delgado, R. (1999). *When equality ends: Stories about race and resistance.* Boulder, CO: Westview Press.

Delgado, R., & Stefancic, J. (2001). *Critical race theory: An introduction.* New York, NY: New York University Press.

Delgado Bernal, D., & Solorzano, D. (2001). Examining transformational resistance through a critical race and latcrit theory framework: Chicana and Chicano students in an urban contex. *Urban Education, 36*(3), 308–342.

Delgado Bernal, D., & Villalpando, O. (2002). An apartheid of knowledge in academia: The struggle over the 'legitimate' knowledge of faculty of color. *Equity and Excellence in Education, 35*(2), 169–180.

Delpit, L. D. (1988). The silenced dialogue: Power and pedagogy in education other people's children. *Harvard Educational Review, 58*(3), 280–298.

Delpit, L. D. (2012). *"Multiplication is for White people": Raising expectations for other people's children.* New York, NY: New Press.

Dewey, J. (1920). *Reconstruction in philosophy.* New York, NY: Henry Holt & Company.

Dewey, J. (1967). *Democracy and education.* New York, NY: Free Press.

Dingus, J. (2003). *Let the circle be unbroken: Professional socialization of African-American teachers from intergenerational families* (Unpublished doctoral dissertation). University of Washington, Seattle, WA.

Donahue, D. M. (2000). Charity basket or revolution: Beliefs, experiences, and context in preservice teachers' service learning. *Curriculum Inquiry, 30*(4), 429–450.

Donnor, J. K., & Shockley, K. G. (2010). Leaving us behind: A political economic interpretation of NCLB and the miseducation of African American males. *Educational Foundations, 24,* 43–54.

DuBois, W. E. B. (1935). Does the Negro need separate schools? *Journal of Negro Education, 4*(3), 328–335.

Duncan-Andrade, J. M. R., & Morrell, E. (2008). *The art of critical pedagogy: Possibilities for moving from theory to practice in urban school.* New York, NY: Peter Lang.

Echevarría, J., Vogt, M., & Short, D. J. (2013). *Making content comprehensible for English learners: The SIOP model.* Boston, MA: Pearson.

Editorial Projects in Education Research Center. (2011, July 18). Issues A-Z: Adequate yearly progress. *Education Week.* Retrieved from http://www.edweek.org/ew/issues/adequate-yearly-progress

Edmundson, M. (2014). *Why teach? In defense of a real education* (Reprint ed.). New York, NY: Bloomsbury.

Elenes, C. A., & Delgado Bernal, D. (2010). Latina/o education and the reciprocal relationship between theory and practice: Four theories informed by the experiential knowledge of marginalized communities. In E. G. Murillo, S. A. Villenas, R. T. Galvan, J. S. Munoz, C. Martinez, & M. Machado-Casas (Eds.), *Handbook of Latinos and education: Theory, research and practice* (pp. 63–90). New York, NY: Routledge.

Elsbree, A. R., Hernández, A. M., & Daoud, A. (2014). Equitable instruction for secondary Latino English learners: Examining critical principles of differentiation in lesson design. *AMAE Journal, 8*(2), 5–16.

Executive Summary Explaining the Academic Performance Index (API). (1999). California Department of Education. Retrieved from http://www.cde.ca.gov/ta/ac/ap/documents/apiexecsummary.pdf#search=what%20is%20the%20API&view=FitH&pagemode=none

Fasching-Varner, K. J. (2009). No! The team ain't alright! The institutional and individual problematic of race. *Social Identities, 15*(6), 811–829.

Fasching-Varner, K. J., Eisworth, H. B., Mencer, T. H., Lindbom-Cho, D. R., Murray, M. C., & Morton, B. C. (Eds.). (2013). *Student teaching: A journey in narrative.* Rotterdam, The Netherlands: Sense Publishers.

Feagin, J. R. (2006). *Systemic racism: A theory of oppression.* New York, NY: Routledge.

Fenstermacher, G. D., Soltis, J. F., & Sanger, M. N. (2009). *Approaches to teaching* (5th ed.). New York, NY: Teachers College Press.

Fernandez, L. (2002). Telling stories about school: Using critical race theory and Latino critical theories to document Latina/Latino education and resistance. *Qualitative Inquiry, 8*(1), 45–65.

Fisher, D., Frey, N., & Lapp, D. (2009). *In a reading state of mind-brain research, teacher modeling, and comprehension instruction.* Newark, DE: International Reading Association.

Flanagan, N. (2014, February 12). *Teacher of the year, Nancy Flanagan, touts the power of self-reflection.* Retrieved April 8, 2015, from http://education.cu-portland.edu/blog/teaching-strategies/the-power-of-self-reflection

REFERENCES

Flowers, C., Ahlgrim-Delzell, L., Browder, D., & Spooner, F. (2005). Teacher's perceptions of alternative assessment. *Research and Practice for Persons with Severe Disabilities, 30*(2), 81–92.

Ford, D. Y. (2010). Underrepresentation of culturally different students in gifted education: Reflections about current problems and recommendations for the future. *Gifted Child Today, 33*(3), 21–35.

Fowler, D. (2011). School discipline feeds the "pipeline to prison." *Phi Delta Kappan, 93*(2), 14–19.

Frankenberg, R. (1993). *The social construction of whiteness: White women, race matters.* Minneapolis, MN: University of Minnesota Press.

Freire, P. (1973). *Pedagogy of the oppressed.* New York, NY: Continuum.

Fuller, B., Wright, J., Gesicki, K., & Kang, E. (2007). Gauging growth: How to judge no child left behind? *Educational Researcher, 36*(5), 268–278.

Gabbard, G. O. (2011). Why I teach. *Academic Psychiatry, 35*(5), 277–282.

Ganihar, N. (2015). A study of quality indicators from the perspective of heads of secondary schools. *International Online Journal of Education & Teaching, 2*(1), 43–52.

Garcia, L.-G. (2012). Making Cultra count inside and out of the classroom: Public art and critical pedagogy in South Central Los Angeles. *Journal of Curriculum and Pedagogy, 9*(2), 104–114.

Garcia, L.-G. (2015). Empowering students through creative resistance: Art-based critical pedagogy in the immigrant experience. *Dialogo, 18*(2), 139–149. Retrieved from http://via.library.depaul.edu/dialogo/vol18/iss2/13

Garrett, T. (2014). *Effective classroom management: The essentials.* New York, NY: Teachers College Press.

GATE Teacher Certification. *Teaching certification* [Web article]. Retrieved from http://www.teaching-certification.com/GATE-teacher-certification.html

Gay, G. (2000). *Culturally responsive teaching: Theory, research, and practice.* New York, NY: Teachers College Press.

Gay, G. (2002). Preparing for culturally responsive teaching. *Journal of Teacher Education, 53*, 106–116.

Gayles, J. G., & Ampaw, F. D. (2011). Gender matters: An examination of differential effects of the college experience on degree attainment in STEM. *New Directions for Institutional Research, 2011*(152), 19–25. doi:10.1002/ir.405

Genzuk, M. (2011). *Specially Designed Academic Instruction in English (SDAIE) for language minority students.* Retrieved from http://www.usc.edu/dept/education/CMMR/DigitalPapers/SDAIE_Genzuk.pdf

Ghaemi, F., & Piran, N. A. (2014). Critical pedagogy in SLA: A state of the art study. *International Journal of Social Sciences & Education, 5*(1), 18–27.

Gilborn, D. (2005). Education policy as an act of White supremacy: Whiteness, critical race theory and education reform. *Journal of Education Policy, 20*(4), 485–505.

Gilborn, D. (2010). Full of sound and fury, signifying nothing? A reply to Dave Hill's race and class in Britain: A critique of the statistical basis for critical race theory in Britain. *Journal for Critical Education Policy Studies (JCEPS), 8*(1), 78–107.

Gilderhus, M. (2007). *History and historians: A historiographical introduction.* Upper Saddle River, NJ: Prentice-Hall.

Goldberg, D. T. (1993). *Racist culture.* Cambridge, MA: Blackwell Publishers.

Goldhaber, D. D., & Brewer, D. J. (2000). Does teacher certification matter? High school teacher certification status and student achievement. *Educational Evaluation and Policy Anaysis, 22*(2), 129–145.

Gollnick, D. (1995). National and state initiatives for multicultural education. In J. A. Banks & C. A. M. Banks (Eds.), *Handbook of research in multicultural education* (pp. 15–40). Old Tappan, NJ: Macmillan.

Gonnerman, J. (2004, November 9). The neighborhood costs of American prison. *Village Voice.* Retrieved from http://www.villagevoice.com/2004-11-09/news/million-dollar-blocks

Gonzalez, N., Moll, L. C., & Amanti, C. (2005). *Funds of knowledge: Theorizing practices in households, communities and classrooms.* New York, NY: Routledge.

Gordon, J. A. (2000). *The color of teaching.* New York, NY: Routledge.

Gordon, L. M. (2012, June 6). *Good teaching matters, teachers matter, and teacher education matters.* Los Angeles, CA: Occidental College.

Gorski, P. (2013). *Reaching and teaching students in poverty: Strategies for erasing the opportunity gap.* New York, NY: Teachers College Press.

Greene, M. (1977). Toward wide-awakeness: An argument for the arts and humanities in education. *Teachers College Record, 79*(1), 119–125.

Grodner, A. G., & Rupp, N. R. (2013). The role of homework in student learning outcomes: Evidence from a field experiment. *Journal of Economic Education, 4*(2), 93–109.

Guinier, L., & Torres, G. (2003). *The miner's canary: Enlisting race, resisting power, and transforming democracy.* Cambridge, MA: Harvard University Press.

Hallahan, D. P., Kauffman, J. M., & Pullen, P. C. (2015). *Exceptional learners: An introduction to special education.* New York, NY: Pearson.

Hand, M. (2008). What should we teach as controversial? A defense of the epistemic criterion. *Educational Theory, 58*(2), 213–228.

Hargrove, B., & Seay, S. (2011). School teacher perceptions of barriers that limit the participation of African American males in public schools gifted programs. *Journal for the Education of the Gifted, 34*(3), 434–467.

Harris, C. (1995). Whiteness as property. In K. Crenshaw, N. Gotanda, G. Peller, & K. Thomas (Eds.), *Critical race theory: The key writings that formed the movement* (pp. 276–291). New York, NY: The New Press.

Hayano, D. (1979). Auto-ethnography: Paradigms, problems, and prospects. *Human Organization, 38*(1), 99–104.

Hayes, C. (2014). What I know about teaching I learned from my father: A critical race autoethnographic/counternarrative exploration of multi-generational transformative teaching. *Journal of African American Male Education, 5*(2), 247–265.

Hayes, C., & Fasching-Varner, K. J. (2015). Racism 2.0 and the death of social and cultural foundations of education: A critical conversation. *Journal of Educational Foundations, 28*(1), 103–119.

Hayes, C., & Juarez, B. G. (2012). There is no culturally responsive teaching spoken here: A critical race perspective. *Democracy and Education, 20*(1), 1–14.

Hayes, C., Juárez, B. G., & Cross, P. T. (2012). What we can learn from Big Mama? *Critical Education, 3*(1), 1–24. Retrieved from http://m1.cust.educ.ubc.ca/journal/index.php/criticaled/issue/archive

Heitzeg, N. A. (2009). Education or incarceration: Zero tolerance policies and the school to prison pipeline. *Forum on Public Policy Online, 2009*(2), 1–21.

Heybach, J. (2009). Rescuing social justice in education: A critique of the NCATE controversy. *Philosophical Studies in Education, 40*, 234–245.

Hildebrandt, S. A., & Swanson, P. (2014). World language teacher candidate performance on edTPA: An exploratory study. *Foreign Language Annals, 47*(4), 576–591.

hooks, b. (1989). *Talking back: Thinking feminist, thinking Black*. Boston, MA: South End Press.

hooks, b. (1995). *Killing rage: Ending racism*. New York, NY: Henry Holt & Company.

hooks, b. (2004). *We real cool: Black men and masculinity*. New York, NY: Routledge.

Hughes, R. L., & Bonner, F. A. (2006). Leaving Black males behind: Debunking the myths of meritocratic education. *The Journal of Race & Policy, 2*(1), 76–90.

Hughes, S. A. (2008). Maggie and me: A Black professor and a White urban school teacher connect autoethnography to critical race pedagogy. *Educational Foundations, 22*(3), 73–95.

Hytten, K., & Warren, J. (2003). Engaging whiteness: How racial power gets reified in education. *International Journal of Qualitative Studies in Education, 16*(1), 65–89.

Ishiyama, J. (2002). Does early participation in undergraduate research benefit social science and humanities students? *College Student Journal, 36*(1), 380–387.

James, C. (2002). Achieving desire: Narrative of a Black male teacher. *Qualitative Studies in Education, 15*(2), 171–186.

Jarrett, D. (1999). *Teaching mathematics and science to English-language learners: The inclusive classroom*. Retrieved April 3, 2015, from http://educationnorthwest.org/sites/default/files/11.99.pdf

Jarvis, M. J. (2014). Finding a space for art. *International Journal of Education Through Art, 10*(1), 85–98.

Johnson, B., & Johnson, D. (2007). An analysis of NCATE's decision to drop "social justice." *Journal of Educational Controversy, 2*(2), 1–9.

Johnson, H., Watson, P. A., Delahunty, T., McSwiggen, P., & Smith, T. (2011). What it is they do: Differentiating knowledge and literacy practices across content disciplines. *Journal of Adolescent & Adult Literacy, 55*(1), 100–109. doi:10.1002/JAAL.00013

Johnson, J., Yarrow, A., Rochkind, J., & Ott, A. (2008). Teaching for a living. *Pedagogy, Culture, and Society, 16*(1), 85–99. Retrieved from http://0-search.ebscohost.com.leopac.ulv.edu/login.aspx?direct=true&db=aph&AN=48123368&site=eds-live&scope=site

Johnson, J., Yarrow, A., Rochkind, J., & Ott, A. (2010). Teaching for a living: How teachers see the profession today. *Education Digest: Essential Readings Condensed for Quick Review, 75*(5), 4–8.

Jones, J. J. (2014). Purple boas, lesbian affection, and John Deere hats: Teacher educators' role in addressing homophobia in secondary schools. *Teacher Education & Practice, 27*(1), 154–167.

Jordan Irvine, J. (1999). The education of children whose nightmares come both day and night. *Journal of Negro Education, 68*(3), 244–253.

Juárez, B. G. (2008). The politics of race in two languages: An empirical qualitative study. *Race, Ethnicity, and Education, 11*(3), 231–249.

Juárez, B. G. (2013). Learning to take the bullet and more: Anti-racism requirements for White allies and other friends of the race, so-called and otherwise. In N. D. Hartlep & C. Hayes (Eds.), *Unhooking from whiteness: The key to dismantling racism in the United States* (pp. 33–51). Rotterdam, The Netherlands, NY: Sense Publishers.

Juárez, B. G., & Hayes, C. (2010). Social justice is not spoken here: Considering the nexus of knowledge, power, and the education of future teachers in the United States. *Power and Education, 2*(3), 233–252.

Juárez, B. G., & Hayes, C. (2011). An endarkened learning and transformative education for freedom dreams: The education our children deserve. *The Journal of Educational Controversy, 6*(1), 1–17. Retrieved from http://www.wce.wwu.edu/Resources/CEP/eJournal/v006n001/a007.shtml

Juárez, B. G., & Hayes, C. (2012). On the battlefield for social justice: Teaching about differences and its consequences in teacher preparation programs. In C. Clark, M. Brimhall-Vargas, & K. Fasching-Varner (Eds.), *Occupying the academy: Just how important is diversity work in higher education?* (pp. 183–193). New York, NY: Rowman & Littlefield Publishers.

Juarez, B. G., & Hayes, C. (2014). On being named a Black supremacist and a racist against your own kind: The problem of White racial domination and the domestic terrorism of White supremacy in U.S. teacher education and colleges of education. *Urban Review, 46*(2), 2–20.

Juárez, B. G., Smith, D. T., & Hayes, C. (2008). Social justice means just us White people: The diversity paradox in teacher education. *Democracy and Education, 17*(3), 20–25.

Kamenetz, A. (2014, November 8). *5 great teachers on what makes a great teacher*. Retrieved March 7, 2015, from http://www.npr.org/blogs/ed/2014/11/08/360426108/five-great-teachers-on-what-makes-a-great-teacher

Karelitz, T. M., Fields, E., Levy, A. J., Martinez-Gudapakkam, A., & Jablonski, E. (2011). No teacher left unqualified: How teachers and principals respond to the highly qualified mandate. *Science Educator, 20*(1), 1–11.

Kelley, R. (1997). *Yo mama's disfunktional!* Boston, MA: Beacon Press.

Kim, C. J. (1999). The racial triangulation of Asian Americans. *Politics & Society, 27*(1), 105–138.

Kim, C. Y. (2009). Procedures for public law remediation in school-to-prison pipeline litigation: Lessons learned from Antoine v. Winner school district. *New York Law School Law Review, 54*(4), 955.

King, J. E. (2005). *Black education*. Mahwah, NJ: Lawrence Erlbaum Associates.

King, K. L., Houston, I. S., & Middleton, R. A. (2001). An explanation for school failure moving beyond Black inferiority and alienation as a policy-making agenda. *British Journal of Education Studies, 49*(4), 428–445.

King, M. L. (1947). The purpose of education. *Morehouse College Student Paper, The Maroon Tiger*. Retrieved from http://www.drmartinluthurkingjr.com/thepurposeofeducation.htm

Kirst, M. (2014). *A look at California's progress with common core implementation*. Retrieved from https://ed.stanford.edu/spotlight/look-californias-progress-common-core-implementation

Knaus, C. B. (2009). Shut up and listen: Applied critical race theory in the classroom. *Race, Ethnicity, and Education, 12*(2), 133–154.

Kohli, R. (2009). Critical race reflections: Valuing the experiences of teachers of color in teacher education. *Race, Ethnicity, and Education, 12*(2), 235–251.

Kraus, S. (2013). Is truthiness enough? Classroom activities for encouraging evidence-based critical thinking. *Journal of Effective Teaching, 13*(2), 83–93.

Lachuk, A. J., & Koellner, K. (2015). Performance-based assessment for certification: Insights from edTPA implementation. *Language Arts, 93*(2), 84–95.

Ladson-Billings, G. (1994). *The dream keepers: Successful teachers of African American children*. San Francisco, CA: Jossey-Bass.

Ladson-Billings, G. (1998). Just what is critical race theory and what is it doing in a nice field like education? *International Journal of Qualitative Studies in Education, 11*(1), 7–24.

Ladson-Billings, G. (2000). Fighting for our lives: Preparing teachers to teach African American students. *Journal of Teacher Education, 51*(3), 206–214.

Ladson-Billings, G. (2005). *Beyond the big house: African American educators on teacher education*. New York, NY: Teachers College Press.

Ladson-Billings, G. J. (1999). Preparing teachers for diverse student populations: A critical race perspective. *Review of Research in Education, 24*, 211–247.

Landorf, H. (2007). Creating permeable boundaries: Teaching and learning for social justice in a global society. *Teacher Education Quarterly, 34*(1), 41–56.

Lee, S. (1996). *Unraveling the model minority*. New York, NY: Teachers College Press.

Lefevre, C. (1965). Why teach? *The Elementary School Journal, 66*(3), 121–125.

Leonardo, Z. (2009). *Race, whiteness, and education*. New York, NY: Routledge.

Leonardo, Z. (2013). *Race frameworks: A multidimensional theory of racism and education*. New York, NY: Teachers College Press.

Lerman, J., & Hicks, R. (2010). *Retool your school: The educator's essential guide to google's free power apps*. Eugene, OR: International Society for Technology in Education.

Lim, W., Stallings, L., & Kim, D. J. (2015). A proposed pedagogical approach for preparing teacher candidates to incorporate academic language in mathematics classrooms. *International Education Studies, 8*(7), 1–10.

Lincoln, A. (2005). The Gettysburg address. In R. P. Basler (Ed.), *The collected works of Abraham Lincoln*. New Brunswick, NJ: Rutgers.

Lindsay, G., Cross, N., & Ives-Baine, L. (2012). Narratives of neonatal intensive care unit nurses: Experience with end-of-life care. *Illness, Crisis, & Loss, 20*(3), 239–253.

Lipsitz, G. (2006). *The possessive investment in whiteness: How White people profit from identity politics*. New York, NY: Routledge.

Liston, D. P., & Zeichner, K. M. (1991). *Teacher education and the social conditions of schooling*. New York, NY: Routledge.

Livingston, J. (2010). Preparing our students for the 21st century. *Academic Leadership, 8*(3), 170–171.

Lord, T., & Baviskar, S. (2007). Moving students from information recitation to information understanding: Exploiting bloom's taxonomy in creating science questions. *Journal of College Science Teaching, 36*(5), 40–44.

Love, B. J. (2004). Brown plus 50 counter-storytelling: A critical race theory analysis of the "majoritarian achievement gap" story. *Equity & Excellence in Education, 37*(3), 227–246.

Manak, J. J., & Gregory, Y. (2014). Incorporating undergraduate research into teacher education: Preparing thoughtful teachers through inquiry-based learning. *Council on Undergraduate Research Quarterly, 35*(2), 35–38.

Manski, C. F. (1987). Academic ability, earnings, and the decision to become a teacher: Evidence from the national longitudinal study of the high school class of 1972. In D. A. Wise (Ed.), *Public sector payrolls* (pp. 291–316). Chicago, IL: University of Chicago Press.

Marable, M. (1993). Beyond racial identity politics: Towards a liberation theory for multicultural democracy. *Race and Class, 35*(1), 113–130.

Maring, E. F., & Koblinsky, S. A. (2013). Teachers' challenges, strategies, and support needs in schools affected by community violence: A qualitative study. *The Journal of School Health, 83*(6), 125–134.

Marquis-Hobbs, T. (2014). Enriching the lives of students in poverty. *Education Digest, 80*(4), 34–39.

Martin, R. J. (Ed.). (1995). *Practicing what we teach: Confronting diversity in teacher education*. Albany, NY: State University of New York Press.

Martin, R. J. (2001). *Listening up: Reinventing ourselves as teachers and students*. New York, NY: Routledge.

Martínez, A. G. (2008). Complexity and education. *Complexity and the Universe of Education, 4*, 32–44. doi:10.4324/9780203764015

Marzano, R. J. (2003). What works in schools: Translating research into action. *Adolescence, 38*(149), 195.

Masunaga, H., & Lewis, T. (2011). Self-perceived dispositions that predict challenges during student teaching: A data mining analysis. *Issues in Teacher Education, 20*(1), 35–45.

Matias, C. E., Henry, A., & Darland, C. (2017). The twin tales of whiteness: Exploring the emotional roller coaster of teaching and learning about whiteness. *Taboo: The Journal of Culture and Education, 16*(1), 29. Retrieved from http://digitalcommons.lsu.edu/taboo/vol16/iss1/4

McCray, A., Sindelar, P., Kilgore, K., & Neal, L. (2002). African American women's decisions to become teachers: Sociocultural perspectives. *Qualitative Studies in Education, 15*(3), 269–290.

McKnight, K. S. (2014). *Common core literacy for ELA, history/social studies, and the humanities: Strategies to deepen content knowledge (grades 6–12)* (1st ed.). San Francisco, CA: Jossey-Bass.

McLaren, P., & Farahmandpur, R. (2001). Teaching against globalization and the new imperialism: Toward a revolutionary pedagogy. *Journal of Teacher Education, 52*(2), 136–150.

Media Literacy Ed. *National association for media literacy education*. Retrieved from http://namle.net/publications/

Meiners, E. R., & Winn, M. T. (2010). Resisting the school to prison pipeline: The practice to build abolition democracies. *Race, Ethnicity, and Education, 13*(3), 271–276.

Millar, R. (2006). *Improving subject teaching: Lessons from research in science education*. New York, NY: Routledge.

Mills, C. W. (1997). *The racial contract*. Ithaca, NY: Cornell University Press.

Milner, H. R. (2015). *Start where you are, but don't stay there*. Cambridge, MA: Harvard Education Press.

Mizzi, D. (2013). The challenges faced by science teachers when teaching outside their specific science specialism. *Acta Didactica Napocensia, 26*(4), 1–6.

Monaghan, P. (2002). Colonialism's lasting impact on indigenous societies in the Americas. *The Chronicle of Higher Education, 48*(19), A12. Retrieved from http://0-search.proquest.com.leopac.ulv.edu/docview/214708107?accountid=25355

Moore, R. (2008). Academic procrastination and course performance among developmental education students. *Research & Teaching in Developmental Education, 24*(2), 56.

Moreno, J. F. (Ed.). (1999). *The elusive quest for equality: 150 years of Chicago/Chicana education.* Boston, MA: Harvard Educational Review, Harvard University Press.

Muth, K. D., Polizzi, N. C., & Glynn, S. M. (2007). Case-based teacher preparation for teaching controversial topics in middle school. *Middle School Journal, 38*(5), 14–19.

National Center for Education Stastistics. (2002). *NCES digest of education statistics.* Retrieved from http://nces.ed.gov/programs/digest/d02/dt068.asp

National Council for the Social Studies (NCSS). (1994). *Expectations of excellence: Curriculum standards for social studies.* Washington, DC: National Council for the Social Studies.

National Summit on Diversity in the Teaching Force. (2002). *Losing ground: A national summit on diversity in the teaching force, summit proceedings document.* Washington, DC: National Summit on Diversity in the Teaching Force.

Neely, S. R. (2015). No child left behind and administrative costs: A resource dependence study of local school districts. *Education Policy Analysis Archives, 23*(26), 12–31.

Newbrey, M. G., & Baltezore, J. M. (2006). Poster presentations: Conceptualizing, constructing & critiquing. *American Biology Teacher, 68*(9), 550–554.

Noguera, P. A. (2000). *City schools and the American dream: Reclaiming the promise of American education.* New York, NY: Teachers College Press.

Noguera, P. A. (2003). Schools, prisons, and social implications of punishment: Rethinking disciplinary practices. *Theory into Practice, 42*(4), 341–350.

Noguera, P. A. (2008). *The trouble with Black boys and other reflections on race, equity, and the future of public education.* San Francisco, CA: Jossey-Bass.

Nuangchalerm, P., & Prachagool, V. (2010). Influences of teacher preparation program on preserves science teachers' beliefs. *International Education Studies, 3*(1), 87–91.

Ober, D. L. (2013). *Education: Pathways to superior content knowledge in preservice teachers* (Unpublished thesis). Old Dominion University, Norfolk, VA.

O'Connor, C. (2006). Chapter 16 the premise of Black inferiority: An enduring obstacle fifty years post-brown. *Yearbook of the National Society for the Study of Education, 105*(2), 316–336.

O'Donoghue, D., & Berard, M. (2014). Six qualities of socially engaged design: Emerging possibilities for K-12 art education programs. *Art Education, 67*(6), 6–10.

Oliva, M., Rodriguez, M. A., Alanis, I., & Quijada Cerecer, P. D. (2013). At home in the academy: Latina faculty counter-stories and resistances. *Educational Foundations, 27*(1–2), 91–109.

Oliver, H. (2011). Lessons learned from the implementation and assessment of student-centered methodologies. *Journal of Technology and Science Education, 2*(1), 1–2.

Oulton, C., Day, V., Dillon, J., & Grace, M. (2004). Controversial issues: Teachers' attitudes and practices in the context of citizenship education. *Oxford Review of Education, 30*(4), 489–507.

Papatraianou, L. H., & Le Cornu, R. (2014). Problematising the role of personal and professional relationships in early career teacher resilience. *Australian Journal of Teacher Education, 39*(1), 15–32.

Parsons, J., & Schroder, M. (2015). *Tools for teaching social studies: A how to handbook of useful ideas and practical solutions* (2nd ed.). Edmonton: Brush Education.

Patrick, H., Ryan, A. M., & Kaplan, A. (2007). Early adolescents' perceptions of the classroom social environment, motivational beliefs, and engagement. *Journal of Educational Psychology, 99*(1), 83–98.

Penrose, A., Perry, C., & Ball, I. (2007). Emotional intelligence and teacher self-efficacy: The contribution of teacher status and length of experience. *Issues in Educational Research, 17*(1), 107–126.

Peters, D. L., & Daly, S. R. (2013). Returning to graduate school: Expectations of success, values of the degree, and managing the costs. *Journal of Engineering Education, 102*(4), 244–268. doi:10.1002/jee.20012

Phelps, G., Weren, B., Croft, A., & Gitomer, D. (2014). *Developing content knowledge for teaching assessments for the measures of effective teaching study* (ETS Research Report No. RR-14-33). Princeton, NJ: Educational Testing Service. doi:10.1002/ets2.12031

Pittenger, A. (2015, January 31). Brief: Free college prep workshops for elementary students' parents. *Arizona Daily Star*.

Porter, A., McMaken, J., Hwang, J., & Yang, R. (2011). Common core standards: The new U.S. intended curriculum. *Educational Researcher, 40*(3), 103–116.

Porter, A., McMaken, J., Hwang, J., & Yang, R. (2011). Response to comments: Assessing the common core standards: Opportunities for improving measures of instruction. *Educational Researcher, 40*(4), 186–188.

Porton, H. D. (2013). *Teaching the standards: How to blend common core state standards into secondary instruction*. Lanham, MA: Rowman & Littlefield Publishers.

Pruitt, S. (2014). The next generation science standards: The features and challenges. *Journal of Science Teacher Education, 25*, 145–156. doi:10.1007/s10972-014-9385-0

Quicke, J. (2010). Narrative strategies in educational research: Reflections on a critical autoethnography. *Educational Action Research, 18*(2), 239–254.

Quijada Cerecer, P. D., Alvarez Gutierrez, L., & Rios, F. (2010). Critical multiculturalism: Transformative educational principles and practices. In T. K. Chapman & N. Hobbel (Eds.), *Social justice pedagogy across the curriculum: The practice of freedom* (pp. 144–163). New York, NY: Routledge.

Raden, B. (2015, March 18). What if education reform got it all wrong in the first place? *Pacific Standard*. Retrieved from http://www.psmag.com/books-and-culture/what-if-education-reform-got-it-allwrong-in-the-first-place

Raley, J. (2013). *Lecture on democracy in education 2/19/13*. Santa Barbara, CA: University of California.

Rebora, A. (2013, October 14). *Instructional coaches dissect classroom-management challenges*. Retrieved from http://www.edweek.org/tm/articles/2013/10/14/cm_coaches.html

Reeve, J., Bolt, E., & Cai, Y. (1999). Autonomy-supportive teachers: How they teach and motivate students. *Journal of Educational Psychology, 91*(3), 537–548. doi:10.1037/0022-0663.91.3.537

Richardson, P. W., & Walt, H. (2005). I've decided to become a teacher: Influences on career change. *Teaching and Teacher Education, 21*(5), 475–489.

Richert, A. E. (2012). *What should I do? Confronting dilemmas teaching in urban schools*. New York, NY: Teachers College Press.

Riggs, M. L., Verdi, M. P., & Arlin, P. K. (2009). A local evaluation of the reliability, validity, and procedural adequacy of the teacher performance assessment exam for teaching credential candidates. *Issues in Teacher Education, 44*(3), 13–38.

Riley, B. (2014, March 25). *Why I support common core standards*. Retrieved May 7, 2016, from http://www.nationalreview.com/article/374112/why-i-support-common-core-astandards-bob-riley

Riley, T., & Ungerleider, C. (2012). Self-fulfilling prophecy: How teachers' attributions, expectations, and stereotypes influence the learning opportunities afforded aboriginal students. *Canadian Journal of Education, 35*(2), 303–333.

Ritchel, M. (2011, September 3). *In classroom of future, stagnant scores*. Retrieved from http://www.nytimes.com/2011/09/04/technology/technology-inschools-faces-questions-on-value.html?

Robb, L. (2003). *Teaching reading in social studies, science, and math*. New York, NY: Scholastic Professional Books.

Roberts, S. R. (2014). Effectively using social studies textbooks in historical inquiry. *Social Studies Research & Practice, 9*(1), 119–128.

Robnett, R. D., Chemers, M. M., & Zurbriggen, E. L. (2015). Longitudinal associations among undergraduates' research experience, self-efficacy, and identity. *Journal of Research in Science Teaching, 14*(1), 12–16. doi:10.1002/tea.21221

Roessingh, H. (2006). BICS-CALP: An introduction for some, a review for others. *TESL Canada Journal, 23*(2), 91–96.

Ross, D. D., Bondy, E., Gallingane, C., & Hambacher, E. (2008). Promoting academic engagement through insistence: Being a warm demander. *Childhood Education, 84*(3), 142–146.

Sadler, I. (2012). The challenges for new academics in adopting student-centered approaches to teaching. *Studies in Higher Education, 37*(6), 731–745. doi:10.1080/03075079.2010.543968

Saltali, N. N. (2013). The teacher student relationship as a predictor of preschoolers' social anxiety. *Mevlana International Journal of Education, 3*(4), 118–126. doi:10.13054/mije.13.66.3.4

Sanchez, G. B. (2007, June 12). Parents applaud plans for Naylor: 'Failing' middle school will see improvements. *Arizona Daily Star*.

Sander, J. B. (2010). School psychology, juvenile justice, and the school to prison pipeline. *Communique, 39*(4), 4.

Sandoval-Lucero, E., Shanklin, N. L., Sobel, D. M., Townsend, S. S., Davis, A., & Kalisher, S. (2011). Voices of beginning teachers: Do paths to preparation make a difference? *Education, 132*(2), 336–350.

Sarles, P. (2013). The common core ELA assessments: What we know so far about the performance tasks. *Library Media Connection, 32*(1), 10–13.

Scherer, M. (2012). The challenges of supporting new teachers. *Educational Leadership, 69*(8), 18–23.

Schick, C. A. (2000). By virtue of being White: Resistance in anti-racist pedagogy. *Race, Ethnicity, and Education, 3*(1), 85–102.

Schroeder, C. C. (1993). New students: New learning styles. *Change, 25*(5), 21–26.

Schutz, P. A. (2001). *The development of a goal to become a teacher*. Worcester, MD: American Psychological Association.

Schwind, J. K., McCay, E., Lapum, J., Fredericks, S., Beanlands, H., Romaniuk, D., LeGrow, K., & Edwards, S. (2014). The experience of developing a faculty research cluster using the creativity of the narrative reflective process. *Creative Nursing, 20*(3), 164–170.

Shah, C. C. (2010). Critical thinking: What it is and why it matters to emerging professionals, an ASM emerging professional's perspective. *Advanced Materials and Process, 168*(5), 61.

Shaw, B. (1903). *Man and superman: A comedy and a philosophy*. Cambridge, MA: The University of Massachusetts Press.

Shelly, B. (2008). Rebels and their causes: State resisitance to no child left behind. *Publius, 38*(3), 444–468.

Sindhi, S. A. (2013). Creating safe school environment: Role of school principals. *Tibet Journal, 38*(1–2), 77–89.

Sleeter, C. E. (2001). Preparing teachers for culturally diverse schools: Research and the overwhelming presence of whiteness. *Journal of Teacher Education, 52*(2), 94–106.

Sleeter, C. E., & Delgago Bernal, D. (2002). Critical pedagogy, critical race theory, and antiracist education: Implications for multicultural education. In J. A. Banks & C. A. M. Banks (Eds.), *Handbook of research on multicultural education* (2nd ed.). San Francisco, CA: Jossey-Bass.

Smith, C. (2009). Deconstructing the pipeline: Evaluating school-to-prison pipeline equal protection cases through a structural racism framework. *Fordham Urban Law Journal, 36*(5), 1009–1049.

Smith, D. T., Jacobson, C. K., & Juarez, B. G. (2011). *White parents, Black children: Experiencing transracial adoption*. New York, NY: Rowman & Littlefield Publishers.

Smith, J. (2013, June 26). *The best and worst-paying jobs in education*. Retrieved April 8, 2015, from http://www.forbes.com/sites/jacquelynsmith/2013/06/26/the-best-and-worst-paying-jobs-in-education

Smith, W. A. (2004). Black faculty coping with racial battle fatigue: The campus racial climate in a post-civil rights era. In D. Cleveland (Ed.), *A long way to go: Conversations about race by African American faculty and graduate students* (pp. 171–190). New York, NY: Peter Lang.

Soloman, R. P., & Palmer, H. (2004). Schooling in Babylon, Babylon in school: When racial profiling and zero tolerance converge. *Canadian Journal of Educational Administration and Policy, 33*, 1–13.

Solorzano, D., & Yosso, T. (2001). Critical race methodology: Counter-storytelling as an analytical framework for education research. *Qualitative Inquiry, 8*(1), 23–44.

Southern Education Foundation. (2010). *A diverse new majority: Students of color in the south's public schools*. Atlanta, GA: Southern Education Foundation.

Spooner, M., Flowers, C., Lambert, R., & Algozzine, B. (2008). Is more really better? Examining perceived benefits of an extended student teaching experience. *Clearing House: A Journal of Educational Strategies, Issues and Ideas, 81*(6), 263–270.

Spring, J. H. (2001). *The American school, 1642–2000*. New York, NY: McGraw-Hill.

Stenhouse, V. L., & Jarrett, O. S. (2012). In the service of learning and activism: Service learning, critical pedagogy, and the problem solution project. *Teacher Education Quarterly, 39*(1), 51–76.

Stephan, J. J. (2008). *Census of state and federal corrections facilities*. Washington, DC: Bureau of Justice Statistics.

Stewart, M. G. (2014). Enduring understandings, artistic processes, and the new visual arts standards: A close-up consideration for curriculum planning. *Art Education, 67*(5), 6–11.

Stockwell, C. (2014, August 13). *The top 10 lowest paying college majors*. Retrieved April 8, 2015, from http://college.usatoday.com/2014/08/13/the-top-10-lowest-paying-college-majors

Stoddart, T. (1990). Los Angeles unified school district intern program: Recruiting and preparing teachers for urban context. *Peabody Journal of Education, 67*(3), 84–122.

Szente, J. (2007). Empowering young children for success in school and in life. *Early Childhood Education Journal, 34*(6), 449–453.

Tan, E., & Barton, A. C. (2010). Transforming science learning and student participation in sixth grade science: A case study of low-income urban, racial minority classroom. *Equity and Excellence in Education, 43*(1), 38–55.

Tate, W. F. (1997). Critical race theory and education: History, theory, and implications. *Review of Research in Education, 22*, 195–247.

Tate, W. F. (Ed.). (2012). *Research on schools, neighborhoods, and communities: Toward civic responsibility*. New York, NY: Rowman & Littlefield Publishers.

The 50 Most Inspirational Quotes for Teachers. (2015, January 1). Retrieved March 7, 2015, from http://www.curatedquotes.com/quotes-for-teachers/

Thornburg, D. D. (2009). *Five challenges in science education*. Mountain View, CA: Creative Commons.

Tobias, J. L. (2004). Assessing assessments of school performance: The case of California. *The American Statistician, 58*(1), 55–63.

Toldson, I. A. (2010). The happy bell curve: How misguided research on race and achievement is duping Black progressives and liberal Americans into accepting Black inferiority. *Journal of Negro Education, 79*(4), 443–445.

Tough, P. (2013). *How children succeed: Grit, curiosity, and the hidden power of character* (Reprint ed.). New York, NY: Mariner Books.

Tulman, J. B., & Weck, D. M. (2009). Shutting off the school-to-prison pipeline for status offenders with education-related disabilities. *New York Law School Law Review, 54*(3), 875.

Tuzzolo, E., & Hewitt, D. T. (2006). Rebuilding inequity: The re-emergence of the school-to-prison pipeline in New Orleans. *High School Journal, 90*(2), 59–68.

Udesky, L. (2015, February 4). *Classroom coaches critical as teachers shift to common core*. Retrieved from http://www.edsource.org/2015/Classroom-Coaches-Critical-as-Teachers-Shift-to-Common-Core

Ujifusa, A. (2014). Resistance to common core mounts. *Education Week, 33*(29), S34–S36.

ULV Teaching Credential Program Catalog. (2015). Retrieved from http://laverne.edu/catalog/program/program-teaching-credential/

Unknown Author. (2013). *A first look: 2013 mathematics and reading, national assessment of educational progress at grades 4 and 8* (nces.ed.org). Retrieved from http://nces.ed.gov/nationsreportcard/subject/publications/main2013/pdf/2014451.pdf

Unknown Author. (2015). *High school dropout statistics* (Statisticbrain.com). Retrieved from http://www.statisticbrain.com/high-school-dropout-statistics/

Urban Education: Teacher Certification. (n.d.). Retrieved April 8, 2015, from http://sitemaker.umich.edu/rosman.356/teacher_certification

Van Roekel, D. (2013). *Getting to the core of common core: Change is hard – not necessarily bad*. Retrieved from http://www.nea.org/home/53977.htm

VanTassel-Baska, J. (2015). Arguments for and against the common core state standards. *Gifted Child Today, 38*(1), 60–62.

Venosdale, K. (2010, September 20). *Why do you want to teach?* Retrieved April 8, 2015, from http://venspired.com/why-do-you-want-to-teach

Vickers, R., Field, J., & Melakoski, C. (2015). Media culture 2020: Collaborative teaching and blended learning using social media and cloud-based technologies. *Contemporary Educational Technology, 6*(1), 62–73.

Vogt, M. E., & Echevarria, J. (2008). *99 ideas and activities for teaching English learners with the SIOP model.* Boston, MA: Allyn & Bacon.

Wacquant, L. (2000). Deadly symbiosis: When ghetto and prison meet and mesh. *Punishment and Society, 3*(1), 95–134.

Wagoner, J. L. (2004). *Jefferson and education.* Chapel Hill, NC: Thomas Jefferson Foundation and University of North Carolina Press.

Wallerstein, N. (1983). *Language and culture in conflict: Problem-posing in the ESL classroom.* Reading, MA: Addison-Wesley Publishing.

Wang, M., & Sheikh-Khalil, S. (2014). Does parental involvement matter for student achievement and mental health in high school. *Child Development, 85*(2), 610–625. doi:10.1111/cdev.12153

Ware, F. (2006). Warm demander pedagogy: Culturally responsive teaching that supports a culture of achievement for African American students. *Urban Education, 41*(4), 427–456.

Westin, A. F. (1964). *Freedom now! The civil-rights struggle in America.* New York, NY: Basic Books.

Whiting, G. W. (2006). From at risk to at promise: Developing scholar identities among Black males. *The Journal of Secondary Gifted Education, 17*(4), 222–229.

Whiting, G. W. (2009). Gifted Black males: Understanding and decreasing barriers to achievement identity. *Roeper Review, 31*, 224–233.

Wilkins, J. (2014). Good teacher-student relationships: Perspectives of teachers in urban high schools. *American Secondary Education, 43*(1), 52–68.

Wilkinson, L. C., & Silliman, E. R. (2001, February). Classroom language and literacy learning. *Reading Online, 4*(7), 3–7.

Williams, J. P. (2014). Who is fighting for common core? *U.S. News Digital Weekly, 6*(9), 6.

Winant, H. (2002). Racial formation theory. In P. Essed & D. T. Goldberg (Eds.), *Race critical theories: Text and context.* Malden, MA: Blackwell Publishers.

Winn, M. T., & Behizadeh, N. (2011). The right to be literate: Literacy, education, and the school-to-prison pipeline. *Review of Research in Education, 35*(1), 147–173.

Winters, M. (2011). *Measuring teacher effectiveness: Credentials unrelated to student achievement* (Issue Brief No. 10). New York, NY: Manhattan Institute for Policy Research.

Wise, T. (2005). *White like me: Reflections on race from a privileged son.* Brooklyn, NY: Soft Skull Press.

Wong, H. K., & Wong, R. T. (2014). *The classroom management book.* San Francisco, CA: Harry K. Wong Publications.

Woodson, C. G. (1933/2000). *The mis-education of the Negro.* Chicago, IL: African American Images.

Zamudio, M. M., Russel, C., Rios, F. A., & Bridgeman, J. L. (2011). *Critical race theory matters: Education and ideology.* New York, NY: Routledge.

Zarate, M. E., & Conchas, G. Q. (2010). Contemporary and critical methodological shifts in research on Latino education. In E. G. Murillo, S. A. Villenas, R. T. Galván, J. S. Muñoz, C. Martínez, & M. Machado-Casas (Eds.), *Handbook of Latinos and education: Theory, research and practice* (pp. 90–108). New York, NY: Routledge.

Printed in the United States
By Bookmasters